More People's Guide to J.R.R. Tolkien

Though very few printed journals of imagination exist any more, the web has provided a whole new generation of readers, writers, and editors with a forum for the liberal arts, properly understood, and the culture of the imagination. For that is exactly what Green Books of TheOneRing.net is: a journal of the imagination. The women and men who write for it—Anwyn, Tehanu, Turgon, Ostadan, and Quickbeam—are the new Women and Men of Letters. Green Books is the 21st-century equivalent of the great journals of culture and imagination of Tolkien's day: *The Criterion*, *The Dublin Review*, and *Colosseum*. The writers of Green Books take Tolkien's "majestic whole" and serve as the "minds and hands, wielding" the pen and the keyboard, manifesting the will of the soul and the imagination.

—From the Introduction by Bradley J. Birzer,
author of *Tolkien's Sanctifying Myth*

ABOUT THE AUTHORS

Anwyn, Cynthia L. McNew, is mother to her son Christopher and a copy editor. She received her B.M. in music education from Butler University and her M.M. in choral music from the University of Illinois at Urbana-Champaign. In her spare time ... actually, with a small son and her job, she has no spare time to speak of, but she enjoys music, movies, and books. A founding member of Green Books at TheOneRing.net, she is very pleased to be a part of the web phenomenon that is TheOneRing.net and proud to have served as editor in chief for this book.

Quickbeam, Cliff Broadway, is a Los Angeles-based filmmaker/writer/actor. His first play, *Elevator*, a claustrophile comedy first produced in 1998, was a critical smash. You can hear his voiceover work on TV and radio, including Samwise Gamgee in Black Label Games' *The Fellowship of the Ring* video game and his (now infamous) appearance on the WB network's hidden-camera show, *The Jamie Kennedy Experiment*. Since 1999, Cliff has used the pseudonym Quickbeam as a writer and roving Hollywood reporter for TheOneRing.net, helping to found the Green Books online magazine. Cliff coauthored the bestseller *The People's Guide to J.R.R. Tolkien*, published in 2003, and is also producer/co-screenwriter for the feature documentary *Ringers: Lord of the Fans*, exploring the past fifty years of the Tolkien phenomenon. His special interests include Dragon Dice, off-road hiking, animation, and fat purring black cats. And, yes, it really is his last name.

Turgon, David E. Smith, first read Tolkien in the 1960s, when the U.S. editions sported some supremely awful covers. He is a librarian and lives in a Chicago suburb with his family. He is also the editor of *The Tolkien Fan's Medieval Reader* (2004), published by Cold Spring Press.

Tehanu, Erica Challis, was born in New Zealand and grew up there and in Australia. A degree in English from the Victoria University of Wellingham was followed by a year spent living in Spain. On her return to New Zealand she gained the position of second horn in the Auckland Philharmonia, where she has played full-time for the past eleven years. An accidental meeting on the internet with "Xoanon" led her to start reporting on *The Lord of the Rings* film project, and shortly afterwards Erica became one of the founders of the fan website TheOneRing.net, where she writes under the name "Tehanu." Erica served as editor in chief for 2003's *The People's Guide to J.R.R. Tolkien.*

Ostadan, Michael Urban, is a lifetime native of Los Angeles and a graduate of UCLA with a master's degree in computer science, supplemented by classes in medieval Welsh, philosophy, and other esoteric matters. He works as a computer systems programmer and has been on the internet since its ARPANET days in the 1970s. Since discovering Tolkien's work in the 1960s, he has been active in organized fandom for over 30 years, including a stint as treasurer of the Mythopoeic Linguistic Fellowship. He began writing for Green Books late in 2000.

More People's Guide to J.R.R. Tolkien

By Cliff Broadway, Erica Challis, Cynthia L. McNew, Dave Smith, and Michael Urban
of TheOneRing.net

Cynthia L. McNew, Editor-in-Chief

Cold Spring Press
P.O. Box 284, Cold Spring Harbor, NY 11724
E-mail: Jopenroad@aol.com

Library of Congress Control No. 2004113791
ISBN 1-59360-026-7

Printed in the United States of America

The authors would like to thank the dedicated staff of TheOneRing.net for their support and encouragement, Dr. Brad Birzer and Mr. Peter S. Beagle for their kind introductory words, Jonathan Stein at Cold Spring Press for the chance to do it all again, and the worldwide Fellowship of admirers of J.R.R. Tolkien, Peter Jackson, and *The Lord of the Rings*.

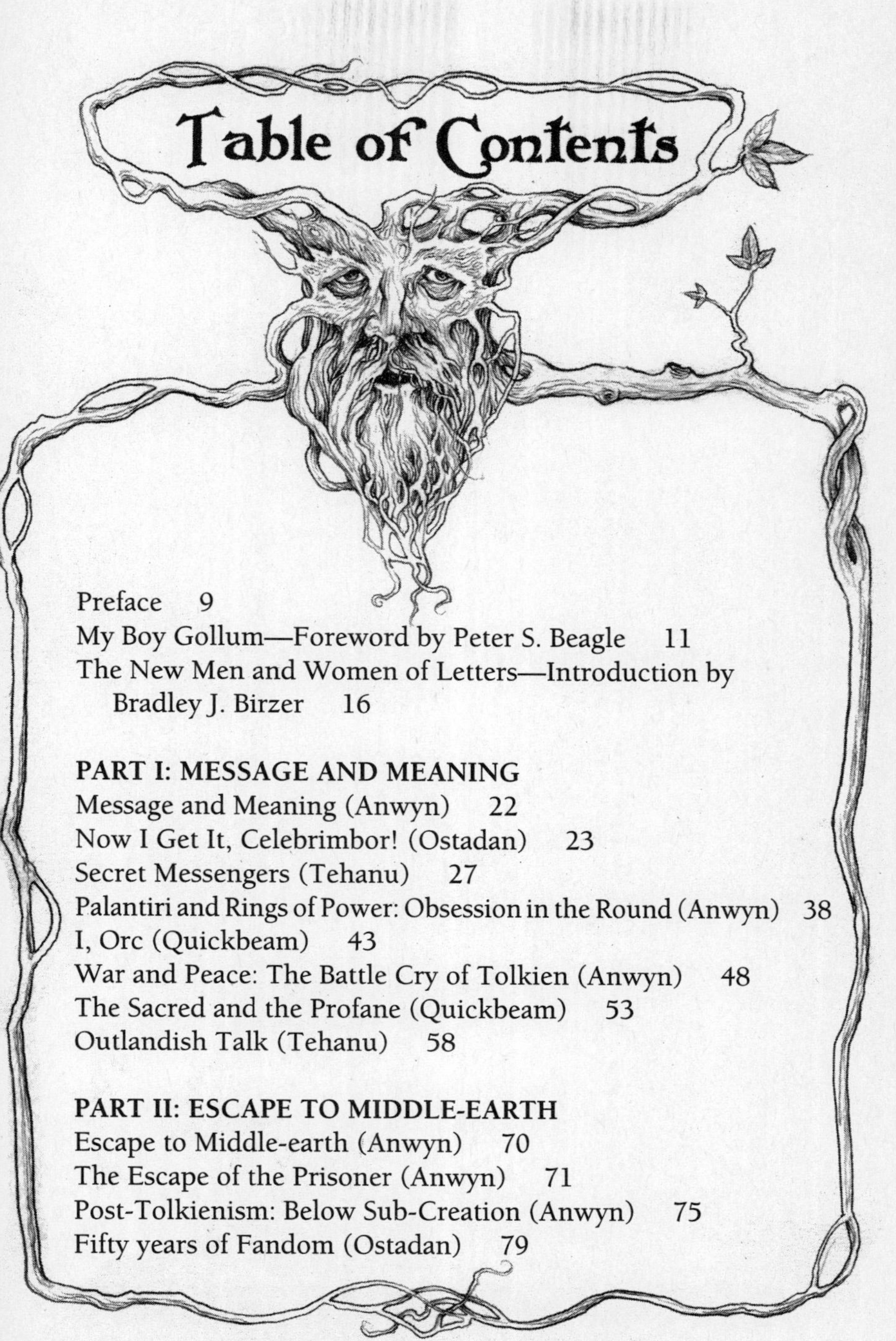

Table of Contents

Illustrations

More People's Guide to J.R.R. Tolkien

Preface

Boy, did we pick the right author.

How many authors out there wrote a work that is both great literature and a popular fireside tale? How many authors were both serious scholars and tremendous fiction writers? How many authors whose work outlasts the century in which they live can claim the kind of mass following that Tolkien's work still enjoys, more than 50 years later?

In this book, we happily delve once more into the minutiae of what makes us, Tolkien's vast readership, stay with Middle-earth as with no other imagined realm. We'll talk escapism and scholarship, orcs and hobbits, rivers and mountains, language and film. But the one constant, as it as always been for us at TheOneRing.net, is of course Professor Tolkien.

How does a mild-mannered, middle-aged Oxford don become the most famous and revered author of dragons, elves, dwarves, and … what were those little guys again … hobbits? … in the world? Well, how does a struggling British single mother shoot to the top of bestseller lists around the globe with a story of a boy wizard, or a young American farmwife become universally beloved for stories of her childhood, or a Canadian orphan garner lasting renown for her stories of another Canadian orphan? Authors have something to say that a large section of the populace can relate to. Successful authors don't rest until that something is said on the grand stage. And famous authors, well, what they have to say relates to a larger section of the populace than usual.

And Tolkien? His influence just seems to keep growing. With the introduction of Peter Jackson's live-action films, Tolkien's readership and realm of fans has grown exponentially, and it doesn't look like stopping any time soon.

We at TheOneRing.net are honored to be a part of this most recent boom of Tolkien fandom. I expect in another couple of decades, something will happen that will create another boom—maybe nothing more than our children coming of age and discovering as we did the wonder that is Middle-earth, maybe something more pan-cultural. However it happens, we are proud to say "we were there..." when Peter Jackson began filming *The Fellowship of the Ring*... when New Line Cinema and the production crews discovered there might be advantages in working with an online fan group instead of shunning them... when *The Return of the King* earned a clean sweep of its Oscar nominations... when hundreds and thousands of new fans learned *What is a hobbit?* and of the perils of the Ring... when we suddenly had a world stage and the privilege of sharing our insights with other fans.

For first, last, and foremost, we are fans. Not scholars by trade or pundits by profession, authors mostly by avocation, not vocation, we are fans of J.R.R. Tolkien, fans of *The Lord of the Rings*, and by extension, fans of Peter Jackson. Thank you for joining us in being there. Tolkien fandom is a special group unlike any other, and we are proud to be a part of that group that serves as a connection—a connection between fans and films, between readers and moviegoers, between fan fiction writers and poets and artists and an admiring internet audience. Long live Tolkien fandom!

—Anwyn
Ostadan
Quickbeam
Tehanu
Turgon

My Boy Gollum

Foreword by Peter S. Beagle

I'm honored and deeply flattered by the request from TheOneRing.net to write this foreword, but for all I know, it may yet get me burned in effigy, or—at very least—force me to change my e-mail address. I have read and loved the work of J.R.R. Tolkien since 1958, well before it was generally known in this country, and I still reread him with great pleasure—not only *The Lord of the Rings* and *The Hobbit*, but most of the dozen *History of Middle-earth* volumes and anyway some of the available philological work. And while I am a long way from being a scholar of any sort—it's a highly intimidating honor to follow Tom Shippey in introducing the second volume of this series—I do feel reasonably justified in sharing one reconsideration, no matter how much debate it may provoke. Here it is: J.R.R. Tolkien and *The Lord of the Rings* present abiding proof that one need not be a genius to create a work of genius.

If anything, sometimes it may be a handicap.

The genius of Middle-earth lies in the miracle of its very existence: in the fact that it exists so solidly and truthfully, on so many levels. No other secondary world (to use Tolkien's phrase) that I know of offers anything like its depth and scope; his friend C.S. Lewis's Narnia is a cartoon by comparison, Lloyd Alexander's Prydain a genial G-rated *Mabinogion*, and brilliant one-shots like E.R. Eddison's *The Worm Ouroboros* and R. Tappan Wright's *Islandia* are just that—unique, unsustainable sports. But *The Lord of the Rings* was made from the inside out, over fifty years and more, and a good deal of blood, grief, loss and erudition went into its foundation. Definitely union work.

Tolkien possessed a first-class mind, a first-class education, and a truly superb gift for storytelling. He was also, however, a second-class stylist—in a crisis he invariably fell back on Biblical cadences and locutions—and his characterizations are most often extremely adept variations on their classical and legendary origins. It's not that he writes—as he was so often accused of doing—in a *Boys' Own Paper* British public-school mode; that's pure slander. But the man's internalized boundaries ("*Tom's country ends here, he will not pass the borders / Tom has his house to mind...*") show in many ways, perhaps most obviously in his handling of his two significant female characters, Galadriel and Eowyn. One is an elf-queen who appears only in the Lothlorien sequence, the other a lovelorn woman warrior who certainly affects the story's finale drastically by taking Merry along with her to the Battle of the Pelennor Fields, but who, after that, has nothing much to do but give up on Aragorn, marry Faramir and live happily ever after. Tolkien has a screenwriter's unfailing feel for the dramatic, but very little gift for genuine tragedy. He sets our blood tingling, or freezes the back of our necks, without even trying. He absorbs us completely in a tale or a ballad that has next to nothing to do with his main narrative—but he cannot break our hearts. In that crucial aspect he falls short of greatness, because the truly great ones do *that* without trying.

And with that said (are we rumbling yet?), I offer the one character with whom Tolkien transcends every one of his limitations and at least establishes a summer bungalow on Parnassus: Gollum, *née* Sméagol.

I have no idea how Tolkien came up with Gollum. In concept as in character, he is a thing apart. He has no ancestors in the Elder Edda or the *Kalevala*; indeed, I can find no scholarly antecedents for him at all. I can envisage Tolkien realizing that Gollum's ring of invisibility—rather dubiously acquired by Bilbo in the original version of *The Hobbit*—was in fact the key to the vast epic of which *The Hobbit* wasn't originally meant to be a part. That far my professional imagination can tail along, even to envying that moment of discovery; but the idea of bringing Gollum out of his dank and wretched lair to follow his "precious" to torture in Mordor, back to the Mines of Moria and the Golden Wood of Lothlorien, and so to his—and the Ring's—inevitable end...No, I don't know how Tolkien created and nurtured so astonishing a reinvention. I'm not sure *he* knew himself, not entirely. Charles Dickens, up against the deadline for the newspaper serial that was to become his first novel, could only say of his own similar breakthrough, "Then I thought of Mr. Pickwick." I suppose your *karma* has to be in apple-pie order to get one of those.

All the pathos of *The Lord of the Rings* is centered in Gollum. He can't be trusted—he can't trust his utterly fragmented self—and yet he *must* be trusted; repulsive as he is, it is impossible not to pity him, yet he's as dangerous a cannibal as Hannibal Lecter, and with distinctly less charm. He can never determine whether he hates or loves Frodo Baggins, and still he yearns toward Frodo's natural decency as a stunted, starved, withered flower still turns its distorted bloom to face the sun. At the last, of course, the Ring matters infinitely more to Gollum than even this skeletal friendship—as it has to, if Tolkien's mighty narrative is to end as it has to end. In that sense, he is certainly the most important character in the entire work.

The small moment when he—meaning ruined Gollum and the still-vulnerable shadow of Sméagol who yet survives in him—debates the question of betraying Frodo and Sam is, for me, the artistic high point of *The Lord of the Rings*. Tolkien never before or after wrote a scene as *humanly* poignant as that one: brief as it is, it encapsulates the doom that lies at the heart of the story and makes the destruction of the Ring so vital to the survival of Middle-earth. There is no one—*perhaps* excepting Tom Bombadil and the Ents—whom the Ring cannot reduce to the common denominator of Gollum, according to the individual's native stature and power. Saruman becomes one version—Boromir would have been another—the nine Nazgûl, once mortal kings, would surely all turn out to be sundered, shattered Gollum/Sméagols themselves, if you met them for lunch. For that matter, the Ring's Master, Sauron, the Dark Lord himself, behind the threatening façade of his vast power...well, it's just a thought—we'll never know.

And even Frodo, at the very last, is becoming Gollum in all but diction, unable to separate his own will from that of the terrible "Precious," until Gollum takes a hand (pun intended) and attains the antiheroic glory he was so sorrowfully born for. Without Gollum, Middle-earth might very well have ended as a world of Gollums—hobbits, men and elves alike enslaved to the One Ring, at times vaguely and briefly recalling that once they were other than the Ring. Generations of their descendants will owe an incalculable debt to Gollum, unaware.

Tolkien brushes fleetingly against a kind of Shakespearean tragedy in a few of the Middle-earth legends—most notably in the tale of Beren One-Hand and Luthien. But only with Gollum does he realize something that the Greek dramatists would have applauded, for all that he violates several of the most basic commandments of classic Greek theatre. Gollum/Sméagol in his beginnings is no king, but an insignificant, hobbitlike creature with no great height to fall from, no *hubris* to offend the gods—unless, of course, you count his slaying of his cousin Déagol to acquire the One Ring. Nor does the action of the story take place within twenty-four hours; nor does any of its violence take place decently offstage. Yet Gollum, for my money, is a truly tragic figure, in the simplest, fullest sense of the word. Doomed and already destroyed from the moment we meet him, he is still distantly capable of something like affection, capable of recognizing kindness when he sees it offered, but long past any real hope of accepting it. If he were all hate and fear and devouring, helpless hunger, he wouldn't be remotely as affecting a character as he is. (As he *becomes,* rather; there's no indication in the first version of *The Hobbit* that Tolkien has any feeling for him, except as a children's-book bogey.) Only those who have borne the Ring—Frodo, Bilbo, and even Sam, who loathes him and is implacably loathed in return—have the slightest understanding of what it is to be Gollum. Yet throughout *The Lord of the Rings* he inspires at least some compassion in almost everyone west of Mordor. And that unquestionably includes his creator.

The gods truly have it in for Gollum: murderer or not, he has suffered far beyond his deserving, and Sméagol knows it. When he shakes his bony fist at the Nazgûl wraiths flying across the moon and cries out, "We won't! Not for you!" it's a grand and moving moment, even—no, *especially*—if he does collapse into blubbering terror immediately afterward. No Terry Brooks, Robert Jordan, Mercedes Lackey, Katharine Kurtz, or any of *their* trilogy-hawking imitators can match it. No way in the world. I'm not sure even my beloved T.H. White, master of so many heartbreaking artistic epiphanies, could have achieved that one.

From Sir Mordred to Iago and Richard III down to Dracula, Steerpike, Tom Ripley and the Duke of Coffin Castle ("We all have flaws, and mine is being wicked"), villains have always ranked among the greatest glories of English-language literature. But the villain who somehow manages to evoke sympathy—as distinguished from a certain fellow-feeling—is the rarest of the breed. Becky Sharp is one, as are Captain Hook and Walter Scott's Brian de Bois-Guilbert, and I must confess that my favorite character in *The Forsyte Saga* remains the appalling Soames Forsyte, who has both the courage of his villainy and the agonizing awareness of its futility. Push comes to shove, though, I'll back my boy against any of them. Tolkien wrought better than I think he can have known when he created poor, dreadful Gollum.

The New Men and Women of Letters

Introduction by Bradley J. Birzer
Hillsdale College, Michigan

The day of the printed journal of imagination—dealing with ideas, literature, and poetry—seems to be fading. To be sure, it has been fading rather dramatically ever since the second world war. Politically and ideologically oriented magazines, specialized academic journals packed full of discipline-specific jargon, and even the so-called bestsellers have replaced the journals of imagination. As many of our most prominent scholars have declared since the advent of the Cold War and beyond, everything has become political. The literature of imagination and poetry seems, therefore, passé and merely romantic. Certainly, most would argue, such journals have nothing to do with the everyday reality of Wall Street or of the post-9/11 international scene.

In Tolkien's day, especially in the 1920s, '30s, and '40s, journals of the imagination abounded. In England, one could read, to name just a few, T.S. Eliot's *The Criterion*, Bernard Wall's *Colosseum*, Tom Burns's *Order*, or Christopher Dawson's *Dublin Review*. These reviews contained poetry, short stories, and learned articles on politics, history, literature, economic, law, and everything else under the sun. Even Tolkien wrote for the *Dublin Review*, publishing his inspired short story about purgatory, "Leaf by Niggle," in the January-February-March issue of 1945. Christopher Dawson, the editor of the *Dublin Review* during World War II and a fellow parishioner of Tolkien's at St. Aloysius's Church in Oxford, had recorded in his personal notebook that he would include anything in his journal written by Tolkien, C.S.

Lewis, or Charles Williams. And while Tolkien published only "Leaf by Niggle" in the *Dublin Review*, Charles Williams published an article or book review in almost every issue under Dawson's tenure. Lewis never did, but he was a friend of Dawson's. And to look at the January-February-March issue of 1945 of the *Dublin Review* reveals much about the nature of such journals. In addition to Tolkien's short story, scholarly articles on Sir Thomas More, the Roman Empire, the Christian tradition in England, John Henry Newman, and Czechoslovakia also appeared.

The editors and the writers for these reviews, for the most part, were not academics in the strict modern sense. Rather than specializing in one or two minor subjects within a larger specialty, focusing on trivial minutia, and drowning in one's own subjective reality, the men and women who wrote for such journals were well rounded and broadly educated in the liberal arts. They believed, in general, that culture and literature preceded politics, economics, and legal systems. The latter, indeed, grew out of the former. To change society dramatically and permanently, one must first change the culture and the ideas that shape and mold that culture, then later turn to the dry subjects of law, politics, and economics. Passing a new law or a new subsidy or developing a new bureaucracy might provide a short-term solution to whatever problem might arise, but one would do better to change the culture first, thus permanently influencing the way in which people thought about their world. These broadly educated editors and writers were simply known as Men and Women of Letters.

Tolkien was a Man of Letters. Though, of course, he was an expert in his own subjects of the Anglo-Saxon world and *Beowulf*, he also read thoroughly and deeply in the classics and especially in mythology. It be would impossible to read any of Tolkien's works without feeling the depth of learning and conviction that went into each character, each situation, each idea, each battle, each evening, each morning, and each day of his legendarium. Tolkien brought his general, classical learning—as well as his specialized linguistic and historical training and his own philosophical and metaphysical beliefs—to fruition and culmination in the sub-created world of Middle-earth. And in his own letters, Tolkien invites others to join in his sub-created world. "I would draw some of the great tales in fullness, and leave many only placed in the scheme, and sketched. The cycles should be linked to a majestic whole, and yet leave scope for other minds and hands, wielding paint and music and drama." Then in a moment of humility, Tolkien concluded the thought in a word: "Absurd." (*Letters*, p. 145.) And yet it is not absurd. What Tolkien described in the early 1950s is at the essence of liberal arts and the culture and understanding of the Men and Women of Letters of the inner-war period: A structure of reality exists, too large for any one of us flawed and finite beings to comprehend fully, and we—each unique in time and space—fill in our little (but vital) parts. In this one passage, Tolkien could also be describing creation, time, and space and each individual's place within it. Such is the obvious brilliance of J.R.R. Tolkien.

What does all of this have to do with the book you hold in your hand at this moment? Well, everything. Though very few printed journals of imagination exist any more, the web has provided a whole new generation of readers, writers, and editors with a forum for the liberal arts, properly understood, and the culture of the imagination. For that is exactly what Green Books of TheOneRing.Net is: a journal of the imagination. The women and men who write for it—Anwyn, Tehanu, Turgon, Ostadan, and Quickbeam—are the new Women and Men of Letters. Green Books is the 21st-century equivalent of the great journals of culture and imagination of Tolkien's day: *The Criterion*, *The Dublin Review*, and *Colosseum*. The writers of Green Books take Tolkien's "majestic whole" and serve as the "minds and hands, wielding" the pen and the keyboard, manifesting the will of the soul and the imagination.

As Plato first taught us, the imagination comes from outside of one's self as a form of divine madness—"a mind beside itself." And as Tolkien most recently taught us, one's imagination is a gift to be used for *enchantment*, that is, the bettering of the created order. Our gifts are not for us, but for others. *Magic*, though, is the desire to have power over the created world, the "domination of things and wills" (Tolkien, "On Fairy Stories," 73). It is the old story and struggle of grace and will. The former helps order the world appropriately; the latter disorders the soul and, consequently, the world. In the long run, we know, the imagination, properly understood, will conquer politics, legal systems, economics, and all other such dreary and calculated things of modernity and post-modernity. The graciousness and sacrifice of the Frodos, Gandalfs, and Aragorns will overturn the pride of the ever-returning Sarumans and Saurons of the world.

Therefore, to these new Men and Women of Letters of Green Books, I offer a hearty and soul-filled congratulations on this second success. May there be many more. Long live their imaginations and the imaginations of others.

Or, as Tolkien best said it in 1958, "I look East, West, North, South, and I do not see Sauron; but I see that Saruman has many descendants. We Hobbits have against them no magic weapons. Yet, my gentlehobbits, I give you this toast: To the Hobbits. May they outlast the Sarumans and see spring again in the trees" (Carpenter, *Tolkien*, 225-26).

Message & Meaning

Message and Meaning

Anwyn

J.R.R. Tolkien is rapidly becoming an author whose work stands up to the scrutiny of time as much as more ancient writers. The present boom of Tolkien scholarship is unprecedented, and any discipline can take part. History, mythology, sociology, psychology, philology (of course!), philosophy, religion, and even astronomy, physics and mathematics all play their part in Middle-earth—one of the very reasons why it is so successful as a secondary reality. The topics are endless, and we at TheOneRing.net never tire of exploring them.

Ever thought about the constellations of Middle-earth and how they correspond to our own? About the significance of the number three in Tolkien's mythology? About the social hierarchy of orcs? About the psychology of Ring addiction? Are hobbits Christians even though they don't go to church? These are the human questions for which we love to seek the answers in our most beloved legend. And that right there may be the ultimate answer: *human* questions. A drum I beat quite a lot is that Tolkien captured far more of the human condition than his critics would like to admit. He lived that same human condition every day of his own life, and no matter how far above ordinary life an author might like to go, ultimately we are bound by our own experiences. He certainly has painted characters more noble, more divine, more evil, more nasty than any that you or I are likely to meet down the street, but they are still human characters, from the highest elf right down to the lowest orc. And the humanity always shines through.

Now I Get It, Celebrimbor!

Ostadan

Recently, we received this question:

"Hello! You guys are great. Why are the Elves of the Second Age so concerned about delaying the passage of time and healing the hurts of the world that they fall prey to Sauron as Lord of Gifts; whereas the Elves of the First Age lived many, many years in Beleriand without seeking such devices (as Rings)?" —Rick

Since Tolkien never adresses this directly, any answer requires speculation on Elvish psychology, drawing inferences (as usual) from whatever Tolkien does say about the Elves.

First, it is important to remember that the Noldor, who alone among the Elves had the craft to create the Three, were in Beleriand in revolt against the Valar, intending to overthrow Morgoth, retrieve the Silmarils, and found new kingdoms in Middle-earth. They might have been more interested in tools of conquest like the One Ring than in tools of preservation and healing like the Three—an alarming thought. Perhaps only in the fastness of Gondolin was the idea of preservation and healing given much importance; it may be significant that in Tolkien's sketchy history of the Elessar seen in *Unfinished Tales*, it is in Gondolin that the jewel-smith Enerdhil wrought the original Elessar, a stone with properties of preservation and healing that would prefigure and inspire Celebrimbor's eventual creation of the Three.

But the atmosphere of the Second Age was different. Morgoth had been overthrown, and judging from the account of life in the Shire in the year after Sauron's fall, it is very reasonable to suppose that the first years (and, indeed centuries) of the Second Age, culminating in the foundation of Eregion by the Noldor in S.A. 750, must have been a true golden age before Sauron's shadow began to appear once again. So it is in this environment (and, perhaps, recognizing that this golden age would fade in time) that, in the tale of the Elessar, Galadriel comes to Eregion and tells Celebrimbor: "I am grieved in Middle-earth, for leaves fall and flowers fade that I have loved, so that the land of my dwelling is filled with regret that no Spring can redeem."

Wielding the power of Nenya, Galadriel made Lórien a place where, as Sam observes, not much seems to happen and nobody minds it that way. Indeed, Sam completely loses count of the days; when he sees the moon after leaving Lórien, he surmises that time does not seem to matter inside. In effect, Galadriel's realm exists out of Time, or in a time of its own. And, as Galadriel tells Frodo, if he succeeds and the power of the Three is lost, Lothlórien will fade, and *time* will abolish the land forever.

Personally, for many years, I did not feel that the Elvish desire to stop Time was a particularly strong or convincing part of Tolkien's mythos. The rather melancholy and nostalgic Noldor that we see in *The Lord of the Rings* seemed to me something of a contrivance. Their dissatisfaction with the "changefulness" of Middle-earth seemed particularly unconvincing; after all, would not the worst thing about immortality be the possibility of boredom, living century after century in much the same way? Surely the changes in the world would be a relief for the sameness of immortality.

But recently, I celebrated my fiftieth birthday (thag you very buch) by attending a Renaissance Faire.

Now, I must explain that I was a regular performer at the RenFaire throughout the 1980s and once had many friends there. Now, attending the Faire for the first time in years, I found that almost all the people I knew back then were gone—passed away, or moved on to other things—and others had aged alarmingly. Even though I am myself quite "well-preserved," to coin a phrase, and indeed had a very enjoyable day with the present cast, feeling much as I did at 30, I was disheartened by seeing how much everything else around me had changed. My heart yearned for it to still be 1982, my own "golden year" at Faire. For the first time, in other words, I felt what the Elves must have felt, trying to make their own golden age last beyond its time. And for some reason, knowing that Celebrimbor was as deceived as the mortal men who became enslaved by the Nine, and that trying to stop time is a trap (and, in any case, impossible) was little comfort for me. After all, there weren't really any Elves; how can one learn from the experiences of a fictitious people? I spent much of September in a rather melancholy mood.

But then I remembered: in a way, the Elves *are* real: they were a product of Tolkien's imagination, and their own nostalgic melancholy was Tolkien's work as well. Did Elvish psychology have some basis in Tolkien's own experience? In the foreword to *The Lord of the Rings*, Tolkien tells us that by the end of the first World War, all but one of his close friends were dead, and he tells us more of the shabby destruction of the country in which he lived during childhood, including a thriving corn-mill beside its pool whose destruction is reflected in "The Scouring of the Shire." Tolkien was himself conservative in his habits, suspicious of modern technologies, and thought it quite reasonable to seek to escape, at least in literature, from "progressive things like factories, or the machine-guns and bombs that appear to be their most natural and inevitable, dare we say 'inexorable,' products" ("On Fairy-stories"). Yet Tolkien knew that one could not, and should not, attempt to stop Time. In a letter to Michael Straight (*Letters* #156, ca. 1956), he wrote,

> Mere *change* as such is not represented as "evil": it is the unfolding of the story and to refuse this is of course against the design of God. But the Elvish weakness is in these terms naturally to regret the past, and to become unwilling to change: as if a man were to hate a very long book still going on, and wished to settle down in a favourite chapter. Hence they fell in a measure to Sauron's deceits: they desired some "power" over things as they are … to arrest change, and keep things always fresh and fair.

Surely Tolkien himself had felt that same longing for the past many times, but he knew with a certainty that the story of our lives should not be stopped, even if they could be. If he had had the power to stop Time and live forever in the golden years before the Great War, he would not have had the experience of his marriage to Edith; of the rearing of his children; of the germination and flowering of his mythology of Middle-earth; of his friendship with the Inklings; of the publication of *The Lord of the Rings*; and of the vindication of his theories of the fairy-story by the immense popularity that his work enjoyed in his lifetime. The Elves must, indeed, pass and fade, but the story goes on in the work of Men, whose deeds, as Legolas tells Gimli, will outlast dwarves and Elves.

Everyone reading this doubtless has had their own special times that they wish could have gone on forever; for some, the present years of 2002-2003, with the appearance of Jackson's films and the immense growth in the Tolkien community, are the best of times and will be thought of with much fondness in the future. My own happy years of the past may be a fine place to visit, but to live there, I would not be willing to trade away the friends I have made since then, nor the excitement and pleasure I have enjoyed in the recent years of working with the wonderful people at TORn. Like Tolkien, I may dream of a year like the Shire's Great Year of Plenty, with "an air of richness and growth, and a gleam of a beauty beyond that of mortal summers that flicker and pass upon this Middle-earth" (a passage that grows more poignant with each passing year; trust me on this, kids), but the years yet to come will have their own joys—and sorrows—that I cannot foresee.

Secret Messengers

Tehanu

In this part of the country at least, the running waters are nothing like the streams and rivers of Middle-earth. The rain can seem endless and the creeks are milky brown with torn-up soil and the tannin of fallen leaves. And yet, even when the rain is falling hardest and the small domestic creek behind my house has risen up in a muddy torrent, I like to walk out and feel something coming off the moving waters. There is energy there, and the promise of change carried along with the tumbling branches and the odd bits of rubbish the water has found somewhere. The creek cleans and scours its own bed, and I breathe in the spirit of life renewed. It is like a message from the world to me.

People often say there is not much religion in *The Lord of the Rings*, or at least little sign of outward worship. No temples and no public religious ceremonies. Only the Elves seem to have the habit of calling the names of the Valar when they call on a greater power. One wonders how much the general populace—the Shirefolk, for instance—knew of the Valar or of Eru who made Middle-earth. When Sam and Frodo reach the end of their tether—Frodo at the Ford of Bruinen, and Sam as he confronts Shelob—both of them call on Elbereth. I always wonder how that seed of knowledge was planted in them, giving them that name of power in time of utmost need. They've heard the Elves singing in Rivendell, and Tolkien tells how the music seemed to call up visions and stories to the hobbits' minds even though they could not understand the words. And they would sing songs about Elbereth all night, as Bilbo commented to Frodo. But in moments of great danger, why did that name come to Sam unbidden? Facing Shelob, he remembers Galadriel who gave him the star-glass with the light of Eärendil, and he calls on the name of the Vala who is Queen of the Stars: Varda, who is also known as Elbereth. And then, apparently as a result, words come to him in a language he does not know. He is chanting in Elvish and his courage and strength are renewed as if by magic. Or in Middle-earth, where words are power and Quenya the most powerful language of all, maybe no more explanation is needed.

Tolkien created a Middle-earth in which religion is not obviously present, but I don't think he meant to leave its denizens stranded without a sense that there was a greater purpose at work. Gandalf, Elrond, and others of the Wise all comment on the unlikeliness of events such as Bilbo's finding of the Ring or the coincidence that has brought representatives from so many lands to Rivendell just at the time that Frodo arrives with the Ring. Just in time for the Council of Elrond, in fact. In their view it is more than chance—such apparent coincidences are a gift to be used for the good.

They need every bit of help they can get, because for most of the history of Middle-earth, the Valar who are its "guardian angels" seem unreachably distant and uninvolved in the struggles of Elves and Men. *The Silmarillion* tells how the Ainur arrived in Arda and became part of the world (after which time they are called the Valar). There they labored to build it, rule it and guide its development. But to say they "rule" Arda is not quite right. They are loath to use their power to coerce anyone or anything, and most of the time they just let be.

I am reminded of a most unusual film by Wim Wenders called *Wings of Desire*. This film has always reminded me of Tolkien's Valar in a way that no other film or book filled with overt magic has ever done. *Wings of Desire* does not refer to Middle-earth in any way and is set in present-day Berlin. But angels overlook the city, silently, solemnly, with endless patience. The camera swoops between single lives and multitudes, and faces are alight with the mystery and wonder of humanity on the grandest scale. Hollywood remakes have seized on the least important element of this film, the plot, in which an angel falls in love with one person rather than all humanity and resolves to become corporeal. The remakes miss the dreamlike serenity and reverence of the original. The angels, like Tolkien's Valar, exist to bear witness. They have been there since the beginning of time, and like the Valar, they don't fully know the future or their god's plan for the world. They describe their surprise and delight when the first human beings ran across the savannah towards them, shouting the first words of language they had ever heard spoken. Humans, with their chaotic freedom and mysterious fate, are infinitely fascinating to the angels.

In the film, the angels pass unseen through the busy human lives around them, turning from one stream of consciousness to another like a radio listener flicking between stations. Sometimes they lay a consolatory hand on a lonely shoulder or put their arms around a dying person. That person might feel a mysterious lightening of spirit for a moment—or they might feel nothing. The angels record moments of kindness and joy, keeping an accounting that has lasted thousands of years. But they cannot intervene in the lives of the people they watch over—except very rarely.

Tolkien's Valar seem to watch and love the Children of Ilúvatar in the same way. Why are they so powerless to protect them? One of the things that constrains them is their own goodness. They are reluctant to risk destroying *any* of the good and innocent even if it is the only way to defeat the greater evils of Melkor and Sauron, who are bound by no such restrictions. Evil can act recklessly to pursue its own desires, whereas Good has to intervene with great care.

The "Ainulindalë" in *The Silmarillion* nibbles around the edges of that problem. The wars with Melkor have thrown the earth into such an upheaval that the Valar fear all life may be extinguished if they continue fighting. As it is, they could only attack Melkor and chain him up again once the Elves had been discovered on Middle-earth and it was known where they were. During that cataclysmic war, a protection was laid on the area around Cuiviénen where the Elves first dwelt, and the ruptures and tempests of the great war passed them by. In later times, once Elves and Men had spread over much of Middle-earth, it was very difficult to make war on Melkor without many innocent deaths. Much later, at the petition of Eärendil, the Valar finally did come out and overthrow Melkor. Tolkien does not speak of the casualties among noncombatants, but there must have been many, for the world was changed by the fury of the battle, with the sea pouring in through chasms, the northern regions torn asunder, rivers changed, mountains flattened and the land of Sirion gone forever. Perhaps the Valar always knew that this terrible battle must happen, but they put it off as long as they could, awaiting the sign or a call that released them to act.

For much of Middle-earth's history, then, the Valar stay in Valinor, which they have made into a paradise of light and beauty. To the creatures left in Middle-earth, it must have seemed like a grave and hopeless desertion. The inertia of the Valar looks terribly similar to complacency, because whatever their reasons, the actual state of affairs is that the Valar are living in a safe and beautiful pleasure garden while the small frail creatures of Middle-earth live in fear of Melkor and later Sauron.

In order that people continue hoping and working for some ultimate good in a world where there is much magic but few miracles, it seems necessary for the Valar to leave symbols and secret signs for people to follow. There had to be a way that people could have knowledge of the Valar, or at least a conscience guiding them towards Good. People could steer a course through their lives if they paid attention to those distant voices. Even if they didn't know what they were or where they came from, people could recognize them. These signs existed in the light, the air, and especially the waters of Middle-earth.

At the beginning of *The Silmarillion,* Tolkien describes the making of Arda, of which Middle-earth is a part. He tells how the angelic Ainur first see the world that they built with their great song, the world that Eru then brought into being. Interestingly, their initial delight and wonder at its colors and forms is tempered by disquiet when they behold the roaring sea. The same disquiet they feel when they regard Ilúvatar's second children, the Men whose changefulness and free will turns them so often astray.

The sea has its own music. The Eldar say in *The Silmarillion* (p. 19), "in water there lives yet the echo of the Music of the Ainur more than in any substance else that is in this Earth; and many of the Children of Ilúvatar hearken still unsated to the voices of the Sea, and yet know not for what they listen." In all of Tolkien's writings, the sound of it and even the smell of it seems to bear a message. We're all familiar with Legolas's talk of gulls and sea-yearning in *The Lord of the Rings*. He says that the sea-longing lives deep in the heart of all his kin. But it's not just the Elves who are stirred by the sea. To the Ainur themselves it is a source of fascination—and unease. I find it interesting how the action of water—and the spirit of Ulmo, the Lord of Waters—moves through Middle-earth and speaks to its inhabitants.

Of the three main symbols that serve Good, air and light act in more straightforward ways than water. Light is the obvious symbol for good. In Tolkien, so many of the characters have a light shining about them either by their nature (remember the Gildor's company of Elves in the Shire, with a glimmering like moonrise that falls about their feet as they walk?) or at moments of power and inspiration. The light of stars is especially important, most of all to the Elves. The stars were kindled by Varda Elentári before the Sun and Moon were created, and she placed bright new constellations in the sky to announce the war against Melkor. In that time the Elves awoke in the place of their creation, and they loved the stars from the first. The Seven Stars that the Númenoreans and the Men of Westernesse take as their insignia form the constellation Valacirca, the Sickle. It is the crown of stars that Varda put high in the northern sky before the war in which the Valar chained Melkor. The Light of Eärendil is an important symbol that wards off evil too. The star that Eärendil bears, which is both a Silmaril and the Evening Star, was set in place to symbolize the Valar's intervention in the War of Wrath against Melkor.

The leader of the Valar is Manwë, and he is Lord of the Air. In *The Silmarillion,* Tolkien tells us about Manwë's power over and knowledge of all things of the air—the winds, the clouds, and all strong-flying birds, most especially the eagles. Now, of all the miraculous pieces of good luck that happen in Middle-earth, it's surprising how many of them are brought about by eagles. In *The Silmarillion,* Fingon prays to Manwë when he sees how hopelessly his kinsman Maedhros is imprisoned. It is Manwë's eagle that lifts Fingon up the mountainside to release him. Eagles watch and help guard the borders of the hidden city of Gondolin, and as Turgon's people flee from the sack of that city, eagles help drive off the Balrog that attacks them. Again the eagles appear in time to rescue Beren and Luthien outside the walls of Morgoth's citadel when they have taken the Silmaril from there. A massed phalanx of eagles appears as a sign and a warning in the last days of Númenor.

These eagles continue their unpredictable involvement into the Third Age. They rescue Bilbo, Gandalf and the Dwarves from being burnt to death by orcs and Wargs in *The Hobbit,* and they turn the tide in the Battle of Five Armies at the Lonely Mountain. In *The Lord of the Rings*, they rescue Gandalf from the tower of Orthanc where Saruman has him imprisoned and from the peak of Celebdil after he kills the Balrog. Finally they take Sam and Frodo off the side of Mount Doom after the Quest is finished. Of all the good fortune and help that is given in Middle-earth, it seems to me that the Eagles are the most unpredictable. They are indeed the *deus ex machina* and almost the only one that is allowed to intervene so directly at dire need. I get the feeling that these eagle interventions were too rare to be relied upon: the Middle-earth equivalent of Moses parting the Red Sea. Just sometimes, when a person had struggled against evil with all their strength, the Eagles might come and tip the balance in their favor. Ordinary people couldn't hope for such rescues very often. However the knowledge that occasionally miracles *can* happen helped people know that their efforts against Sauron and Morgoth *meant* something.

But even when not rescued outright by agents of the Valar, the people of Middle-earth are not completely alone. At other times there are subtler forms of help that we might ascribe to the Valar. For instance, could Manwë have caused the change in the wind that Ghân-buri-Ghân smells in the air, before the Battle of the Pelennor Fields? Not only is the wind changing—when Wídfara confirms the change in the wind a while later, he tells Théoden that it carries the sea-tang. Is even the smell of the sea a message of hope? It's noticeable how everyone's heart is lifted by that wind driving back the dark clouds out of Mordor. Everyone gets the message, if message it is: the Riders of Rohan, massing to charge, and the two hobbits far away in Mordor. They all feel a moment of hope, and it affects the way they act.

Water is the third symbol of good, and it is governed by Ulmo. Through it Ulmo is aware of and present to the people of Middle-earth, and I think his presence is more constant and reliable than any other. When Tolkien writes about water, very often there is magic nearby.

When Ilúvatar showed the created world of Arda to the Valar, Ulmo was the one who took it upon himself to study and understand as much as he could about water, the mysterious and changeable element. Ulmo was also the Valar to whom Eru taught the most about music. From then on, Ulmo delighted in the ability of water to make music. Fountains, streams, rain, and the sea itself—Tolkien writes of them as though they had each a voice and a song. In Tolkien's imagination, music has the power to create—it is the foundation of the creation of Middle-earth and it upholds the power of all the magic in it. Water has its own varied music, and it is also free and difficult to confine. It seeps through the smallest crack, wafts away as vapor, tears up rocks and hillsides as a flood, and freezes solid as ice. Thus it has both freedom and power.

Again and again in *The Silmarillion,* Tolkien mentions how Ulmo's spirit spreads secretly through Middle-earth and how he refused to abandon Men and Elves to their fate. At times he would travel to the shore or even up the rivers of Middle-earth to make music on his great horns of shell, and the sound filled people with longing for the sea. More often he would speak with the voice of water, "For all seas, lakes, rivers, fountains and springs are in his government." (*The Silmarillion,* p. 27.) Even when Melkor appeared to have dominated Middle-earth entirely, Ulmo's power "...coursed still through many secret lodes, and the Earth did not die; and to all who were lost in that darkness or wandered far from the light of the Valar the ear of Ulmo was ever open..." (*The Silmarillion,* p. 40) Whereas for his part Melkor hated the sea, and his creatures would not use it to travel upon. "Water all his servants shunned, and to the sea none would willingly draw nigh." (*The Silmarillion,* p. 120.) Thus the Elves were never attacked from the Sea.

And on the other side, when Tolkien wants to show us that evil has really gained control, he shows us places where water is defiled and polluted. The foul pool where the Watcher in the Water lives should warn us of the state of affairs within Moria. Around Mordor the water is foul, oily and full of scum if it exists at all. The hobbits feel it as a terrible desecration of the natural order of things, and it troubles them as a terrible sign of evil. They encounter it again when they return home to the Shire and find that Ted Sandyman has the new Mill pouring filth into The Water.

And where water is absent? The very dryness of Mordor is an evil, and the sea in the middle of it, which has no outlet to the open ocean, is described as "bitter," "dark," and "sad." One feels that the voice of Ulmo cannot reach across the desert to the landlocked Sea of Núrnen.

Going back in history a little more: The sound of water was the first thing the Elves heard in the moment of their creation at Cuiviénen, so they loved it as they loved the stars they saw there first. Water was a familiar voice to them, a secret messenger that they heard before any of the other Valar found them. Ulmo seems to have wanted the Elves to stay in Middle-earth and receive more protection there. He spoke against the plan to have the Elves migrate to Valinor for protection instead. (*The Silmarillion,* p. 52.) He was overruled in this, but continued being the secret helper to those who remained or were exiled there. He guided Turgon to the place where he would build the hidden city of Gondolin, and the waters of the river Sirion protected it, for Ulmo's power was there also. Ulmo planned to send a messenger to warn Turgon when the city was no longer safe. Tuor was that messenger, and he was guided by the sea-longing in his heart until he found the deserted Elven city of Nevrast on the shore. There Ulmo spoke and sent him to Gondolin at last. But Turgon ignored the warning, though it came from Ulmo himself. Once again, the Valar could only let the Children of Ilúvatar ruin themselves—they would not constrain their free will to make choices, whether for good or ill.

When Varda made the Sun and Moon, the first Men awoke in Middle-earth. The new light was for their protection too, but none of the Valar came to them to teach them about the world—except Ulmo, who sent messages to them along the waters. Men did not understand the messages, yet their hearts were stirred by the water nevertheless.

And water remained in some circumstances magical, and throughout *The Lord of the Rings* it's worth paying attention whenever water is mentioned. A real journey from Hobbiton starts once one is across the Water, and a journey from the Shire once one has crossed the Brandywine. As Sam crosses on the ferry for the first time, Tolkien records his strange feeling that his old life is falling away to lie in the mists behind him and some dark, dangerous future lies in wait on the opposite bank. But the river is more than a dividing line—it's the place where Drogo Baggins and his wife drowned, leaving Frodo an orphan—and thus free to become Bilbo's heir.

There is another reason that Frodo should inherit Bilbo's Ring and become part of the chain of circumstances that destroy it. He has, according to Tolkien, always had dreams and visions, even when he was just living quietly in the Shire. Sometimes he dreamed of mountains that he had never seen, sometimes of things that were really happening far away (as in the House of Tom Bombadil, where he dreams of Gandalf on top of Orthanc, though he doesn't realize that is what it is), but most interestingly, he dreams of the Sea, which he has never seen. It's mentioned right at the end of the chapter "A Conspiracy Unmasked," and we're told that the sound of the sea had *often* come into his dreams. In Middle-earth terms, if Frodo was born hearing the voice of Ulmo, he must surely be singled out for some special fate.

How strange that the Ring should have traveled to the roots of the mountains where it lay so long forgotten until Bilbo found it! But maybe not so strange, if you consider that Ulmo's power was surely in the River Anduin where it fell, and that it was Ulmo's streams that Gollum followed until they brought him to his cave under the Misty Mountains. Somehow, a power was working to remove the Ring from where it could do harm for a long time. That power could have been Ulmo.

Water collaborates in the magic of Gandalf and Elrond when they raise the river against the Ringwraiths outside Rivendell, and the river is under Elrond's power—one of the forces that protects Rivendell. Gandalf's added touch—the white horses of foam—look like a nod to the Greek sea-god Poseidon, for horses were his creatures according to Greek myth. Ulmo is a kind of Poseidon figure in Tolkien's mythology. As for Rivendell itself, the roaring of a waterfall is the first thing Frodo hears when he awakes in the House of Elrond, and the sound of water pervades every corner of the place like the unseasonal summer scent of trees and flowers. Wherever the hobbits walk, they hear the waters of the River Bruinen running through Rivendell: it may be part of the power that protects it.

Other characters openly use the power of water. Galadriel carries Nenya, the Ring of Adamant. But in the Appendices of *The Silmarillion,* we are told that Nenya is also the Ring of Water. And Lothlórien is bounded by rivers—the Anduin on one side, Nimrodel and the Silverlode on another. When the Fellowship crosses the Nimrodel, Frodo feels his weariness wash away—there is some power in the water. When he crosses over the Silverlode, he feels as if he is walking in a place that no longer exists. The sense of sundered time occurs again as their boat bears them down the Silverlode out of Lothlórien. The river is a demarcation point, and magic surrounds it.

When Sam and Frodo look in the Mirror of Galadriel, she works the magic of her visions in a hedged garden with a silver stream fed by a fountain. They are under the light of Eärendil, the evening star. The Mirror is filled with water from the stream. Thus two powerful symbols are there at once: starlight (and Earendil's star is a particularly powerful one) and water.

Much later when Sam and Frodo are alone in Mordor, darkness oppresses them and thirst torments them. Sam wishes Galadriel could hear them now—he'd petition her for a bit of light and some water, and that would be better than any jewels. Soon after, they see the wind rise up and turn back Sauron's pall of darkness, and not long after, they come across a small trickle of precious water. It's like a prayer answered. To Sam, maybe Galadriel is as much a "higher power" as he can know or understand. But in Tolkien's mind, maybe Sam's prayer is heard by Manwë himself, who foreknew and sent down a sweetly falling rain where it would reach the hobbits, forlorn in the Dark Land.

Water spills freely around Tom Bombadil's house too, for the Withywindle tumbles past it as a small stream. As indeed it should—Tom's wife Goldberry is no less than the *daughter* of the River! She can sing down the rain—Bombadil calls it "Goldberry's washing day." Nobody has ever settled for once and for all whether Goldberry and Bombadil are Maiar or not. But we know that the Valar have Maiar that attend them, and not all of them are named. Tolkien tells us of Ulmo's vassal Ossë, who governs the seas of Middle-earth, but there may well be other Maiar with Ulmo who govern the freshwater streams. And we know from the story of Melian and Thingol that sometimes the Maiar have children. Perhaps that is Goldberry's story. In any case, she is there in Middle-earth—magical and good, though her power seems limited to her small river domain. For the hobbits on their dangerous quest, Goldberry and Bombadil's help does more than dispel the immediate danger. The knowledge that they might encounter mysterious and powerful allies along the way must help them to continue when their courage is flagging.

Other "good" characters in Middle-earth value water, and it's often a big element of where they choose to live. The Ents build their homes around water, making springs, pools and waterfalls a central feature. Bregalad and Treebeard go out of their way to get wet and take delight in it. The waterfall that conceals Faramir's hideout in Ithilien seems almost magical, especially when the westering sun turns it into a curtain of rubies. Gondor is built around a fountain, in the court of the White Tree, and Tolkien says that in the reign of Aragorn, the city was regenerated with the planting of trees—and more fountains. These are all places where the fight against evil continues.

Light, air and water: three simple things we all need to live. Tolkien made these common things into symbols and messages of hope. Throughout all his work, air, light and water are subtle forces that encourage and guide the inhabitants of Middle-earth who are paying attention.

It's nice to look out the window at the rain and think of it as more than an annoying wetness. It's much better to see it as Tolkien wanted us to see it: as a sign of life and regeneration. The awareness of beauty and meaning in simple things is one of the great gifts Tolkien gave us to carry around in the everyday world. And so I walk out to the creek and listen with pleasure to its great roar.

Sources:

J.R.R. Tolkien, *The Lord of the Rings,* Houghton Mifflin 1-volume edition 1987/2001.

J.R.R. Tolkien, *The Silmarillion,* Houghton Mifflin Hardback 1977.

Palantiri and Rings of Power: Obsession in the Round

Anwyn

The assumption is that the Ring is completely irresistible, that it will eventually and always be in control. Yet of the characters who handle it in the course of *The Lord of the Rings,* one resists its effects for nearly a full year while carrying it closer and closer to the source of its power, one wields it seemingly unaffected but for a brief vision that he writes off as "only a trick," and one refuses to touch it at all save once, to verify its identity.

But this same Ring produces obsession, madness, and unbridled aggression in three more characters who to their chagrin do not handle the Ring, except the one who hurtles with it into death.

The assumption is that the Palantiri are completely irresistible, that they will eventually and always be in control. Yet of the characters who handle them in the course of *The Lord of the Rings,* one uses his only as a projectile weapon, one is involved only in a brief fling brought on by curiosity, and one wrenches the stone to his will.

But these same Palantiri produce obsession, madness, and unbridled despair in two more characters who think they are in control until the end, including one who takes his with him to his death.

Critics frequently complain of the lack of psychological complexity in *The Lord of the Rings*—black is evil, white is good, and nary the twain shall meet. Yet White is broken and replaced, Black can serve as a camouflage, and there is a wide range of human characterization to be found in the responses each character gives the Ring or a Palantir.

We once received a question from a reader that really struck me. It ran along the lines of, "If everybody succumbs to the Ring eventually, how could the Council ever have had the ghost of a hope that Frodo could complete the Quest?" Gandalf reminds us that it was supposedly only a fool's hope—and yet they sent him anyway. What could they have known about Frodo beforehand that would lead them to do this? The surprising answer is: nothing. You might say they were desperate. Elrond, Gandalf, Glorfindel, Cirdan, and others of the Council sought an end to an ages-old evil, an object that had power and life and self-awareness of its own, and they knew its power well enough that *not one of them dared handle it*. Moreover, each of them had the will to stick with that decision. Gandalf, after his initial testing of it, refused to touch it any more to the point where he would not even hand Frodo the envelope Bilbo had left it in. They knew that it was out of the question for one of them to attempt the task; power frequently begets power, and Gandalf says right out that with the power of the Ring, he would be beyond control.

We also know that there was at least one being over whom the Ring had no power whatsoever. Tom Bombadil plays with the Ring as with a toy. But Tom's very immunity makes him an improper keeper for the Ring. In order that the Ring not do damage to others, one must keep it who has control over it—and for that kind of control, it is necessary for the Ring to have at least an elementary hold on one's mind, so that the keeper always knows where it is.

What is the power that the Ring presents in such great measure to the Wise and which has no lure for Tom? Simply power for its own sake. The Wise walk a fine line: they are powerful, and yet they must use their power for the good of the land and for others or risk ultimate corruption. With the Ring, their power would be redoubled and that corruption no longer resistible. Tom already has all the power he could desire—and has deliberately limited his sphere of influence himself; perhaps through a kind of boredom with unbounded freedom, he has decided to stay within one patch of earth and niggle with the details there. Frodo, then, is a gentle medium. A humble hobbit, without desire for power over others, with enough native strength of his own to resist corruption, at least for a time.

This begs the question, of course, "Why Frodo *specifically*?" Why not Sam? Why not Merry? Leaving aside the bits about Frodo being *meant* to have the Ring for the moment, which is of course the ultimate answer, Frodo exhibits enough of the steady, medium qualities that would make him most likely to resist the Ring the longest. Sam is almost *too* humble. He is like Tom in that the Ring would not necessarily have enough control over him to make him a safe guardian, and in any case Sam's primary purpose is to serve. Merry or any of the other hobbits? Well, shall we consider the fate of one hobbitlike person who did take the Ring for many long years?

We are told that Smeagol once lived above the earth, under the sun and moon, and in the presence of friends and family. A good little river-hobbit, eh? But the presence of friends and family does not automatically confer character on a person. Smeagol fell to the lure of the Ring in scarcely an eyeblink. From the moment he saw it, he coveted it, and within minutes of seeing it, he committed murder to possess it. Murder of his so-called friend, no less. From that act, there was no looking back. What was in Smeagol that made him so different from Frodo though they were of the same heritage?

"Logic! What *do* they teach them at these schools?" I have yet another club to wield over those who claim that Tolkien lacks human subtlety. Clearly, the primary difference between Frodo and Smeagol, between *any* healthy person and *any* addict, is the ability to resist addiction. I will not here debate the nature vs. nurture argument—whether or not some people are hardwired for addiction and for others, addictions just naturally don't take. It's inflammatory and it's moot in this context. What matters is that for whatever reason—natural depravity or conscious choice—Frodo is able to resist, and Smeagol is not. Sam is able to resist, and Boromir, another person of power for whom more power would corrupt, is not. Somehow I hear Nancy Reagan's "Just Say No" ringing in my ears. But is it that simple?

Another Tolkien-created object that inspires addiction in some and resistance in others is the mysterious palantir. Again we have ostentatious examples of completely different reactions to the same object. Aragorn, with the strength of his kingly will, makes the stone bow to his will. Denethor, with the bitterness of his steward's lot, despairs that matters in Gondor will ever improve. And Pippin, with the curiosity of a hobbit in his tweens, gives us the greatest example of Tolkien's position on addiction and human choice. When Pippin steals the stone, it is a brief trespass. Gandalf finds him out, removes the stone, and then says the words that must end forever any supposition that Tolkien does not understand the complexities of human psychology. He tells Pippin that longings such as his for the stone *can be cured*. Moreover, that to achieve this cure, Pippin must *tell* of his problem and *ask* for help! Hark! I hear the sound of 20th-century therapy and rehabilitation echoing in the language of what is essentially a 19th-century author! Denethor's pride and his inability to share with others, to allow others to help him bear his burdens, led to his obsession and madness at the hands of the stone. Pippin, were he to be further troubled with "palantir withdrawal," had only to ask for help, and it would be given. Thankfully, in his case, it was not necessary; curiosity did not kill the cat, as it has with so many drug-addicted teenagers in our society today.

So why *did* the Council think that Frodo could stand the strain of carrying the Ring but not succumbing to it? Perhaps they knew the innate strength of all hobbits—no, not all hobbits; there is still Smeagol. Perhaps they knew the innate strength of Frodo—no, he had already shown even he was not wholly immune to the Ring's call. Perhaps—just perhaps—they didn't really believe he could do it at all, but knew he was their best chance at staving off the end of their game.

We can compare Frodo's journey to Mordor to a person being given a grain or two of cocaine, say, per day, against his will and without his consent. In the end, of course, the addiction to cocaine will win by sheer physical law; in our world, it is the choice not to take the cocaine to start with that separates addicts from healthy persons. But Frodo, though his free choice would have been to resist the responsibility of the Ring, had to take it because he was the only one who could resist these tiny grains of cocaine, so to speak, long enough to see some good done. And as we see played out time and again each time we read the book through, in the end the sheer physical law of the Ring's power overwhelmed Frodo till his will could no longer resist. But before that happened, he had made it far enough that the goal was in sight, and *he had help* to make it back from the brink. Unwitting help in Smeagol, and unfailing help in Sam.

People, whether humans, elves, wizards, or hobbits, have natures that make them more or less prone to addiction, to obsession, to unhealthy behavior of all kinds. And by the way, there's nothing saying Frodo wouldn't have had more trouble with some other form of temptation than he did with the Ring! He happened to be fairly resistant to the Ring, but another lure might have done him in. Human nature, and hobbit nature, is not just one way or the other. It is in knowing our own nature, and in choosing accordingly, that we escape the traps or are drawn in, to the hurt of ourselves and others. It is in knowing ourselves and allowing others to know us—as Gandalf knew Frodo and Pippin—that we can stand up against horrifying downfalls and pits laid to trap us. Help is always there, if we but seek.

"I, Orc"

Quickbeam

We have read all about Orcs in Tolkien's books, certainly leading the youngest among us to have nightmares about the "scary orc hiding under the bed." They sing a great deal of the time in the Rankin/Bass cartoons, like a chorus line on Broadway. We've read the details in *Dungeons & Dragons* books—where Orcs can serve as stalwart player-characters in the game. All good Tolkien fans knows their Moria goblins from their Uruk-hai. But what have we really learned about Orcs as a race? After all these years, I still have a few unanswered questions.

What kind of society did Orcs have? How did the light of individuality shine on a single Orc? Is such a notion even possible?

The basic concepts of sociology have never been applied to the Orcish denizens of Middle-earth, as far as I can tell. There are desperately few clues in the text to support the idea of a unique Orc society. But there is enough to start some healthy debate. And if there is one thing Ringers love to do...

Fast-tracking through the history lesson: According to the published version of *The Silmarillion*, Orcs originated when Melkor/Morgoth captured some of the earliest Elves that first appeared in Arda. Maybe he captured a considerable number of them, trotting them off to Utumno in the north. By the evil arts of magic, torture, and exposing them to the horrors of his power, the first Dark Lord corrupted them over time, twisting them into a different breed. After the completion of *The Lord of the Rings*, the Professor went back to the subject of Orcs and struggled to reconcile their origin with his later thoughts on the most basic "mythic structures" of his secondary world. In *The History of Middle-earth, Vol. X, Morgoth's Ring*, we learn that Tolkien considered

Orcs coming from a base stock of Men instead. He even considered that Melkor/Morgoth merely started the job, leaving Sauron to finish with the details. Here's a shocking idea—perhaps their origin began with lesser Maiar spirits corrupted early in the game. But these decisions were never finalized. The Orcs' existence mocked the creations of Eru, just as Melkor intended. Orcs were no longer Elves (or Men or Maia) when placed within the stories. They were base monsters.

Tolkien went further by limiting what could happen with a community of monsters, sociologically speaking. Orcs were slaves and soldiers for the Enemy—bred to hold hatred against all things. That was their main pattern of accepted behavior, a behavior all other Orcs understood: Kill, Burn, Destroy, Loot to Survive, Torture for Fun. Now what kind of a blueprint for living is that? It is essentially a negation of everything *human*. Your sociology teacher might say: "Without culture, society would not function." For the Snaga, Uruks, and other breeds of leathery, cannibalistic, fanged, bow-legged, treacherous, and homicidal Orcs, there was hardly a scratch of real culture beyond the hatred in their black hearts.

In terms of *learned social behavior*, Orcs created a spinning history of ongoing hate that was self-fulfilling. One could argue that their intense capacity and execution of evil acts was not learned at all. How strong the evidence that it's in their very nature! Tolkien considered this point a great deal. Perhaps the spirit of Morgoth was somehow infused into them. Contrast the innate evil of Orcs with our society, where human life is valued. We have an instant guideline for our behavior. Since Orcs don't value any life at all, the concepts of societal structure just don't hold up.

Other questions about Orcs still linger. Did they breed like other mammals? Were there female Orcs? It seems that way, yes, but we don't know for sure. Did Sauron run a "mad scientist" laboratory underneath Utumno? A case of genetic splicing run amok? Test-tube Orcs crawling out of holes in the walls? Again, we are left to assume. Tolkien himself remained far from conclusive.

Somehow these monsters were not wholly unreasoning "animals" unable to think for themselves. They possessed speech, though not much by way of original language was to come from them. Of course creatures like crows and Wargs have speech, too, as do the "dull and lumpish" trolls who originally had "no more language than beasts" but had been taught some language. And speaking of language, Tolkien uses it to show the fragmentary nature of Orcish society, displayed in their bastardized bits of dialect here and there. They didn't record any of their own history that we know of. They did form packs and "tribes" when not directly in thrall under a Dark Lord, with mismatched linguistic structures within each, no doubt. But Tolkien says the tribes of the Misty Mountains had their own capital in Mount Gundabad. So at one point, it seems, Orcs had a rudimentary template of society, fractured one from the other, feuding and desperate.

Fear was often used to fuel their hate. There you have Morgoth's methods in a nutshell. Sauron's too. The Orcs feared their masters with every fiber in their being, and it was enough to control their self-destructive tendencies. It was no small feat that Sauron managed to later create a functioning army out of them, made from different tribes and assembled groups that would normally slice each other to bits. The cohesion born of their fear would sometimes dissipate, as it happened in Cirith Ungol, where they mostly did themselves in before Sam arrived at the front gate.

There's something to learn from the two Orcs who track the hobbits in the chapter "The Land of Shadow." After escaping from Shagrat's Tower, our heroes are almost cornered by a tracker and a fighter-orc in the Morgai valley. The orcs threaten each other. The larger one would report to the Nazgûl the tracker's name and number, in an effort to quell his "rebel talk." So we know there was a numbering system for Sauron's slaves. There was evidently an ongoing problem with rebellious orcs and deserters. I would bet that working in the human resources department of Mordor was probably the worst job imaginable. What a mess!

Is that the extent of an orc's social status? A number? I've read in the books about Orcish differentiation by military rank. Some held positions of authority assigned to them. The larger Uruks always seemed dominant over the smaller breeds. But the complexities stop there. Theirs is no more "society" than a pack of wolves—except wolves are more likely to cooperate with their own. In reality, we humans have many ways of stratifying social groups. Mostly based on a hierarchy—the stratum each person falls into will greatly affect their life chances to achieve things desirable by society. But I just can't see how this applies to Orcs the same way.

The most fascinating conversation between these creatures, where Tolkien lets them actually talk to each other at length (this doesn't happen much in *LotR*) is the one between Shagrat and Gorbag. Remember all that dialogue? We learn heaps about the separation of Sauron's forces and Shelob's eating habits. But we also see a tiny shade of individuality coming across. These two fellows seem to have individual thoughts of self-preservation. Gorbag enthuses that he and his buddy could make off, without any "big bosses" telling them what to do. With a few "trusty lads" they could walk free in the world, just like the good old days. They are slaves to the Eye, but hate their Master beyond measure, and therefore these Orcs show they are not mindless automatons. They somehow want to be free. This is a very odd thing indeed for a race characterized as "homogenized evil" by many of Tolkien's critics.

Yes, critics have complained about the way Tolkien uses Orcs as disposable adversaries. They are just faceless guys who take a hit during the big "action sequences." A Trekkie would refer to them as "red shirts." George Lucas used armies of anonymous stormtroopers, later extending the idea by showing us they were just clones under those faceless helmets. The Sardaukar terror troops from Frank Herbert's *Dune* more resemble Orcs than anything else I've seen in genre fiction. Armies without souls. Unquestioning. Hundreds of thousands of them. But we know that Orcs are not exactly like that.

The finest line is drawn in the sand here. Orcs straddle that line, it seems to me. They are monsters, devoid of any moral sense. They are also thinking, rational, real individuals, and they even posses a kind of "future-sense" about themselves. But the only thoughts they bear are evil. They would never show mercy or kindness for anything. *Any* living thing. It is truly horrific to imagine a creature, strong and brutal and ruthless, who has no compunction. No shred of "humanity" to be found within—but somewhere in his *Letters* Tolkien also suggests that Orcs are little (or no?) worse than the worst of humanity. We see here the fulfillment of Melkor's greatest malice towards the Children of Ilúvatar. Corrupted from the unfortunate first Elves, Orcs are the ultimate perversion of Life itself—something so beautiful twisted into something so ghoulish. Maybe they are a spiritual vacuum. Maybe the Enemy found a way eradicate the Orcs' very souls. Imagine the nightmare of the Eldar: To be pitted against soulless fiends who are the antithesis of their own existence. It makes me shiver.

Do Orcs even have souls? Could they be immortal too, considering their origin? These are metaphysical questions I cannot answer.

Tolkien was undecided on this for years, and *Morgoth's Ring* is filled with the different directions of his thought.

At least we know one thing with certainty—they don't break out into song and dance numbers as they march to war.

War and Peace: The Battle Cry of Tolkien

Anwyn

The trenches of 1916 were a hard place to learn war. Death not at the end of a missile trajectory, but at arm's length; close acquaintance not with computerized weapons technology but with the bayonet; deployment not to a peacekeeping force or to patrol duty, but to the front lines of defense against a determined invader with designs of conquest. J.R.R. Tolkien, a man of imaginative vision, depth of soul, and sensitivity of feeling, watched his comrades blown literally into pieces, saw the filth of trench life, and felt firsthand the bitter irony of the killing of his fellow men with whom he had no personal quarrel, men who, like himself, were following the orders of their government. With the utmost deference to our modern armed forces and respect for the missions they carry out, I submit however that far fewer of the world's fighting men today are called upon to witness scenes of horror such as those that presented themselves in the older style of warfare. Is it any wonder that Tolkien should have emerged from his war experiences, after the deaths of two of his three closest friends, somewhat in conflict about the nature and justice of war?

We see this conflict played out in many forms, both in his letters to his children serving in World War II, in the comments of his biographer Humphrey Carpenter, and, of great interest to us, in the characters of *The Lord of the Rings*. Though Carpenter has well recounted Tolkien's dislike of the school of literary "criticism" that proposed to plumb the depths of an author's works by examining that author's biography, the reverse, the process of shedding light on an author's life experiences by looking for the meaning in his writings, has a certain value that cannot be discounted. Tolkien himself knew that his writing sprang from the wells of his experiences as well as his imagination, and he talked often of the great tree whose roots were founded down in the dark mould of experiences taken in, composted, and allowed to sift together and recombine until not even he knew what might next rise to the top. Certainly his seemingly several views of war and peace were rooted in his experiences in the war as well as his intellectual judgments of the world around him.

So what are these conflicts of Tolkien's? Most obvious is the quandary of many if not most reasonable people: the desire for peace and safety against the defense of "life, liberty, and the pursuit of happiness." Add to that a belief in the justice of one's position against a hatred of the atomic bomb ("fighting Sauron with the Ring") and of air battles ("infernal combustion engines")—essentially a thoughtful concern for the rightness of the battle vs. a perceived wrongness of the method of fighting it—and a deep natural melancholy that colored all of Tolkien's opinions, and a picture begins to emerge of a cautious moderate, a man who believed in justice and freedom but knew firsthand the costs, sometimes, of obtaining them.

After the battle of Helm's Deep, Saruman and Théoden had words to the effect that the war was all Théoden's fault, that Saruman certainly did not desire it, that moreover he desires peace. Théoden's response is sterling: that they will indeed have peace when Saruman and all his works are no more. What stands out like a beacon from this passage is Tolkien's rejection of the "peace at any price" dogma. Éomer comments on Saruman's words, saying that the trapped prey would speak to the predator thus if he could. Thus also would many a dictator and invader speak to his victims: if you go to war against me, it's not because I desired it! No doubt he did not desire it! Clearly Saruman's preference, as the preference of Hitler, of Wilhelm, of Napoleon, of King George III, would have been for Théoden to have sat in Meduseld ignoring his enemy's encroachment until it was too late and Saruman would have gained dominion over the lands of Rohan and undoubtedly would have tried to spread his influence to Gondor. By implying that Théoden himself could have prevented war, Saruman is simply saying in effect "If you had let me take over as I wanted, none of your people would have been killed." But even that is a lie; before Théoden ever lifted a hand, Saruman's orcs had been at work burning and killing in the fields of Rohan. Thus the words of a traitor and a liar. Tolkien knows, and tells us through Théoden, the truth of the old words that those who buy peace with their freedom shall have neither freedom nor peace.

Contrast Théoden's hard-won knowledge of this fact with Frodo's position at the end of *The Return of the King*. When it becomes clear that the Shire has been occupied while Frodo, Sam, Pippin and Merry were gone, Frodo is adamant that even if it comes to fighting, the killing is to be kept to a bare minimum, that he himself will take no part in it, and that at the end of all, Lotho Sackville-Baggins and even Saruman and Wormtongue are to be spared, at least spared any actions of his.

Compare this outlook of Frodo's with the beginning of *Fellowship*, where he complains to Gandalf that Bilbo did not kill Gollum when he had the chance! Frodo has undergone a great change in the course of the book, much as Tolkien's own experiences in WWI shaped him: after having seen death and destruction firsthand, Frodo now desires to prevent it as much as possible. But make no mistake: despite his "no-killing" policy, Frodo was able to accept the loss of life, both ruffian and hobbit, in defense of the Shire. Tolkien tells us his part in the battle was preventing the hobbits, "in their wrath at their losses, from slaying those of their enemies who threw down their weapons." It seems perfectly clear that what Frodo abhorred most was *unnecessary* or *cold-blooded* killing. Thus his attitude towards Saruman and Wormtongue: despite the injuries done by them to the Shire, he was willing to let them depart in peace, if they would. Even after Saruman attempted to stab Frodo himself, Frodo still would have allowed mercy, though Sam and the other hobbits did not. It is entirely open to question whether or not, if Frodo had not been wearing the mithril coat that turned Saruman's blade, he would have drawn sword to defend himself. These passages seem quite a struggle between Tolkien's belief in justice (i.e. defense against attack, with death for the attacker if need be) and his earnest desire to avoid killing. Wishful thinking, perhaps? Idealization of the real world (the thought that perhaps Saruman and Wormtongue would depart in peace) mixed with the bitter reality of human nature (Saruman's attempted stabbing and Wormtongue's actual killing of the wizard)? Regardless, Frodo clearly presents a second face of Tolkien's views of fighting.

And Tolkien gives us a third on the fields of the Pelennor. When he describes the coming of the Rohirrim to the City of Gondor, he says they *sang* as they slew, for the *joy* of battle was upon them. How's *that* for a change from Frodo's sad earnestness?

A partial answer to all these conflicts lies in Humphrey Carpenter's excellent biography of Tolkien's friends, *The Inklings*. In an imaginary conversation between the friends where their lines are taken from their writings, both published and unpublished, the Inklings discuss pacifism, most repudiating the doctrine of "peace at any price" and going on to state that one irritating outgrowth of pacifism is the school of thought that says if you must fight your enemy, you should do it as if you are ashamed of it, with a long face, even if you feel your cause is just. Clearly Tolkien, through the Rohirrim above, rejected this idea. It seems he felt that if the cause is just, the method correct—you are willing to meet your enemy face to face to decide the matter in a conflict of arms—then you are justified in feeling joy that you are taking part in a great conflict, one that will decide a part of the battle of the Good vs. Evil.

So it seems that at the bottom of the matter, all of Tolkien's characters, even Frodo the seeming pacifist of the end of the story, held to the belief that if their cause was right, war and even killing could be justified. But there is a great difference between such things in story and such things in the real world, as Tolkien well knew. His innate melancholy tendencies colored his views of all of these matters, until he was writing to his sons that "Wars are always lost, and The War always goes on, and it is no good growing faint!" By which he seems to have meant simply that the struggle between Good and Evil will always go on, and no matter how dark you feel, you must not lose heart. Further, he hoped that "in after days the experience of men and things, if painful, will prove useful. It did to me." He understood that painful experiences were a part of life and strove against his natural darker tendencies to make good use of them.

Always in any question of justification, right and wrong, or Good and Evil, there is the question of surety. How can you be sure that your cause is just, that you are free from wicked motives? Here again, Tolkien seems to have idealized reality in *The Lord of the Rings*. I have spoken at length elsewhere on the black and white nature of his good and evil characters. They leave no room for doubt. But this was, as I say, idealization, and Tolkien knew it. He wrote to Christopher: "[The wars of 'romance'] are still derived from the 'inner war' of allegory in which good is on one side and various modes of badness on the other. In real (exterior) life men are on both sides: which means a motley alliance of orcs, beasts, demons, plain naturally honest men, and angels. But it does make some difference who are your captains and whether they are orc-like per se!" The ideals of Tolkien's imagination were at constant war with the reality he found all around him of corrupted motives even on the "good" side, of "plain naturally honest men" among the invading Germans, and the stark finality of the atomic bomb. We see this struggle purified in *The Lord of the Rings*, free of taint and doubt, Good vs. Evil, just vs. injustice, right vs. wrong.

J.R.R. Tolkien was a man who desired peace, but who had seen war firsthand. He desired life and growing things, but saw death and destruction. He was wary of judging his fellow creatures, but saw evil human beings in the world. Through his characters in *The Lord of the Rings*, we see clearly his many conflicting thoughts about war and peace, but though his views take different roads, they arrive at the same destination: justice in war, forbearance in peace, and mercy for all men—even the wickedest.

The Sacred and the Profane

Quickbeam

Many years ago someone asked our Q&A department about churches and organized religion in Middle-earth. The very thoughtful Anwyn took up the gentle query and correctly identified the scarcity of such things in the pages of *LotR*. The Elves had many songs of praise for the great Valar of Aman, she also noted. But you really have to wonder what Tolkien was up to. You don't find churches in Bree. You never hear mention of them in the cities of Dwarves or Men. Here we find a great puzzlement within the "Secondary World" created by a man we know was a devout Catholic. A man who lived his life obeying the structure and dogma of the Church had decided, through the laborious process of writing, that he would not exhibit such religiosity in the pages of his sub-creation. A paradox, perhaps?

Matters of worship and religious behavior are only mentioned at three points during *The Lord of the Rings*. There is a passing reference to Gollum worshipping the monstrous Shelob. This does not prove the "Church of Shelob" in any way whatsoever. It seems rather that Gollum's extremely servile attitude saved his life, but he had no intention of deifying Her Ladyship. We also know the Oathbreakers of the Dwimorberg previously worshipped Sauron outright—an occurrence that might be unique in Middle-earth. And of course, there was the evening meal with Faramir, Frodo, and Sam in Henneth Annûn. They all share a moment of silence, Faramir's assembled men facing the West, almost as if in prayer. Frodo feels quite awkward and uneducated when he's caught unawares by this Gondorian custom, which speaks interestingly towards his character. Faramir, in turn, finds it odd the hobbits have no such reverential practices in their culture (frankly, so do I).

Come now, this is a really massive book. It already has so much going on, thematically and plotwise; why not add a few more layers of complexity? There were many opportunities for Tolkien to take various religious messages and lay them on thick. But unlike his friend C.S. Lewis, Tolkien avoided them every step of the way. We, the readers, are not hammered over the head with obvious Christian apology like the "Aslan-died-for-your-sins" thing in the *Narnia* books. I find myself wondering anew about Tolkien's legends functioning without the overriding presence of "Absolute Authority" or an omnipotent deity being so intrinsically involved. During our interview for the *Ringers* documentary, Sir Ian McKellen reminded us the heart of the story is "a group of people who are trying to do the right thing—without the benefit of a deity who's telling them what to do. God doesn't appear in this story. It's up to each person to decide what they're going to do with their life as Gandalf says." Then again, at certain crucial points (like when Gandalf is "sent back" to finish his work), it all comes back to Eru, Ilúvatar, who is the equivalent of a Judeo-Christian God.

So why would the Professor not supply his characters with structured religious elements of human expression? His stories carry forward several facets of spiritual belief, that much is clear, but no larger system exists. Very often, especially in *The Silmarillion*, the interaction between the Divine and the Mortal fuels the mythology. But nowhere do we find worship was required by Ilúvatar or the mighty Valar. Middle-earth was designed to function without the cultural impact of organized religion. Was the storyteller defining his world as secular? The case here could go either way.

Tolkien comments on this directly in a drafted letter to Peter Hastings (*Letters*, No. 153) that was never sent out. He decided it was taking things too seriously in discussing aspects of Elves' reincarnation and defending Tom Bombadil as not being "God" within the stories. But there is a remarkable footnote where Tolkien states the "good" people of his world had very little or no religion, period. If a character calls on the assistance of any Vala, it was loosely comparable to how a Catholic would call on a Saint for help. As the author envisioned Middle-earth to be a "primitive age," it was unseemly for the Children of Ilúvatar to have a refined, worshipful relationship with the Valar. Neither did they want such obeisance, it seems.

Now back to Númenor we go. Meneltarma was the mountain's name among the Eldar. Men called its peak the Pillar of Heaven; and it was a "holy mountain" in Eru's eyes. Tolkien says clearly in Letter 153 that the Numenoreans were monotheists, that they invoked Eru, the One, or God, and praised him privately and publicly. This kind of overt religion, limited in scope, seems to be a singularity in the overall histories of Middle-earth. The open temple was later defiled and corrupted when Sauron planted himself in the King's heart, to become a horrific site of human sacrifice in the name of Morgoth. Under Sauron's influence, the Númenóreans sought to refuse the Gift of Eru to Men and seek for immortality in the undying lands. After the downfall and destruction of Atlantis—oops, I mean, Númenor—the holy Mountain was never replaced. Such traditions as the Faithful had held went under the waves as well.

We can clearly see adulation, sacrifice, and worship as one of Morgoth's and Sauron's favorite games—a twisted game meant to mock Eru. The Oathbreakers, doomed to spend the ages within the Paths of the Dead, no doubt furthered the gravity of their evil by worshipping Sauron. Perhaps Isildur was more inclined to bring the curse upon them as retribution for their "sacrilege." That's a funny word to use when talking about Tolkien's stories, isn't it? The word never comes up anywhere in *LotR*. Proof yet again of how careful the writer was in choosing his words. Tolkien delineated the sacred and the profane very carefully, almost subliminally, in his work.

After returning to Mordor, Sauron may indeed have required worship from many others in his thrall, for all we know. I sense a warning here in the text. A warning against worshipping false gods, yes, but that's only the surface. There is also a suggestion that Middle-earth itself was a better place without the infusion of religion. Perhaps this was the best way for Tolkien's sub-creation to work effectively, by peeling off such layers of the Primary World we live in, making the Secondary World unique.

But on the other hand, the entire race of Elves was a filter of spiritual ideals. Their reverence towards the Valar (and Eru/Ilúvatar) bears a resemblance to Native American spirituality and belief systems. There is a connection here. Elves of all types lived their lives as a celebration of the Valar—and by that I mean a celebration of living things, a joy in the innate power of nature and the environment around them. Elves taught the Ents to speak, did they not? They sing songs to the Valar, owing them a lifetime of beautiful works, song, and artistry. The most basic characteristics of Native American spirituality are strikingly similar to this, with the exception of ceremony and ritual being more prevalent across the huge diversity of North American tribal practices than it ever was with the Eldar. Still, the common underlying "spiritual celebration" of the natural world reminds me of Elves a great deal.

The other Free Peoples of Middle-earth were removed from this. We have no clear idea if the Dwarf-lords had shrines or temples built in honor of Aulë. Perhaps they did, carefully keeping them secret. But Hobbits and Men had a subtle response to the spirituality of the Elves. When the story of *LotR* comes primarily from the Hobbits' point of view, the Elves become almost venerated. They are saintly, ephemeral, unworldly—these creatures have the light of Aman in their faces. The way everyone reacts to Galadriel is a fine example of spiritual power bringing a dose of "awareness" to the lives of mortals who otherwise would not be exposed to it. Watching the way Hobbits respond to the Elves seems like Tolkien's way of saying: "Look at the difference between those with spiritual awareness and those without." It never occurs to our wee heroes what the light in her eyes must mean. Perhaps to Frodo it does.

No, Tolkien did not give his characters the cultural function of religion. Without the forces of orthodoxy having an impact, Middle-earth history unfolds in a distinctive way. Religion would not have served the greater story. The Professor's aim was to very finely and discreetly put spiritual ideas, layer by cautious layer, into the work. Some of the Angelic Powers are there, hovering in the background of the tapestry. Many of the main characters never see them, nor care to notice. Samwise comes quite close to his own spiritual epiphany, though he doesn't recognize what it is, when he looks up from the waste of Gorgoroth and sees the solitary star above him.

Throughout Middle-earth one may find reverence towards the Unseen, particularly where Elves are concerned, but for everyone else, the equation of life is all about choices, choices, choices. Each character makes his or her own choices in service of Good or for the advancement of Evil. And these choices are made without kneeling at a pew. Without guidance from beyond. The lines are drawn in each person's heart. The moral compass is drawn between choices of freedom against slavery. Peace against war. Kindness against cruelty. Love against fear. Tolkien has given us a secondary world where one's free will is continually tested (not so different from ours). It's about how you choose—and facing the consequences of your choice. The function of Free Will is still very much the dominant exercise in the story. So the absence of churches notwithstanding, the sub-creation that Tolkien so meticulously crafted has much of his own personal and fundamentally religious impressions layered into it.

This was a deliberate choice to let the world of Middle-earth exist on its own secular terms. By doing so, Tolkien greatly amplifies his characters' choices—and the consequences—by somehow isolating them spiritually. But the Unseen forces still operate, somewhere out on the margins, whether the characters accept, reject, or even know of such things. It is a concept that might benefit those of us in the Primary World. We are reminded how the Universe might work from another point of view. Without the guiding hand of religious culture, without having any relationship with a Higher Power, the characters make choices that strongly define who they are. Each forward step they take resonates in their own hearts. And in ours.

Outlandish Talk

Tehanu

When I look at children today and the books they read, the games they play, and hear the language they use, I am reminded that Tolkien's world is, like Lothlórien, slipping backwards in time. Not only do the characters of Middle-earth speak the Common Tongue in their own particular way; Tolkien, speaking and writing as himself, also talks in his own particular way when he is simply narrating events. He uses words like "hythe" and "dwelt" and speaks of "the hither shore." To a new reader his language must seem formal, stilted, and old-fashioned, and in the normal course of things this would be an increasing gulf between his work and the modern reader.

Of course, we know that Tolkien has a powerful new ally: Peter Jackson's *The Lord of the Rings* films are unquestionable successes, and because of them we can be certain that interest in Middle-earth will not die out for a long time to come. But will the films supersede the books? Will the films become long-lived classics while the books dwindle into curiosities that few will bother to explore?

To a greater or lesser degree, all of us have had our visual images of Middle-earth supplanted by those that the films provide. But the words, the dialogue, the language that Tolkien used: will these things be lost to history?

I think the answer is no, for two reasons: because older forms of language are kept alive by more than just the written word, and because so many of us respond with curiosity to unusual ways of speaking.

Through the *Rings* films, millions of people have been exposed to a bit of Tolkien's style, because it is used verbatim or used as a template for a great deal of the dialogue in the film. The taste for this kind of language will be kept alive for a very long time as a result, and we need have less fear that Tolkien's writing will become impenetrably old-fashioned to a new reader. But before that could happen, the screen-writers had to do a delicate job of judging how much "high English" (for want of a better term) moviegoers new to Tolkien could hear without being turned off.

Luckily, formal English is far from dead. The survival of "high English" is helped by the fact that some of its old-fashioned stylistic quirks have been kept alive in other fields, so this language isn't read solely in Tolkien and his imitators. For instance, think of all those passages in *Lord of the Rings* full of "Yea" and "Behold," and those chains of sentences beginning with conjunctions: "Then they came unto...Then it is told that...Thus it came to pass that...But ever after it was said...And so the day came...And none who were there re-called..." These sound rather biblical. Take Genesis; this is from the King James version:

> Now the serpent was more subtle than any beast of the field which the Lord God had made. And he said unto the woman, Yea, hath God said, Ye shall not eat of every tree of the garden?
>
> And the woman said unto the serpent, We may eat of the fruit of the trees of the garden:
>
> But of the fruit of the tree which is in the midst of the garden, God hath said, Ye shall not eat of it, neither shall ye touch it, lest ye die.
>
> And the serpent said unto the woman, Ye shall not surely die...

People still do read the Bible, so this construction sounds rather familiar. There is no doubt, in his biblical-sounding passages, that Tolkien means us to take the events utterly seriously. If you want a good example, read "The Steward and the King" in *The Return of the King*. The episode where Faramir seeks out Éowyn at the Houses of Healing, and the section where Gandalf takes Aragorn up to find the scion of the White Tree on the slopes of Mt. Mindolluin are passages constructed almost entirely in that way. Oaths, prophecies, marriages, dynasties: The story moves from plot and character to the stuff of epic mythology. Subconsciously we recognize what this *type* of language is about, from hearing the biblical rhythms in it.

A more formal language thrives on the airwaves. Like Tolkien himself (who read so much of his work aloud to an audience while he was working on it), radio storytellers find the vocabulary and rhythm of old-fashioned speech better suited to the listening ear. For people who still have time to listen to the radio, there are such gems as the *Prairie Home Companion* or (until recently) Alistair Cook's *Letter from America* that still speak very differently, and in a measured and graceful way.

Politicians do their bit to keep old forms of speech alive. In the kind of oratory that accompanies politics, speechwriters commonly plunder centuries-old poetry for its lexicon of rolling, sonorous phrases. It gives a speaker an air of weight and authority. I can scroll through old "State of the Union" addresses online and pick up phrases that sound quite comfortably Tolkienian. This is from George W. Bush's 2002 State of the Union Address: "I will not wait on events, while dangers gather. I will not stand by, as peril draws closer and closer." Or "We stand for a different choice, made long ago, on the day of our founding. We affirm it again today… Steadfast in our purpose, we now press on."

It reminds me of Tennyson's *Ulysses*: "To strive, to seek, to find, and not to yield." It also sounds like Kipling:

> No easy hope or lies
> Shall bring us to our goal,
> But iron sacrifice
> Of body, will and soul.
>
> (From *For all we have and are*)

This kind of poetry is still being read today, in school and out of it, so this formal, high-flown language is far from dying out. Of course it was highly popular in Tolkien's day too and was familiar language to him.

So we don't find it too hard to move into Tolkien's style, even though the rhythm and language he uses seem peculiar to a modern speaker of English.

In any case I think a lot of us are born with what I can only call a "questing ear," which means that whenever we hear an odd dialect or intonation, it fascinates us. Quite soon we may even find ourselves imitating it. How often have you been to see a movie—perhaps a small independent movie made with actors who speak with their local accent—and been delighted with the music of the speech? Maybe it's the lilting Irish of a film like *The Commitments*, or the Yorkshire accents in *Calendar Girls*, or the fascinating rural American accents in films like

Raising Arizona or *Forrest Gump*. A lot of people here in New Zealand wandered around trying to say "choc-lit" in the same way as Tom Hanks after seeing that latter film. Likewise, a generation of American children grew up trying to mimic the accents they heard on Monty Python.

If you have the questing ear, you'll happily listen to BBC World's broadcasts as much to enjoy the voices of the foreign correspondents as for the actual content. You may find yourself listening to radio programs in languages you can't even identify simply because the sound of them piques your curiosity. I think a lot of people are struck the same way by the way Tolkien's characters speak. It's strange—and therefore interesting.

And sometimes you may hear a kind of speech that calls to you like the gulls of Pelargir called to Legolas, and it stirs something in you.

Only Spanish was spoken in my home until I began to learn to talk, and after that my parents always spoke English. Spanish was an extremely rare language where I was brought up, so I almost never heard it in later life. But whenever I do—right up to this day—it creates an indescribable yearning in me. It's as though there's a whole other life, another person, who is me—a shadow person—who understands every word and is totally at home in that language. But for many years I couldn't understand more than a few words and would be wrung with frustration because it all seemed to be just out of reach at the tip of my comprehension. Until later when I learned it out of books, I could never reach that tantalizing other world where I would be at home in Spanish. Whenever I hear it unexpectedly, it is a shock, like discovering I have a different home from the one I thought was mine. The language reminds me of how it feels to be about one year old and perfectly at home in the center of my own universe. That language was "home" to me even when I couldn't understand it.

I suppose that Tolkien, with his hypersensitivity to language, felt that way intensely about certain kinds of speech. Orphaned at an early age, he put down roots any way he could. In particular, he felt drawn to some dialects of Middle English with which he had an ancestral connection—they were in his blood. In his *Letter # 165* he talks about his identification with the counties of the West Midlands upon the Welsh Marches, from which came his forebears on his mother's side. Because we know Tolkien by his father's surname, we tend to forget how little influence the Tolkien side of his family really had compared to his mother's folk, the Suffields. In *Letter #44,* Tolkien writes that he is a Suffield by nature, not a Tolkien, and that their corner of the world is home to him as no other place is.

It was his mother who first taught him languages and who pursued hobbies as an artist, calligrapher and a pianist. You could say that her hobbies were very Elvish: Music, language, art. Maybe it was the Suffield women whom Tolkien had in mind when he talks about Bilbo's ancestors, the "three remarkable daughters of the Old Took," and how one of the Tooks had reputedly had a "fairy wife," (*The Hobbit,* Chapter 1). According to the hobbits, the Took clan were prone to adventurousness as a result. I think this is an apt description of the Suffield women and of Mabel, who married into the Tolkien clan. An astonishingly little known fact about his mother surfaces in Leslie Ellen Jones's *Myth and Middle-earth:* "Before her marriage, Mabel had worked as a governess, she and her sisters had undertaken missionary work in the harem of the Sultan of Zanzibar, and she had sailed to South Africa to marry Arthur [Tolkien] completely on her own."

Tolkien attributes his interest in Anglo-Saxon and Western Middle English to his ancestry. To him, place, ancestry and language were an absolutely vital part of understanding one's origins. Moreover, he felt an urge—part of his urge to create a mythology for England—to give us a vision of this lost past, and of an even more remote past that he imagined came before it: The world of Middle-earth. He used the most powerful tool he had, language, to give us a kind of experience of that vanished world and its values.

Tom Shippey puts it this way in his book *J.R.R. Tolkien: Author of the Century*.

> ...Tolkien was the holder of several highly personal if not heretical views about language. He thought that people, and perhaps as a result of their confused linguistic history especially English people, could detect historical strata in language without knowing how they did it. They knew that names like Ugthorpe and Stainby were Northern without knowing they were Norse; they knew Winchcombe and Cumre must be in the West without recognizing that *cwm* is Welsh. They could feel linguistic style in words...

Shippey talks about the way Tolkien constructed his languages—Elvish or Black Speech—so that they would convey beauty or ugliness.

He believes this is the reason why Tolkien has his characters speak in their own languages and leaves them untranslated.

> The point, or a point, is made by the sound alone—just as allusions to the old legends of previous ages say something without the legends necessarily being told.
>
> ...But Tolkien also thought—and this takes us back to the roots of his invention—that philology could take you back even beyond the ancient texts it studied. He believed that it was possible sometimes to feel one's way back from words as they survived in later periods to concepts which had long since vanished, but which had surely existed, or the words would not exist.

I've spoken elsewhere about the idea of "home" in Tolkien's works: what makes a place homely and the degree to which Tolkien's characters are involved in a search for home. Throughout his life he would encounter languages that fed a kind of appetite in him—those particular dialects of Middle English from his favorite ancestral corner of England, as well as Welsh, Finnish and Spanish. I guess that they felt like home to him from the moment he encountered them. They satisfied his ear and hinted at a time and culture that he admired more than the present age. More than that, it was as if he wanted to use his stories to lead his readers to that home too. I think that Tolkien's very language was intended to lay out a mythic "home" where people spoke and thought in a certain way.

It's an interesting exercise to pick almost any character in *The Lord of the Rings* and analyse what sets their speech apart from all others. Take Sam, for instance. He is perhaps the finest representative of a kind of rural simple-heartedness that Tolkien admired. He has an understated steadfast goodness. To Tolkien's mind, this was the ancient, natural character of rural England, strongest where least touched by invading history. Sam's speech is handed down from a time before the Normans brought an influx of southern European language and ideas. Yet there is a paradox here—the Anglo-Saxons were certainly invaders too, and Tolkien is playing favorites when he prefers them to the indigenous Celts or the not-unrelated Normans. Tolkien's point of view has supporters. A recent book called *The Year 1000* by Robert Lacey and Danny Danziger makes a good argument for considering Anglo-Saxon England as a kind of golden age. They've spoken to many people who research the period and communicated *why* so many people find it rewarding to study.

Be that as it may, if you read Sam's every utterance from beginning to end of the *The Lord of the Rings*, you will find Tolkien has been as consistent as possible in keeping Sam's speech free of Latinate or Greek-derived words. It makes him sound like a country bumpkin, as Tolkien intended. But more than that: to Tolkien's mind—and as a philologist, he'd be in a position to know—Sam's background has escaped almost all influences from outside the Shire (Britain). So his speech remains as closely descended from Anglo-Saxon speech as possible. His speech is not just simple or unlearned in its grammar. Sam's vocabulary constantly prefers words like "seemingly" and "mostways" to Latinate equivalents like "apparently" or "usually." Few authors have the alertness, knowledge, or the ear for niggling detail required to keep this up for a thousand pages.

In the Rohan chapters, Tolkien drops us into an older world with different virtues: the world of *Beowulf* and its heroes. He starts drawing from the actual language and rhythms of Old English. If Sam had a model in real life among the farmers of the countryside where Tolkien grew up, then the Rohirrim sound like that farmer's Anglo-Saxon forebears from a time before the England of hedgerows and watermills. Not only names and words are drawn from Old English, but the characters and Tolkien's descriptions of the place start to sound like the alliterative poetry of the time. Here's an example from the Old English poem *The Wanderer:*

> …A man who on these walls wisely looked
> Who sounded deeply this dark life
> Would think back to the blood spilt here,
> Weigh it in his wit. His word would be this:
> 'Where is that horse now? Where are those men? Where is the hoard-sharer?
> Where is the house of the feast? Where is the hall's uproar?…'
>
> (*trans. Michael Alexander)*

That sounds very familiar to us if we recall the Rohirric song Aragorn sings as they approach Edoras for the first time, "*Where now the horse and the rider?*" However in that song, which Aragorn is translating into the common speech, he has cast it into rhyming poetry—exactly as we might translate foreign poetry into modern

English and put it in our habitual mode, which is rhyme. Tolkien was ever alert to the way languages actually mix. The native poetry of the Rohirrim is, like that of the Anglo-Saxons, alliterative and rhythmic. The ends of the lines do not rhyme. Instead, each line is divided by a sort of pause in the middle, with an equal number of stressed syllables on either side. There are usually four of these "beats" to a line, two on either side of the midline break. The most common pattern in the poetry of the Rohirrim has the first three stressed syllables starting with the same sound (alliteration), and the last one with a different one. Quite often one of the vowel sounds in the last half-line is echoed in the next half-line:

> *Out of **doubt**, out of **dark** / to the **day's rising***
> *I came **singing** in the **sun**, / **sword unsheathing**.*

The first line has the alliteration on the "d" and the second on the "s." The vowel sound of "day's" is echoed in the next line, "came." The number of syllables in each line is variable. But if you read the "Rohan" passages of *The Lord of the Rings* you start to notice that even in the course of narrating the story, alliteration starts sneaking in. Éomer on the fields of Pelennor thought to "...fight there on foot till all fell." Or at Snowmane's burial: "Green and long grew the grass on Snowmane's Howe, but ever black and bare was the ground where the beast was burned." Now that you're looking out for it, that line starts to sound like Anglo-Saxon poetry, but in fact Tolkien has just snuck it into the background of the storytelling. As Tolkien tells us the story of Rohan's part in the War of the Ring, the language takes on the strong rhythm of Old English. The hidden message from Tolkien has to do with the culture and way of life of both people. Aragorn sums them up in his answer to Gimli's question just before they meet Éomer's troop for the first time: He calls them proud, wilful, truehearted, generous, and bold without cruelty. The alert reader with a questing ear can pick up the strangeness in the language, roll it around the tongue, and receive a flavor of the old heroic code of the past, when courage and loyalty were overriding virtues. Not the stubborn enduring courage of Sam and the hobbits, but a kind of reckless defiance of fate and the expectation of a violent death.

Tolkien also presents us with the Elves and their language, both in their native tongues and the way they express themselves in the

Common Tongue. All their speech in English is graceful, educated, and beautiful, and their speech in Elvish is full of delicate and harmonious sounds. Tolkien means for us to believe in an even more remote past when things were beautiful and filled with wonder. Their lives are full of song and their songs full of ancient history and the joyful appreciation of nature. The Elves have wisdom, he tells us, and they express it through their wide vocabulary (very different from Sam's, for instance, for it includes the Latinate and Greek-derived words which came into English from the languages only "educated" English speakers knew) and courtly speech. But what stays with us most is the mystery of their beautiful language. Hearing it at last spoken in Peter Jackson's films has been a wonderful gift, but I can only imagine what it's like for a Tolkien newbie to read the books and realize how much of that language exists.

Many people are seized with the urge to go out and learn Quenya or Sindarin or explore the fragments of other languages that Tolkien developed. At the moment there are few published resources that are readily available to people wishing to learn these, and students must piece together what is known of Tolkien's languages from a few heroic volunteer efforts on the web and in specialty journals. It's a pity that there have been no publicly available books of grammar and vocabulary that lay out all that can be known or extrapolated from Tolkien's own notes. (At the time of this writing, David Salo's soon-to-be-released grammar of the Elvish language, *A Gateway to Sindarin*, looks set to remedy that lack.) Given the opportunity, the study and practise of Tolkien's languages would surely flower throughout the world wherever language buffs gather.

It would indeed be a pity if Tolkien's own words were to be supplanted entirely by the films, because we would lose so many of the nuances that his language conveys. Every speaker in the books reveals more than just character by their speech. They hint at a whole background and give us subtle cues about the cultures and societies that Tolkien understood. His writing was meant to convey what he loved and admired about those vanished cultures, and we would be sorry to lose that. Somehow I don't think we will, as long as people have the questing ear.

Sources:

The Letters of J.R.R. Tolkien Selected and Edited by Humphrey Carpenter. Houghton Mifflin Company, Boston, 1981.

Myth and Middle-earth, Leslie Ellen Jones. Cold Spring Press 2002.

The Lord of the Rings, J.R.R. Tolkien. Houghton Mifflin one-volume paperback, 1987.

J.R.R. Tolkien: Author of the Century, Tom Shippey. Houghton Mifflin paperback, 2002.

The Year 1000, Robert Lacey and Danny Danziger. Abacus Books, 2003.

The Earliest English Poems, Michael Alexander. Penguin 1977.

Escape to
Middle-earth

Escape to Middle-earth

Anwyn

The rush started practically at the moment of publication. You could almost hear the pounding feet, the whir of the bike chains, the motors of the cars and buses. Those of us left behind furtively scrawled "Frodo lives" on the dank underground walls and waited for our chance. Those who could took flight—to Middle-earth.

The Lord of the Rings was as popular in its day as almost any modern bestseller. Tolkien's fervent fandom developed during his lifetime and partly amused, partly engaged, and partly perplexed him until his death. And periodically it returns to the bestseller lists once more—particularly in the last few years with the explosion of popularity of Peter Jackson's movies.

Those not in the group styling themselves Tolkien fans, hobbit fanciers, or what have you have often leveled criticism at those who are, but the group rolls on. Pundits and scholars label Tolkien with any negative tag you please, but the group rolls on. Opinion of the films can be wildly varied from fan to fan, but the group rolls on.

Join us as we explore the hows and whys of this peculiar group of people. We never tire of asking what makes us return again and again to Middle-earth.

The Escape of the Prisoner

Anwyn

What is "escapism," exactly? Fantasy is an inclusive term that takes in stories of magic, dragons, ghosts, heroes, and basically anything that does not happen in our everyday world. The disparagement hurled most often at lovers of fantasy is that they are "escapist;" those who use this term seem to mean by it that fantasy readers can't handle the real world at all, and so they must escape into one where wizards wave wands and dragons breathe fire, and oh yeah, hobbits put on a Ring and disappear, and kings return to their thrones in glory. But the realm of fantasy includes Stephen King as much as it does Tolkien, and I don't hear as much about "escapism" when people talk about Stephen King. Lots of grown men and women in our country and around the world devote hours per week and great quantities of brain cells to their favorite sports teams—perhaps wishing they could be as physically talented as the players—and nobody accuses them of not being able to handle the real world.

Want to know what I did this week? I worked my "day job," I took care of my child, I finished editing my colleagues' pieces for this book, I wrote some of my own, I began planning my wedding and ordered my wedding dress, I bought my father's birthday present, I talked on the phone at least once a day to both my mom and my younger sister, I went grocery shopping with my baby and my youngest sister, I did five loads of laundry, I loaded and unloaded the dishwasher a few times, and I organized two closets. Who says I can't handle reality?

And moreover, who doesn't occasionally feel imprisoned by that reality and need to escape, take a momentary trip to a higher, sweeter place? Let's face it, folks, there is hardly one among us who doesn't need to disconnect from reality every now and again. Whether your outlet is Tolkien, the Chicago Cubs, a favorite movie or TV show, or simply going out to a club, we all do plenty of things that don't necessarily advance our finances, contribute to our jobs, or clean our houses, but which enrich us nevertheless. Do you think my fiancée would be the person he is unless he could tell you the Cubs' pitching rotation this week, who's on their disabled list, and how he thinks the rest of the season is going to play out (he's frequently right)? Do you think he would think me half the person that I am if I couldn't tell him about some of my views through Tolkien's lens? The things we read and involve ourselves in and think about help make us the people that we are, and we would be mighty dull indeed if our only focus was on the mundane things we humans have to do to get through life. How can anybody be arrogant enough to disparage some time spent away from the humdrum and out of the ordinary?

So why is it that so many of us choose Tolkien as one of our preferred avenues for vacationing for a while from the plain and everyday?

I wrote once of how *The Lord of the Rings* is not a novel, but a story. While it is possible to escape into novels (I love those of Jane Austen, myself), novels are ultimately set in the world we know and therefore there are limits to the escapade. With stories—sagas, myths, legends, noble-truths-disguised-as-fiction—we can leap much farther across the boundaries of our own experiences. True, I've never been an 18th-century daughter of a landowner, so of course I daydream of that experience when I'm reading Jane Austen, but on the other hand I am a daughter, a woman who has had thrills and disappointments in love, so I can relate to her characters because they are still human, still living on Earth within a time frame I can comprehend. I'll tell you what, though, I've never been a hobbit or an elf or a dwarf, and I don't expect I will be. So Tolkien and other "fantasy" writers I admire are capable of taking me much farther beyond the boundaries of my reality, and I enjoy that. Not everybody does. That's fine, but they're not better than me simply because they don't and I do, and that "escapist" label they like to hurl seems to imply they think they are. It's time they were disillusioned.

Why else does story possess such a siren call for many of us? Clearly there are elements to the enjoyment that smack of the danger that tired term "escapism" embodies. There are those who go too far outside reality, so far that they neglect important responsibilities. I'm not condoning that. It's sad, and it's frightening. But listen, if somebody is responsible, does their job well, is reasonably clean and clothed in public, then what do you care if they like to dress up as a Klingon or an Elf on the side? All of this is really just another form of humans' second oldest pastime—hating others just because they are different from oneself. See also Cain and Abel. Have we really not advanced farther than this in the 21st century?

But back to Tolkien. What are the elements inherent in a good yarn that pull us along, that sweep us up? Well, wouldn't you like to be a hero? How many times do you get the chance in your ordinary life? And if you did get the chance, how confident are you that you wouldn't freeze up, that you would *really* know what to do and react in a timely manner? Aragorn and Éomer always react well—they're still alive after how many swordfights? Frodo holds the course even in the face of terror. How well would you do? But you don't have to—you can shiver as Frodo is overtaken by Shelob, but you never have to feel the spider's sting yourself.

The screenplay to the Jodie Foster/Chow Yun-Fat *Anna and the King* contains the following gem: "It is always surprising how small a part of life is taken up by meaningful moments." But it is never surprising how large a part of stories are made up by meaningful moments. Characters are rich, never dull, even the wicked, and they all hold a fascination or charm that can be difficult to find in the people all around us. And those most drawn to fantasy, the shy, the diffident, or the withdrawn, have more trouble than usual in finding the richness in the people that surround them anyway. Small wonder, then, that so many of us are drawn to characters like Tolkien's, and Rowling's, and yes, King's. But even if you're not shy or withdrawn, how many of us have enough faith to go seeking for the goodness, richness, and wit in others without fearing how vulnerable that makes us? In the story the richness is mined out for us. And let's not forget that even when we have meaningful moments, they're not always fun. They can be uncomfortable, inconvenient, even distasteful. In story, we don't necessarily have to bear the distaste, the humiliation, or the inconvenience ourselves. And our timidity is hardly ever a factor in story. The heroes stand up to be counted when it counts, without fail.

Tolkien gave us not only the means but also the license for this escape. When people talked of escapism to him, he commented that it is only jailers who are uptight about people escaping, and said that the means of escape books like *The Lord of the Rings* offer are for the escape of the prisoner, rather than the flight of the deserter. I don't have to abandon my real life to live in Tolkien's world for a time. It's always there waiting for me when I come back. If sometimes I need more of a break than others, well, there is always the danger of being tempted too far, I suppose, and of becoming *a deserter* after all, but it hasn't happened so far. Nor do I know anyone to which it has.

Ultimately, escapism is a coined term for a largely imaginary malady that if it strikes, affects a very few, and usually temporarily. I can't imagine a truthful human being who says there have not been occasions when he or she wanted to be somebody else, and story is one outlet for that desire. Spectator sports are another. There are others, some more dangerous, but those are not my soap box here. If somebody calls you an escapist, smile, because more than likely, that poor soul is not getting enough of a break from his or her very mundane everyday responsibilities. All work and no play makes Jack (or Ronald) a very dull boy indeed, and story is just an area where we can play, no matter how old we may be. Savor those areas where you can play. The work will always be there.

I remember one other thing I did this week. I re-read *Harry Potter and the Order of the Phoenix.*

Post-Tolkienism: Below Sub-Creation

Anwyn

What do you read besides Tolkien? C.S. Lewis? J.K. Rowling? Dennis McKiernan? David Eddings? Tracy Hickman and Margaret Weis? Robert Jordan, perhaps?

What do you recommend to your friends besides Tolkien?

And what do you find that is as good as Tolkien?

On two occasions, two different people, people I regarded as serious Tolkien fans, recommended authors that each claimed were "second only to Tolkien." On a third occasion, a guy I met at random in a bookstore recommended still a third as second only to Tolkien. The first recommendation was the *Dragon Prince* trilogy by Melanie Rawn, the second was the *Wheel of Time* series by Robert Jordan, and the third was *Eye of the Hunter* by Dennis McKiernan. I picked up each of them and read. I enjoyed the Rawn, plowed through the Jordan, and couldn't make it even halfway through the McKiernan. Though I later came back to Jordan and read all he's written so far, still, the claims of my pals and of the stranger in the bookstore continued to ring hollow: *these books were nothing like Tolkien*.

A blurb on the back of the Jordan books burbles that "Robert Jordan has come to dominate the world that Tolkien began to reveal." I cringe every time I catch sight of this utterance on a dust jacket. It is unfair, unbelievable, and untrue. Nobody I have read so far has lived in Middle-earth but Tolkien, and nobody dominates there—well, not since the demise of Sauron, at any rate.

Tolkien is so frequently called "the father of modern fantasy" that it's a bit incredible that so many of these modern authors cannot come up to scratch. Their stories are mostly trite, primarily about 20th-century people set in some magical, dragon-inhabited, no-electricity landscape. If smartly done, the tales engage my mind and emotions, make me laugh and cry a bit and wish I could be a Sunrunner, or an Aes Sedai, or even a solitary traveler with a mysterious quest. But in the end, these are not much more than D&D knockoffs that cater to our desires to live a different life. If I were the "father" of this modern fantasy, I'd be wondering, "Where did I go wrong?"

So what is it exactly that sets Tolkien apart? The ability to write an engaging story is not lacking among the authors I mentioned; dialogue is both pithy and witty, descriptions are vivid, and good characterizations are plentiful. But though each author tries his or her best to create a unique landscape, one with those few elements that are not to be found anywhere else, still their stories lack that organic growth, that flowing quality that make Tolkien's stories so true.

For it is truth that sets Tolkien apart, truth and his method of conveying truth to us through beautiful story. Modern authors may have many goals, but among them, most assuredly, is to write a good-selling book that will keep people coming back for sequels. Tolkien wrote *The Hobbit* as a lark and *The Lord of the Rings* as a natural outgrowth of his great lifelong passion, *The Silmarillion*. He wrote these partly because he could not bear not to, but partly because of his unyielding belief that through stories such as these, he was communicating great human truths that our Maker wishes us to know. He felt, humbly but determinedly, that he was fulfilling his purpose in what he called *sub-creation*, that wondrous and unique idea of his that through stories of his own invention, he was a voice for the universal truth that returns again and again in various forms and at various times, but always for our good.

***

My mother is not a reader by nature. She is a doer. She gardens, she cooks, she crafts, she makes and mends. She is also a devout Christian. The one thing she does read daily is the Bible, and she has lived with its words all her life. But she called me a few months ago after my father, an avid reader who read *The Lord of the Rings* to us all when my sisters and I were children, read aloud to her the Ainulindalë, the creation myth that prefaces *The Silmarillion*. She was almost in tears as she described to me her reaction to Tolkien's retelling of the making of the world. "It gives me a hope beyond death," she said, "hope for all the wrong in the world. The way they created the world with music, and the evil that tried to play louder ... and God was patient and sat quietly by, and basically he says that he will take all these things—the good, the bad, and the ugly—and make something beautiful."

The Ainulindalë says nothing that is not already written in the Bible that my mother has read all her life. It speaks of Divine Creation, of the fall of one of the highest, noblest created beings, and of the consequences of that fall. Yet Tolkien's version affected my mother greatly. It touched her on a different level, but in the same sphere of influence, as does the creation story in the Bible.

***

If Tolkien was a sub-creator, then so far in my experience, he is the only one of his kind. Don't misunderstand me—I enjoy many authors and a wide variety of books, and I don't chuck them into the bin simply because they're not Tolkien. I like a rousing fight between Weis and Hickman's Knights of Solamnia and Dragon Highlords, I like to imagine Rawn's Sunrunners and Jordan's Aes Sedai employing their various arts, and I get a huge kick out of living for a spell (get it?) at Rowling's Hogwarts. And each of these authors does have philosophy of his or her own. Melanie Rawn's *Dragon Prince* books are downright political in many places, and Robert Jordan's biting portrayal of bickering human nature is sometimes too close for comfort. But what sets Tolkien apart is that he was not conveying his opinions of how the world should run on human terms. He was speaking of truth as to how it *does* run on terms not set down by man—that good will always triumph over evil, that good can only triumph through striving, that alone each of us is ultimately helpless, but together we can rise above the powers of the world. And it was because he felt called to this higher purpose that his inventive and linguistic talents—by themselves nearly matched, in some cases, by some of our more recent authors—rise to that higher plane where none that I know of, so far, have followed him.

Sub-creation is not limited to the making of a world. If that were the case, then there would be nothing to set Middle-earth above Rowling's Hogsmeade, Orthanc above Jordan's White Tower, or Sauron above Eddings's Torak. Whereas Jordan, Rowling, Eddings and the rest had a good idea for a book, drew up a philosophy to go with it, and wrote it all down, sub-creation is the conviction that one is taking part in the expression of something created by higher power, not by oneself. When you take the self out of the equation, then your talent can bless people in ways you never imagined, as Tolkien's has done for uncounted thousands of readers over the years.

Don't get me wrong. Jordan is convincing. Rawn is highly entertaining. Rowling is downright addictive! I'm nearing the end of *Harry Potter and the Order of the Phoenix* for the second time and am just as enthralled on second reading as I was on first. I am not saying the fantasy authors who have followed Tolkien lack talent, vision, or purpose. I am saying, however, that they lack Tolkien's determination to express anew the stories that live universally in mankind—the struggle, the striving, the sacrifice for an objective standard that humans will never consistently live up to, despite brief, brilliant flashes of greatness. The key lies in the phrase "objective standard"—ideas not *created* by the author, but merely *expressed* by them. Tolkien took the truth as he knew it and started from the beginning—creation—and took us through the fall, into the pit of evil, and onto the heights again with Frodo's triumph over Sauron. No wonder we can't put down *The Lord of the Rings* after many years and countless readings. No wonder my mother cried. No wonder Tolkien is the father of modern fantasy—but it's a shame that more of his "children" haven't followed in Dad's footsteps. Sub-creation is a difficult standard to live up to, admittedly, but not one to be abandoned on that count. Worldmaking is a beginning; let's realize that however many worlds we make, however, we cannot ultimately escape the truths inherent in this one.

Fifty Years of Fandom

Ostadan

Introduction

From the viewpoint of a newly minted Tolkien fan of the 21st century, it may be easy to suppose that Tolkien's work must always have been as much a part of "mainstream" culture and as well known as it is today, or at any rate as it was before the release of Peter Jackson's hugely successful film adaptations. After all, was *The Lord of the Rings* not named the Book of the Century by the British public in numerous polls? With the legions of fans who show up for Tolkien-related events or participate in online activities, it is hard to imagine a time when Tolkien's fans were a small in-group exchanging their thoughts in mimeographed "fanzines." And yet, so it was.

A fully comprehensive history of the first fifty years of Tolkien fandom—even limited to the United States—would fill a book, and is certainly beyond the scope of this short article. Instead, the purpose is to give a very broad look at the various phases of American Tolkien fandom during those decades.

Hardcover Days

The first two volumes of *The Lord of the Rings* were published in 1954; the third volume did not appear until October 1955. Movie fans who waited impatiently for the second and third parts of the Jackson adaptation can well imagine the reaction of those readers who had to wait a year to find out what would happen to Frodo and Sam in the tower of Cirith Ungol!

Among the most enthusiastic fans of *The Lord of the Rings* in those days were the organized fans of science fiction (many of whom had already become acquainted with Tolkien through *The Hobbit*). These fans already had an extensive communications network through inexpensively printed fanzines produced by mimeograph machines, with artwork drawn directly on mimeo stencils. The science fiction fans held (and continue to hold) annual conventions such as the World Science Fiction Convention (Worldcon), as well as smaller regional conventions, and some clubs such as the Los Angeles Science Fantasy Society (LASFS) have held regular meetings since the 1940s. It was these fans who gave this new fantasy work its biggest word-of-mouth buzz, as fans waxed enthusiastic in their fanzines and at conventions. It was not long before fans had begun to produce artwork and musical adaptations or parodies (known within the hobby as filk songs) based on the world of Middle-earth.

In September 1957, Worldcon XV was held in London, England. The Worldcons are purely a fan phenomenon, run by and for fans of science fiction and fantasy literature. From 1951 through 1957, a jury comprising prominent members of the convention awarded the International Fantasy Award to a deserving fiction work (in later years, the Hugo Awards, nominated and voted on by all the members of the convention, would become more prominent; the *The Lord of the Rings* film adaptations have received Hugo awards for Best Dramatic Presentation in recent years). In 1957, the last year in which the award was given, the sole nominee and winner was *The Lord of the Rings*. This was Tolkien's first encounter with organized fandom. A group of Los Angeles fans took a taxi all the way from London to Oxford to meet Tolkien, after first contacting him by telephone; although he received them graciously, Tolkien was somewhat taken aback as the taxi disgorged a group of "strange men and even stranger women."

It does seem that Los Angeles fans were particularly enthusiastic about Tolkien's work. Ed Meskys, who would become the head of the Tolkien Society of America, wrote in 1997: "Anyhow, at that time the Los Angeles fen would discover one book after another and gush wildly about their greatness in *Shaggy* [the LASFS club fanzine] and their APAzines [amateur press associations]. Enthusiasms of the time included Ayn Rand's *Atlas Shrugged*, John Myers's *Silverlock*, and Tolkien's *LotR*." (*The View from Entropy Hall #12 (1997)*.)

In 1960, Bruce Pelz published the first Tolkien fanzine as the organ of the newly formed Los Angeles fan group, The Fellowship of the Ring: *I Palantir*. It is a notable work in that it contains three articles that are representative of the kinds of Tolkien fan writing that continue to this day: an article on the elven rope *hithlain*, collecting what information could be gleaned from the details of the book and extrapolating and speculating (sometimes rather wildly) on some of the questions it raises; a work of fiction describing the War of the Ring from Sauron's point of view; and a more scholarly article comparing the character of Sam Gamgee to another faithful servant, Sam Weller from Dickens's *Pickwick Papers*. These three formats—fan fiction (and artwork and filk songs); research within the world of Middle-earth; and literary scholarship—have been the mainstays of fan writing for more than forty years.

I Palantir produced only four issues between 1960 and 1966, so Ed Meskys started running much more Tolkien material in about 1964 in his own general fanzine *Niekas* (which would later include the first publication of Robert Foster's guide to Tolkien's work). Other fanzines such as Greg Shaw's *Entmoot* also began to appear at that time. It is often thought that during the First, or Hardcover, Age of Tolkien Fandom, *The Lord of the Rings* was an obscure work. To be sure, it was still a book with a relatively small audience, but it had sold very well up to that time and had developed an enthusiastic following among science fiction fans. But as 1965 dawned, everything changed.

Tolkien on Campus

1965 was a watershed year in Tolkien fandom. In February, high school student Richard Plotz put up a notice on the 116th Street subway station in New York announcing a meeting of a Tolkien fan group on the Columbia campus; seven people showed up for this outdoor meeting on a sub-freezing afternoon. Encouraged, Plotz placed an ad in the April issue of *The New Republic* for a new Tolkien fan organization. The ad netted 70 responses, and the Tolkien Society of America was born. This was the first fan group to grow out of a "grass roots" population (just Plotz and his high school buddy Bob Foster) rather than out of the traditions of organized science fiction fandom. Tolkien was starting to reach an audience on college campuses. In the summer of that year, an inexpensive paperback edition was published by Ace Books; editor Donald Wollheim had discovered a legal loophole that allowed him to publish this legally without an agreement with Tolkien's agents or the payment of royalties, and it was clear that there would be a substantial market for a paperback edition. Ballantine

Books (which had subsidized the publication of one or two issues of the Tolkien Society of America's *Tolkien Journal*) soon after published an authorized edition complete with a note from the author exhorting fans of the book to purchase this edition and no other. The growing network of Tolkien fans spread the news about how fans should support the author by purchasing the Ballantine edition, and before the end of the year, under pressure from both fans and the Science Fiction Writers of America, Ace Books voluntarily decided to pay Tolkien royalties on the books they sold and to cease publication of further copies.

It should be mentioned that Tolkien still interacted directly with the fans during this period. He exchanged letters regularly with Richard Plotz and other fans, including some lore of Middle-earth not found in the published books. But the ranks of Tolkien fandom were about to swell massively, and Tolkien would find it impossible to maintain this kind of communication before long.

It is often thought that the 1960s explosion of Tolkien's popularity was due to the publication of a paperback edition. But it is not so simple; as we have seen, *The Lord of the Rings* had already achieved significant popularity on college campuses even before the paperback publication. The paperback *enabled* Tolkien's audience to expand greatly, but it did not *create* the demand. There are many possible reasons for Tolkien's popularity among young people at that time, and it is not likely that historians and sociologists will reach a consensus. This burst of admiration seems to have arrived at a time when its themes of preserving the beauty of the natural world against the military and industrial might of Mordor and Isengard dovetailed perfectly with the emerging social movements (especially the environmental and anti-war movements) on the college campuses. Or maybe it's just that hippies thought that "hobbits are groovy." Whatever the reasons, the phenomenon was massive and immediate: the Ballantine edition sold a million copies in its first year. John Clossen's "Frodo Lives" lapel buttons (available through the Tolkien Society) were seen on college campuses across the country. As more magazines and newspapers published articles on Tolkien, including the Tolkien Society's address, membership swelled, reaching 2000 members in 1966. The July 2, 1966, issue of the very mainstream *The Saturday Evening Post* ran an article by Henry Resnick, *The Hobbit-forming World of J.R.R. Tolkien* (perhaps the first major publication to use this pun;

alas, not the last). Tolkien had become an official cultural phenomenon.

Even network television began to get in on the act in their typically surrealistic cluelessness: in the summer of 1967, a teen-audience music show on ABC, *Malibu U*, ran a music video with Leonard Nimoy, the now infamous "Ballad of Bilbo Baggins." More importantly, in 1967, a young fan named Glen GoodKnight organized a Bilbo and Frodo's Birthday Party Picnic in the Los Angeles area and announced the formation of the Mythopoeic Society, an organization to be devoted to the writings of Tolkien and his fellow Inklings, C.S. Lewis and Charles Williams. Members held monthly meetings in their homes to discuss one of the authors' works. At just about the same time, Richard Plotz, faced with academic pressures on his time, turned over the Tolkien Society of America to Ed Meskys, who could apply his considerable experience with fanzine publication and distribution to the Tolkien Society.

Tolkien fandom continued to grow. Tolkien costumes were a commonplace at science fiction conventions; many new fanzines appeared, though of small circulation and sometimes running only a single issue. In 1971, Ed Meskys became blind and could not continue to run the Tolkien Society of America, so its assets were merged into the Mythopoeic Society. In 1971, it held its first convention, Mythcon, with the guest of honor, Inklings scholar C.S. Kilby, reporting on his 1966 visit with Tolkien and talking about some of what he had read of the eagerly awaited *Silmarillion*. Tolkien was still alive and writing, although he rarely interacted directly with fans, and there was endless room for speculation on just what he might be writing about. In September 1973, Tolkien passed away. Tolkien's readers would someday read what he had written, but he would write no more.

A Golden Age for Geeks

Ironically, the death of Tolkien coincided with a burst of creativity in the fantasy field. The early to mid-1970s were very much a golden age for fans of imaginative literature. Tolkien's success had shown publishers that there was a market for fantasy beyond the traditional children's books, and Ballantine had already started the ball rolling in 1969 with the inauguration of their Adult Fantasy Series. For five years, this series reprinted some of the finest fantasy stories of the past, including works by William Morris, Lord Dunsany, James Branch

Cabell, and George MacDonald. Previously, such works had been rather hard to find, and only in hardcover editions. Soon, the series would begin to publish new fantasy works by such authors as Katherine Kurtz and Evangeline Walton.

In 1977, the fantasy phenomenon became evident to even the most casual observer, as the posthumously published *Silmarillion* rose swiftly to top bestseller lists; *Unfinished Tales* would achieve considerable commercial success a few years later. The beast fable book *Watership Down* (with its own lapine mythology and language) was hugely successful, as was Stephen Donaldson's *Thomas Covenant* trilogy, itself markedly influenced by Tolkien's work. A group of fans from the Mythopoeic Society founded The Fantasy Association, which throughout the decade published its own fanzine covering the broad spectrum of modern fantasy literature, the widely respected *Fantasiae*.

It is no coincidence, certainly, that in other media, the influence of Tolkien could be seen. Shoppers in 1972 could purchase a Tolkien Calendar for 1973 displaying Tolkien's own artwork; the 1975 Tolkien Calendar featured art from the master's thesis of (formerly) fan artist Tim Kirk, whose work had first appeared in the *Tolkien Journal*. In 1974, Gary Gygax and Dave Arneson published that groundbreaking fantasy roleplay game, *Dungeons and Dragons*, in which players could take the roles of wizards, dwarves, elves ... or hobbits (before the lawyers explained matters to Gygax). In 1977, cinema was forever changed by the science fantasy blockbuster *Star Wars*; in the same year, Rankin and Bass's animated adaptation of *The Hobbit* was televised. And in 1978, Ralph Bakshi's animated adaptation entitled *The Lord of the Rings* opened in movie theatres around the country.

The Mythopoeic Society itself grew throughout the 1970s, adding many new local discussion groups and new activities such as the Inklings II writers' group. In fact, the Society achieved something usually quite difficult in fandom: it managed to maintain its original backbone of local discussion groups while also supporting a large international membership based on journal subscriptions.

Meanwhile, in a few college campuses and government laboratories, the newly invented ARPANET began to take shape and acquire its own subculture. Fans at MIT and UCLA could chat about Tolkien through this new medium, and by the end of the decade, one of the most popular ARPANET mailing lists was the SF-LOVERS list, which covered science fiction and fantasy, including Tolkien topics. Few took notice at the time, but the first electronic communities were being born.

All in all, the mid-1970s were a wonderful time to be a geek, and Tolkien fans had perhaps the best time of all.

Factories for Fantasy

Perhaps it was inevitable, but the creative energy that led to the fantasy boom of the 1970s was soon taken over by a more commercial-minded regime. The idealistic 1960s were long gone, and the more business-oriented Reagan years were at hand. Perhaps the first sign of change was the 1977 publication of Terry Brooks's *The Sword of Shannara*. This was a hugely promoted trade paperback from Ballantine Books with several illustrations by the Brothers Hildebrandt, including a full-color foldout illustration. But the story itself was a mediocrity by any measure, and very obviously influenced by Tolkien (and little else). This, perhaps, was the distinguishing feature of the fantasy books and movies of the 1980s: while earlier fantasists were well acquainted with the literary traditions of myth, epic, history, and romance and were writing out of the same traditions as Tolkien, the knockoff writers of the 1980s only knew these traditions secondhand, filtered through Tolkien or perhaps other modern writers.

So while the 1970s had brought forth *Dungeons and Dragons*, a vital and creative new work, that same company, now grown large and corporate, brought forth books based on roleplaying game scenarios, such as Weis and Hickman's unoriginal *Dragonlance* books. Instead of *Star Wars*, the movie industry stuck to safe and uninspired generic fantasies like *Krull* or *Hawk the Slayer*. General public interest in Tolkien stabilized and perhaps began to stagnate. By the end of the 1980s, it was not uncommon to find young people of the "MTV generation" who found *The Lord of the Rings* to be dull, slow-paced, and even a bit cliché because they did not read it until after they had already been fully dosed with *Dungeons and Dragons*, *Dragonlance*, and other generic fantasy titles that had their roots in Tolkien (and no deeper). The people who would have provided new blood for the "fun" side of fandom—filk songs, art, fan fiction, or costuming—were doing other things.

During this period, there were no further books like *The Silmarillion* to appeal to a general audience. Instead, the 1980s saw the publication of the *History of Middle-earth* series by Christopher Tolkien, a monumental twelve-volume work of Tolkien scholarship, in which the development of Tolkien's world is traced from its beginnings during World War I until Tolkien's death more than fifty years later. Those fans in groups like the Mythopoeic Society, whose interests in Tolkien took a more scholarly bent (either to study matters within Tolkien's created world, such as his languages, or more conventional scholarship seeking to understand Tolkien's work as literature) were vitalized by Christopher Tolkien's work. Mythcons and the Mythopoeic Society journal *Mythlore* took on an increasingly scholarly appearance, and the quality of Tolkien scholarship (and fantasy scholarship in general) increased dramatically. But the public took relatively little notice of these books, which were really specialty items for hardcore Tolkien devotées (some critics, misunderstanding the academic nature of the books, accused Christopher Tolkien of "literary grave-robbing"). And so matters stood until the electronic communities first nurtured by the ARPANET hackers of the 1970s became accessible to the general public in the 1990s.

The Age of the Internet

Two phenomena coincided during the 1990s to once again revitalize interest in Tolkien in the general public and to reenergize Tolkien fandom. Firstly, the baby-boomer generation, the ones who had carried the paperback edition of *The Lord of the Rings* in their hip pockets on college campuses in the 1960s, had started families and had given their children the book to read as they reached a suitable age. Consequently, in the mid-1990s, there was a whole second generation of new readers discovering Tolkien's world. In another time, this would likely have led to a modest upsurge in fan activity as these new fans discovered fannish institutions like the Mythopoeic Society and shared the book with other friends through word of mouth; a kind of echo of the 1960s.

But as every reader of this article knows, the 1990s were also the years when the internet, once the private domain of computer professionals and hobbyists, became a widespread cultural phenomenon, due primarily to the invention of the World Wide Web protocols by Tim Berners-Lee. Of course, whole volumes have been written documenting the social impact of the internet and WWW, and it would be impossible to analyze even such a restricted domain as Tolkien fandom in a few short paragraphs.

Nevertheless, it seems to this author that Tolkien fandom was not so much altered as magnified by the web. Web sites and forums are not very different from the paper fanzines of the past (in which letters of comment from the readers were of great importance); but they have much more rapid turnover and have circulations that are orders of magnitude larger than even the most successful fanzines. Before the Web, one had to accidentally read an article on Tolkien fandom that gave the address of the Tolkien Society or Mythopoeic Society in order to find those organizations; today, a routine web search produces dozens of prospective sites in which to read articles about Tolkien's world and communicate with other like-minded individuals. In 1965, hundreds of Tolkien fans could raise enough of a ruckus to force the Ace paperback off the market; on the modern internet, tens of thousands of fans created the much sought-after "buzz" about the Peter Jackson films on TheOneRing.net and similar sites well before the films hit theatres. A fan artist like Tim Kirk might expect to have had his work seen by perhaps a few thousand people in the 1960s; in 2004, a WWW page for an artist might be seen by tens or even hundreds of thousands of viewers.

And finally, beginning in 2001, a new element was added: the almost impossibly successful film adaptation of *The Lord of the Rings* directed by Peter Jackson. For the first time, substantial numbers of new readers are being brought to Tolkien's world not by word of mouth, or reading an article, but because they have seen and loved the movie. It is too soon to see what the effect of the movies will be on fandom, just as the long-term effects of the internet are still impossible to predict. But as with the internet, perhaps the effect will be more quantitative than qualitative. Tolkien fan activity will be much the same as it has always been; there will be new and insightful writing about Tolkien's world, scholarship about Tolkien's place in literature and fan fiction of widely variable quality that, in the best cases, expands on and enriches Tolkien's creation. There will be artwork (perhaps too often imitative of the movies, at least in the near term). Fans will invent new filk music and wear costumes based on Tolkien's characters. And finally and most importantly, there will always be little gatherings in which Beorn's honey-cakes and mead will be served, where just a few close friends will sit around the fire conversing in good fellowship and marvel anew at the wonder and richness of Tolkien's gift to us all. And this will honor Tolkien's memory the most of all.

Coming Home

Tehanu

One of the things that I've heard over and over from people is that the first time they read *The Lord of the Rings,* they felt like they had come home at last. I remember that feeling myself. It was the first time I'd read a book of that length, and it was such a luxurious sensation to sink into an adventure that went on and on like that, in a world that seemed to get larger as I went on. And it was always there to return to! That's been the pattern since then: every few years it's time to take a holiday from the surrounding world and go home to Middle-earth, where my welcome is assured.

It's funny that we should feel so at home in a fantasy world. You'd think we'd be going there to get away from it all. "Screw this," you think, in the middle of a stressful workday or a boring weekend, "I'll check out of all this for a few hours and go to Middle-earth." But in reality we're looking for the home we really want, the home we secretly wish for, the one we hope we deserve.

Tolkien helps us out in that fantasy by pretending that Middle-earth really *is* our world and that it's part of our collective past. Tolkien pretends that our present world is based on his history, his mythology, and that we've merely forgotten. He's the lonely archaeologist excavating the lost history with torch and trowel. That is how it felt to him, as he explained in his famous *Letter #131* to Milton Waldman. To him it appeared that the stories were waiting to be uncovered, and he was, in his own words, "given" them as he wrote. He states that he always had a feeling of recording information that already existed, not inventing it himself. He persuades us that we're reading our lost past and coming home to our own history.

It's interesting that the subtitle to *The Hobbit* is "There and Back Again." Right from the title page of his first completed tale of Middle-earth, the idea of returning home is put alongside the idea of adventure. It's the shortest possible summary of the archetypal Hero's Tale and states that the adventure includes the return home.

And how the book celebrates "home" right throughout the story! As I reread *The Hobbit* this time I noticed how much of the Shire we see in Peter Jackson's films is actually taken from that book rather than *The Lord of the Rings*. The detailed description of what a hobbit-hole is, from the round door with a yellow brass knob in the middle to the polished and paneled interior of Bag End—that is right on the first page of *The Hobbit*. Later on, when Bilbo is crossing the Misty Mountains, he casts his mind back to the Shire, where it is already summer, summer of haymaking and picnics, berrying and the fullness of harvest. In the film of *The Return of the King*, the writers deftly used this type of thing in Sam and Frodo's dialogue on the slopes of Mount Doom, as they remember and mourn the Shire they believe they will never see again. The film's much-quoted reference to "second breakfast" is from *The Hobbit* too, and the hobbits' love of food is clear from the lovingly detailed inventory of Bilbo's pantry, which his Dwarf visitors enjoy in "The Unexpected Party."

But the it's the key word "comfort" that is repeated again and again. "It was a hobbit-hole, and that means comfort," we learn on the first page. Caught in the rain in the Lone-lands, he dreams of his kettle singing on the hob by a nice fire back in Bag End. Looking back west from the perilous passes of the Misty Mountains, Bilbo looks back to his own land of "safe and comfortable things." Stuck in the dark underground before meeting Gollum, he thinks of himself frying bacon and eggs back in his own little kitchen. Held high in the air in an Eagle's claws, he's asked what could be better than flying. He immediately thinks of hot baths and breakfast on the lawn back home. In fact it is a habit of Tolkien's to have Bilbo dwell on thoughts of a nice loaf of bread and butter, or tea and toast, or some other pleasant meal, in the midst of his most trying adventures. The words "nice" and "little" occur again and again when the Shire is mentioned. *The Hobbit* is a paean to the joys of an ordinary life.

There and Back Again: Clearly, the adventure is not completed, and maybe it has no meaning, until the hero returns home, bringing whatever wealth or wisdom the journey gave him. That is true of Bilbo, returning from the Lonely Mountain and finding he's lost his reputation among respectable hobbits, but on the other hand, he's an Elf-friend, a companion of wizards, a writer of poetry and wealthy to boot. In the very last pages of *The Hobbit*, Tolkien describes Bilbo's remaining years in his comfortable hobbit-hole in glowing terms. His kettle is ever ready on the hearth to offer tea to his many visitors, the more adventurous young Took relatives admire him and seek him out, and his house is a center of hospitality for passing elves, dwarves and wizards. Tolkien doesn't say, but it is possible that from their point of view, Bag End became a kind of "Very Last Homely House" to all such travelers heading West. There they could expect Bilbo to host them, to feed them, to listen to their tales, to swap poems and songs, to try to speak their language, and generally give them whatever time and space they needed while they took a break from their journeys.

The second most notable feature of all these adventures is the importance of peace. The Shire is above all a place that has forgotten war. As the dwarves discuss their plans for tackling Smaug, Gandalf tells the dwarves that there is a shortage of warrior heroes in the Shire. "Swords in these parts are mostly blunt, and axes are used for trees, and shields as cradles or dish-covers." Sitting on Smaug's doorstep much later he dreams of "the quiet Western Land and the Hill and his hobbit-hole under it." Tolkien never lets the story go on too long without contrasting the present peril with the peaceful joys and delights of the home Bilbo has left behind.

The primary hallmark of home, of a home to be wished for and sought after, is its hospitality. Both great adventures, Bilbo's and Frodo's, start with a party where the food is lavish and unstinting: the unexpected tea-party for the dwarves and Gandalf, and the Birthday Party for Bilbo, to which most of the Shire is invited. Then who can forget the hospitality of Rivendell? Rivendell is full of guests always, and when Frodo arrives there it seems as if the singing and dancing and feasting have been going on uninterrupted since Bilbo first visited. For both of them, the hospitality there is the cure for their fear and weariness.

Elsewhere there are other homely houses, like islands of light and cheer in a hostile world Tom Bombadil's house is one, and Beorn's house another. Visitors are fed and entertained and sent on their way with all the help their hosts can offer. However, it couldn't be said that any of the places outside the Shire welcome all comers. The hobbits have to win their right of entry, either by having the magical companion Gandalf along to vouch for them, or by being on a great Quest, or by being "Elf-friends," something that Goldberry detects in Frodo's eyes and speech. All kindly creatures disposed to help the Council of the Wise are on the lookout to help Frodo if they can, and some, like Gildor's folk or Tom Bombadil, do their part.

For restoring the weary traveler, though, nothing can compare to Rivendell—ideal for all moods and all seasons, apparently. Nobody forgets that famous first description of it in *The Hobbit*. It's the perfect place, whether one wants to sit and think and be alone, or to trade stories, or dance, or eat, or walk in the friendly woods where Tolkien says no evil ever came. One could be as sociable or as solitary as one liked.

Presumably many things went on that Tolkien doesn't describe directly, such as the forging of weapons and the making of beautiful things—jewels, maybe, or musical instruments. There would be great kitchens and gardens to supply them. People would be writing books and music. Others would be tending the trees of the woods, watching over them for long years and getting to know them before choosing to the right moment to fell (with what reverence or ritual we can only guess) perhaps one certain tree for fine carpentry, or another that was fitted for making musical instruments. Meanwhile, some would be riding out to gather news or weaving the ingathered news into the history that Rivendell already kept in its great libraries. Lastly, Rivendell was a center of strategy and policy among the loose affiliation of its friends, and it had more active souls who served it as messengers and knights errant. We see Glorfindel, Elladan, Elrohir and Aragorn setting out from and returning to Rivendell in that way, like King Arthur's knights serving and venturing from Camelot. Thus there was room for many kinds of personalities in Rivendell, provided that they were well intentioned. There was comfort and freedom to pursue whatever suited them best.

It's interesting how many people in Middle-earth are engaged in a quest to get home. Bilbo spends most of his journey wishing he were home; like Sam, his attitude seems to be that there is a job to be done before he can finally turn homewards, but no doubt in his mind that home is where he's headed in the long run. But it's not only the hobbits who are obsessed with going home. Bilbo's dwarves, for instance, consider the Lonely Mountain to be their home, and they want to drive the dragon out so they can reclaim it. Their songs in *The Hobbit* are filled with their love of the dark deep places and the sound of them when they were living cities. They delight in the ringing music of their craftsmen's hammers and the light of the shining gems they mined. You can hear how joyfully they worked creating beautiful and cunningly wrought things out of the precious metals they loved. That is the perfect home of dwarves, whether other races would like it or not. In *The Lord of the Rings* Gimli goes further. After he has seen the Glittering Caves of Aglarond he waxes rhapsodical about their beauty. His speech to Legolas tells us that dwarves love the caves and stone for their own sake and would tend the gardens of stalactites reverently.

For their part, the Elves are engaged in a quest to return to Elvenhome across the sea. Some few, such as Galadriel, were born there and partly wish to return, but they are exiled and it is many thousands of years before they are forgiven and may return. The rest know that it is a place made for them, the place appropriate to their magical and immortal nature, and they long to be there. But at the same time, during their thousands of years of life in Middle-earth, they have fallen in love with it and cling to it. They love it, but it cannot entirely be their home. It is one of those things that Tolkien never entirely explains, but which we have to accept as the rule in Middle-earth: the world is fated to change and become the domain of Men, and the magic must fade. Everywhere that the three Elven Rings do not hold sway, the world is falling away from them, losing magic, moving forward to the present day. The Elves are losing their powers.

Frodo sees Lothlórien as a place marooned in time; whether Rivendell and the Grey Havens are the same, Tolkien does not say. Elrond the Half-elven can perhaps be at home in both worlds, and integrate Rivendell into the rest of the world. At the Grey Havens, Cirdan's gift is to make the crossing between Middle-earth and Valinor possible. His ships link the mortal world of Middle-earth with the magical and immortal world of Valinor. In Lothlórien, Galadriel with her ring Nenya holds out the mortal world and denies the passing of time for as long as possible. As Sam notices when the Fellowship leaves Lórien, time within its borders runs at a different rate, and he cannot reconcile the phases of the Moon outside to the apparent length of time the Fellowship has spent inside.

The sadness of the Elves is partly that they have lived in Middle-earth long enough to explore it and inhabit it thoroughly. They once built great cities like Gondolin and Nevrast and Nargothrond, long since abandoned. They once taught the Ents to talk and shaped the mallorn trees to their needs. After much struggle they have finally learnt to live together in peace among themselves, but Middle-earth cannot ever quite be their home. The Elves may know it better than anything else that lives there, but they cannot stay. Their gift of foreknowledge tells them that the Fourth Age must come, and when it does, the magic will go, and they must follow it or become diminished.

Legolas is surely not the only one who is disturbed by the sound of crying gulls and by dreams of gray ships and the sea road to the West. His song on the Field of Cormallen tells us that the days of the Elves in Middle-earth are ending and the voices of his people call him to Elvenhome, the Last Shore, "*the land of my people forever.*" He's never been there, but he yearns to go home. According to the song, all his people feel that longing.

In the end, isn't that the way of it? Sometimes home is a place we've never seen before. We come home to the place where we're understood, where they listen to us and they speak our language, where we're welcomed in and treated with hospitality. For so many of us, Middle-earth has proved to be more than a good book. It's become, for our imaginations, a good home.

Sources:

The Hobbit, J.R.R Tolkien. Houghton and Mifflin Company, Boston, 1994.

The Lord of the Rings. J.R.R Tolkien. Houghton and Mifflin Company one-volume edition, Boston, 1987.

Reading Tolkien Beyond *The Lord of the Rings*

Turgon

One of the most frequent questions I have received from readers of Green Books has to do with what to read by Tolkien after *The Hobbit* and *The Lord of the Rings*. And this is not really a straightforward question. What I find is usually meant by it is how should one approach *The Silmarillion*, *Unfinished Tales*, and the twelve-volume series *The History of Middle-earth*. The truest answer is to read as much, or as little, as you like. But that hardly offers any guidance to what's out there, so I'll attempt to give some brief notes here, considering only Tolkien's Middle-earth writings.

Tolkien wrote in what might be classified as three main styles. The first is the novelistic style, as is found in both *The Hobbit* and *The Lord of the Rings*. The second is more like a chronicle, a distant narration of events. And the third style is essay-like. Both the second and third styles are fairly represented in the Appendices to *The Lord of the Rings*—the chronicle style can be found in Appendices A and B, the "Annals of the Kings" (including the "Tale of Aragorn and Arwen") and the "Tale of Years;" the essay style is used in the other appendices (C, D and E) on calendars, writings, and languages.

The Silmarillion is mostly written in the chronicle mode. It begins with an elvish creation myth, the "Ainulindalë," and an account of the god-like Valar, the "Valaquenta". Both are written in an archaic, almost biblical style. The book becomes far more easily readable once you get to the "Quenta Silmarillion" proper, which is the major portion of the book. Two shorter works conclude the volume, the "Akallabêth," an account of the downfall of Númenor, and "Of the Rings of Power and the Third Age."

Unfinished Tales (actually the full title is *Unfinished Tales of Númenor and Middle-earth*) is just what the title says, but it contains writings by Tolkien in all three styles. Unfortunately, most of these writings are indeed unfinished. So the nearly one hundred pages of the novelistic Tale of the Children of Húrin, the "Narn i Hîn Húrin," is not quite complete, while the history of a Númenorean mariner and his wife, "Aldarion and Erendis," simply breaks off midstream. Other pieces, in both the chronicle and essay modes, were originally intended to be part of the Appendices to *The Lord of the Rings*, but were cut for reasons of length. These include Gandalf's account of how he arranged Bilbo's journey, "The Quest of Erebor," and materials on Celeborn and Galadriel, the Drúedain, the Palantiri, and the Istari (or wizards).

The History of Middle-earth is a twelve-volume series edited by Christopher Tolkien, who basically took the rest of his father's papers relating to Middle-earth and published them chronologically according to when the various items were written. Thus the first two volumes, composing *The Book of Lost Tales*, were written just after World War I when Tolkien was in his twenties, while the final volume contains his last writings on Middle-earth before his death in 1973.

The History of Middle-earth is a grab-bag of miscellaneous and very different types of writings: long poems in rhyming couplets and in alliterative verse, prose narratives and chronologies, short poems and tales and essays, unfinished novels and the early drafts of what became *The Lord of the Rings*. There are many reworkings of various legends of the First Age of Middle-earth, some strikingly different from what is known from the published *Silmarillion*. No short listing here of the contents can do this series justice. In order, the twelve volumes of the *History of Middle-earth* series are as follows: I. *The Book of Lost Tales, Part One*. II. *The Book of Lost Tales, Part Two*. III. *The Lays of Beleriand*. IV. *The Shaping of Middle-earth*. V. *The Lost Road and Other Writings*. VI. *The Return of the Shadow*. VII. *The Treason of Isengard*. VIII. *The War of the Ring*. IX. *Sauron Defeated*. X. *Morgoth's Ring*. XI. *The War of the Jewels*. XII. *The Peoples of Middle-earth*.

To turn back to the question of what to read after *The Hobbit* and *The Lord of the Rings*, this can be answered in part in relation to one's personal reaction to Tolkien's three styles. If you love the chronicles and essays in the Appendices, you have lots of real treats coming, but if you favor only the novelistic storytelling in *The Hobbit* and *The Lord of the Rings*, there is a more limited range of delights. Two shorter works should not be missed by anyone—the "Epilogue" to *The Lord of the Rings* (in volume IX of the *History of Middle-earth* series), in which Sam answers various questions after having read the Red Book to his children. And in volume XII, there is a tantalizing single chapter of a sequel to *The Lord of the Rings* that Tolkien began (and unfortunately abandoned). It is set about a hundred years after the death of Aragorn and concerns the emergence of secret orc-cults. The chapter is called "The New Shadow."

Next I'd say read *The Silmarillion*, bearing in mind that it is a kind of compendious chronology of elvish mythology and of the history of Elves and Men in the First Age of Middle-earth, thousands of years before the events of *The Lord of the Rings*. If the early parts of *The Silmarillion* are found to be difficult or offputting, I'd recommend jumping forward and reading two chapters by themselves: chapter XIX, which tells the story of Beren and Luthien, and chapter XXI, which tell the story of Túrin. These are two of the major stories of *The Silmarillion* and are among the very best parts of the book. They should not be missed by lovers of Tolkien.

If you like the Appendices to *The Lord of the Rings* and have sampled (or even read) *The Silmarillion*, I'd say the next book to tackle is *Unfinished Tales*. It stands as a kind of sampler (though it doesn't really overlap in contents) of just the type of writings you will find in the *History of Middle-earth* series. I feel it is important point to note that, for any level of interest, *Unfinished Tales* and the twelve-volume series need not be read in the order of presentation or publication. Browse any of these books and read whatever interests you at any given time. What might seem uninteresting on first look, you might find utterly engrossing another time. And vice-versa.

Many volumes of the *History of Middle-earth* series contain variant forms of tales and legends found in *The Silmarillion*, but there are a number of different treats as well. Around 1936 Tolkien and his friend C.S. Lewis had a toss-up, whereby one would write a time-travel story, and the other would write a science fiction tale. C.S. Lewis's science fiction novel, *Out of the Silent Planet*, was his entry, while Tolkien never finished his fascinating story of time-travel, "The Lost Road," in which a father-and-son pair recall the downfall of Númenor. Some years later Tolkien tried again with a similar idea, now called "The Notion Club

Papers," with the fictional Notion Club based on Tolkien and Lewis's writers group, the Inklings. I find both of these fragments endlessly interesting. They appear in volumes V and IX.

In the right mood, the sub-series (volumes VI through VIII, along with part of volume IX which is published separately in paperback as *The End of the Third Age*) on the writing of *The Lord of the Rings* is a marvelous look at how Tolkien wrote the book. Can you believe that Frodo was once named Bingo Bolger-Baggins, or Strider was initially a hobbit named Trotter who wore wooden shoes? Yes, Tolkien changed these names for the better, but there are also a number of details in the drafts of *The Lord of the Rings* that do not conflict with the published version and add to the appreciation of it.

And lastly, I'd recommend that you don't neglect the collection *The Letters of J.R.R. Tolkien*, edited by Humphrey Carpenter and Christopher Tolkien. Sure, this is a collection of letters, not stories, but the great bulk of the letters were written to admirers of *The Lord of the Rings* and in the letters Tolkien gives many details about the peoples, legends and history of Middle-earth that are not otherwise available. Most of these letters are written in the style of essays, so again they almost seem like outtakes from the Appendices.

Tolkien's creation of Middle-earth was a lifelong passion, sometimes reaching perfection as in *The Lord of the Rings*, while at other times never even achieving a published form in the author's lifetime. That we have such posthumous publications as are found in the History of Middle-earth series is remarkable, and I encourage readers to sample them to see for themselves the various modes and expressions of Tolkien's genius.

Explorers of
Middle-earth
Dark Lord
Elven Realms
Horse Lords
Little People
MORDOR

Explorers of Middle-earth

Anwyn

In the same way that Tolkien found himself eyed slightly askance by his colleagues for puttering around with mythology instead of focusing wholly on philology, there is a growing number of scholars today who are questioned for engaging in a branch of academia that others may find odd—Middle-earth and its historian.

Tolkien as food for serious study is not a strange idea, but still it is not surprising that those hardy scholars who undertake to carry out that idea can be derided or marginalized. The reason why is not far to seek: timing. Tolkien has been dead only thirty years, the popular focus of his work, *The Lord of the Rings,* published only fifty or so. While it is true that college courses include many works being written today, it is not as often that you find whole branches of academia devoted to current authors. Tolkien himself worked hard to institute syllabus reforms at Oxford that didn't require students to waste time on more recent authors, and the habit of studying only that which is removed from us by a century or more is long ingrained.

But this is a fast age. The internet caters to humankind's innate desire for instant gratification. We as a people no longer wait for time to give a topic, a person, or a work its value. We explore it right away to determine its value for ourselves. Thus the resumes of distinguished scholars may now include that they teach a course on Tolkien, that they have published several books on Middle-earth and Tolkien.

The academics in the following pages—Anne C. Petty, Ph.D. in English literature; Verlyn Flieger, teacher of Tolkien and mythology at the University of Maryland; Douglas A. Anderson, versatile author, annotator, and editor; Jance Chance, professor of English at Rice University; Karen Wynn Fonstad, cartographer of *The Atlas of Middle-*

earth; and Brad Birzer, professor of history at Hillsdale College—have graciously given of their time and insights in conversations with Turgon, Quickbeam, and Anwyn, and we proudly share them with you.

Q&A with Anne C. Petty

Turgon

Anne C. Petty received her Ph.D. in English literature from Florida State University. Her dissertation was published as *One Ring to Bind Them All: Tolkien's Mythology* (1979; reprinted with a new introduction and expanded bibliography 2002). Another book, *Tolkien in the Land of Heroes: Discovering the Human Spirit*, came out in August 2003. And just published is a book that includes a chapter on Tolkien, *Dragons of Fantasy*. Check out her website at www.annepetty.com.

Q: Your first book, *One Ring to Bind Them All: Tolkien's Mythology*, grew out of your Ph.D. dissertation. It covers Tolkien's writings—in particular *The Hobbit* and *The Lord of the Rings*—from a much different perspective than the usual source of studies and literary criticism, approaching Tolkien by way of the methodology of folklorists and of comparative mythologists. For our readers who may be unfamiliar with these approaches, can you give a bit of an introduction to them and how you apply them to Tolkien?

A: Well, let me put the book in context. In the early '70s, when I was a graduate student looking for a dissertation topic, J.R.R. Tolkien was still alive, Shippey's source-based study, *The Road to Middle-earth*, and Flieger's *Splintered Light* wouldn't be written for another 10 years, and in fact, not much in the way of academic research into Tolkien's writings was available. Joseph Campbell was still alive, and his writings and lectures about myth and civilization were quite popular on American college campuses. The field of comparative mythology was relatively new, especially in terms of what Campbell saw as the "comprehensive effect of myths" in literature, the arts, and psychology. I met Campbell when he spoke to our English department during a book tour and asked him what he thought of applying his theories from *The Hero with a Thousand Faces* to the fiction of Tolkien. He was encouraging, and my ideas for a myth-based study of Tolkien's fiction took shape.

As an English literature major with specialization in creative writing and a minor in humanities, I found the study of myth and mythmaking very appealing. I had just finished reading *The Lord of the Rings*, recommended to me by a fellow doctoral student, and I realized there was much more to the work than mere fantasy entertainment. I felt that it was an example of genuine mythmaking, and that Campbell's discussion of the ubiquitous quest myth—departure, initiation, return—put Tolkien's epic into much fuller perspective. I felt then—and still do—that Tolkien was a mythmaker for our modern age. I like Verlyn Flieger's observation that myth "names" and "arranges"—it organizes, but it doesn't necessarily explain. For example, "the splendid mythic resonance of Genesis 1, in which God created the world by speaking it into existence, does not explain either the How or the Why of that world, or God's motive for making it." Tolkien's vision of Middle-earth has that same effect.

Flieger also refers to Campbell's four categories of the major uses of myth: Cosmological, Transcendental, Socio-political, and Psychological. These ideas, along with those of Claude Lévi-Strauss and Vladimir Propp (who categorized the structure underlying many fairy tales), formed the basis for my study of Tolkien as mythmaker. Did Tolkien consciously set out to follow those age-old mythic patterns for his plot? Likely not, but that was my point—what he created was the genuine act of mythmaking, not a surface attempt to write a story according to a set pattern. His mythos of Middle-earth evolved over many years and was still evolving and shifting at his death, as mythologies and the cultures that support them do in real life. To me, the fact that his fiction continues to fascinate and move readers in the 21st century attests to the effectiveness of his "mythic imagination." It appeals to something beyond the literary taste of the moment. The validity of the "Tolkien as mythmaker" approach is illustrated in a recent collection of papers from the International Congress on Medieval Studies edited by Jane Chance under the title *Tolkien and the Invention of Myth*.

Q: More than twenty years passed between your first book on Tolkien and the second, *Tolkien in the Land of Heroes*. Did you go away from studying Tolkien and subsequently return? What was the impetus for the second book?

A: By the time *One Ring to Bind Them All* was published, my writing career had veered off in a different direction, away from literary analysis and more focused on creative writing: fiction, screenplays, and poetry. I also started building up a body of commercial freelance work (articles and photos) in arts, lifestyle, and culture magazines. I did write occasional scholarly articles, but they were mostly about the craft of writing rather than a specific author. Then I got recruited by a private corporation to become their publications director and senior technical editor, which opened up a totally different career path of managing editorial departments and teaching seminars in writing, which I did for several different corporations. At that time I was also involved in helping found the Tallahassee Writer's Association and the Florida Film Association, which gave me the chance to teach seminars in scriptwriting for both commercial and educational formats.

I had some correspondence off and on in the late 1990s with the University of Alabama Press about a second edition of *One Ring to Bind Them All*, but that didn't really get off the ground until a new editor in chief came on board and moved the project into high gear. Peter Jackson's first film was hitting the theaters at about the same time, so it was propitious timing. It also gave me a chance to catch up on current Tolkien scholarship and to see just how much the landscape had changed since my first book was written. Tolkien has now become a respectable component of academia, whereas when I was coming through the system, I had a devil of a time convincing my doctoral committee that the chap in England who wrote those cultish fantasy books about dragons and dark lords was worthy of a dissertation.

After the second edition of *One Ring to Bind Them All* was published, I was approached by Cold Spring Press to write a book on Tolkien that would appeal to a more general readership. Because I had quite a few new ideas about Tolkien's fiction, especially *The Lord of the Rings*—and had learned more about life in the years since my first book—I welcomed the chance to put those thoughts into a new book.

Q: *Tolkien in the Land of Heroes* moves into a more familiar type of discourse on what you call in the introduction "the grand themes" in

Tolkien's writings: "the nature of evil, the use and abuse of power, the joys and sorrows of living, and the need for heroes both great and small." The style is very conversational and readable. Tell us a bit about what you've learned about Tolkien from this thematic approach.

A: The style and content of *Tolkien in the Land of Heroes* came out of two things, I think. First are all the years I've spent as a wordsmith, both teaching people how to write clearly and spending a lot of effort shaping and organizing other people's ideas into readable manuscripts. This produced the conversational tone you mentioned. The second thing is the change in demographics of people who want to read books written about Tolkien. With the popularity of Jackson's movies has come an almost insatiable thirst from old and new fans to understand more about the stories and their larger importance. I wanted to share my views on how the themes of life are richly woven into the substance of Tolkien's fiction, but I wanted to do it in terms that anyone, whether an academic and a general reader, could enjoy. Writing this kind book, one that's scholarly yet user-friendly, was a liberating experience, actually.

Remember those wonderful James Burke *Connections* television programs? My major professor had that same kind of synthesizing mind, one that could see patterns and paradigms and resonances over a wide body of knowledge. I felt that *Tolkien in the Land of Heroes* was in some ways an homage to his influence on me and my ability to think in a straight line while paying close attention to side roads and alternate routes that might crop up along the way. I learned from him how the comparative study of the mythologies of the world brings into focus the commonalities with which humans tell the stories of their cultures, covering everything from creation to the end of the world. These commonalities are the great themes that often form the bedrock of fiction and elevate storytelling to great literature.

Q: In your new book, *Dragons of Fantasy*, Tolkien is covered in only a chapter, but the subject of the book as a whole is certainly one that would have interested him greatly. For you, what is the attraction of dragons?

A: As I say at the end of the book, like "so many others seduced by the Worm, I love the idea of them and the power of Faerie that clings to their hides." I believe it's the volatile blend of terrifying bestiality and raw physical power set against cold intellect and magical empowerment that makes dragons so alluring. I think Tolkien said much the same thing. As a child, I read about them in Andrew Lang's color *Fairy Book* series and stared at pictures of them in illustrated retellings of Germanic myths and legends. I especially remember one very powerful black and white illustration of Fáfnir in mortal combat with Sigurd, where the dragon looms over the hero, dwarfing him with its coils. The dragon seems invincible, yet you know it's doomed. That always struck me as tragic.

I have always loved encountering dragons in fiction, even when they're just animal brutes like J.K. Rowling's tournament dragons, but when there's a cunning mind behind those catlike eyes, the dragonspell just sucks me in. When I was a little kid, my favorite make-believe character to play was a wise old dragon with tourmaline-colored scales that flashed magenta, teal, and ultramarine. I didn't use those color names when I was a first-grader, but I can still vividly see them the way I envisioned my dragon alter-ego in those days. *These* days, I'm working that vision into a fantasy novel with my old scaly loremaster as the main character.

Q: You have divided the book into two main sections—the first covers several modern fantasy writers and their dragons, while the second gives the historical background of beliefs about dragons over the years. That seemed almost backwards to me. Why did you do it that way?

A: I'm laughing as I read this question. That was a marketing decision, based on the assumption that since the book is aimed at general readers, it shouldn't start out like a textbook. So the book begins with Tolkien, Glaurung, and Smaug. As I suggest in the Introduction, if you prefer, there's no harm in reading the Dragonology chapters first and then diving into the chapters on specific writers.

Q: Tell us about your favorite dragons and dragon stories.

A: Smaug is definitely at or near the top of my list. Tolkien just got it right when it comes to turning a monster of myth and legend into a thinking, conniving, fully drawn character. Smaug is by turns frightening, funny, and ultimately vulnerable. I love the way he manipulates the other characters, but is manipulated by them as well. The way Tolkien builds up readers' expectations about Smaug throughout *The Hobbit* until the moment of truth when Bilbo finally steps out of the tunnel and into the dragon's lair is masterful, You can just feel the sweat trickling down his neck as he gets closer to the cavern and it becomes painfully obvious that the dragon is real instead of an often-told legend. I'll be speaking about Smaug and Tolkien's other dragons at this year's Dragon*Con in Atlanta, as part of the Tolkien Track programming.

I'm also intrigued by the dragons in George R.R. Martin's *Song of Ice and Fire* series. The blend of ancient dragon and human lineage is appealing and gets a great send-up in the final pages of *The Game of Thrones*. The book ends with the iconic scene in which Daenerys Stormborn steps into the inferno of her husband's funeral pyre as three rare dragon eggs hatch in the heat. Martin's prose can be turgid and overwrought on occasion, but here he strikes just the right note: "As Daenerys Targaryen rose to her feet, her black *hissed*, pale smoke venting from its mouth and nostrils. The other two pulled away from her breasts and added their voices to the call, translucent wings unfolding and stirring the air, and for the first time in hundreds of years, the night came alive with the music of dragons." Great stuff!

And I must mention the golden Dragon of Romance found in Lord Dunsany's short-short story, "Miss Cubbidge and the Dragon of Romance." I'd gladly trade places with her!

Q: What else have you published on Tolkien?

A: I'm really pleased to have a chapter in the premiere volume of *Tolkien Studies*, the annual hardback collection of Tolkien essays launched in April 2004 and edited by Douglas Anderson, Michael Drout, and Verlyn Flieger. My article, "Identifying England's Lönnrot," looks at the similarities between Elias Lönnrot, the compiler (and some say author) of Finland's *Kalevala*, and Tolkien, especially regarding his work on *The Silmarillion*.

My chapter on *The Hobbit* (titled "Tolkien's Prelude") from *One Ring to Bind Them All* has been published separately in the volume *J.R.R. Tolkien,* which is part of the *Modern Critical Views* series edited by Harold Bloom.

Q: Your website says that you are working on two things, another book on Tolkien titled *Echoes of the Kalevala in Middle-earth*, and a series of speculative fiction novels inspired by mythological tales of the Australian Dreamtime. Tell us a bit about each project.

A: I first read W.F. Kirby's translation of *Kalevala: The Land of*

Heroes when I was in high school and immediately committed whole passages of it to memory, I loved it so much. At the time, the Hiawatha-like singsong rhythm didn't deter me from being transported completely to the spellbound frozen lands of the ancient Finns. I've since read four other translations of it, and by far prefer the version rendered by Eino Friberg. In any case, if you're going to study the *Kalevala*'s influence on Tolkien, you must refer to Kirby's translation because that's the one Tolkien read. I've been thinking about Tolkien's Finnish connection for a number of years, and was actually starting to work on it when I got the green light for the second edition of *One Ring to Bind Them All,* so I put it aside temporarily. Before I could get back to it, I was offered contracts for two books from Cold Spring Press, so it's still waiting for me to gear it up again.

My fiction project is also something I've been working at off and on for several years and is just now coming together. As I said earlier, I have always been a wordsmith, by vocation and avocation, and have been writing fiction and poetry since I was about five or six. When my mother died years ago, I found my first "book" among other childhood artifacts she had saved and packed away in a dresser drawer. It was done on a piece of cardboard folded to make a book, written in orange and red crayon, and titled "The Dog Who Lost His Bark." Inside it said, "Once there was a dog. Who lost his bark. He was sad. Then he found it again," plus illustrations. My mother had written "age 6" on the back. I have to think I've come a long way since then.

Regarding the fiction project, I don't want to say too much about the plot of the first novel in the Wandjina series (four are planned), but I can tell you that it involves encounters with certain Dreamtime entities in a modern-day urban setting.

Q: And finally what are your views on Peter Jackson's three films of *The Lord of the Rings*?

A: As I told Anthony Burdge when he interviewed me for Heren Istarion [See www.herenistarion.org/parmanole/PettyInterview.html], I have a love/hate relationship with the movies. I've seen all three films multiple times in the theater (took part in the Trilogy Tuesday festivities at Ft. Myers, Florida, when *The Return of the King* premiered) and own the extended DVD versions, which I think are far superior to the theatrical cuts. I think all three films are beautiful to look at, the acting is mostly fine, and the music (treating all three films as one long opus) is one of the best film scores I've heard in years. That said, here are my reservations about the films.

Jackson and his creative team got so many things right that when they seriously missed the mark I found it hugely frustrating. The script (again, treating all three as a whole) devised by Jackson, Boyens, and Walsh is to be commended for salvaging many gems from Tolkien's actual dialogue, but it also has some problems, especially concerning character interpretation. If they had just trusted Tolkien's reasons for creating his main characters as you find them in the books, and trusted the movie audiences to "get it," most of these problems would have been eliminated. I guess you could call me a quasi-purist, if there can be such a thing. I didn't really mind the elimination of some characters, such as Tom Bombadil and Glorfindel, but it was the skewing off the plumb of significant characters such as Aragorn, Elrond, and Faramir that kept me from embracing the films. Saddest to me was the excising of all Aragorn's "magical" attributes that attest to the Elvish side of his ancestry and that make him the *true* king (there's a reason Sauron fears a Númenórean revival, and it isn't the fact that Aragorn can kill a dozen orcs with a single sword swipe).

As I've said in other interviews, Jackson's version of Aragorn has lost his aura of otherworldly power. The scriptwriters give him recurring lines that emphasize the weakness that flows in his veins when in fact his bloodline flows straight from High Elven sources that include Thingol (a High Elf) and Melian (a Maia); Lúthien Tinúviel and Beren; Dior (Thingol's heir) and Nimloth; Eärendil and Elwing; and finally, Elros (Elrond's brother) who founds the line of Númenóreans. Jackson's Aragorn is just a brave warrior and a sensitive fellow who can weep on demand, but in the books he is so much more. We are also robbed of the wonderful relationship that develops between Aragorn and Éomer. Unless some unexpected footage shows up in the extended cut of *The Return of the King*, they don't even meet on the battlefield.

Tolkien's Aragorn is clearly worthy of marrying into the Elvish side of the family once he accomplishes the task set for him by his foster father and prospective father-in-law. But not film Aragorn. Did anyone watching the films who hadn't read the books even realize that Aragorn considered Elrond his foster father, which makes their estrangement all the more poignant? Which brings me to the problem with Elrond. Yes, he is stern and demanding of Aragorn, but he also loves him as a son, which was missing from the film. Film Elrond seems more petulant than commanding, more sour and resentful than heartsick over the potential loss of both his Evenstar and his foster son.

And Faramir? Well, he improved somewhat in the third film, but I still feel that the whole encounter with Frodo and Sam in Ithilien got so warped off track that the ripple effect mostly ruined the complex Faramir-Denethor relationship, reducing Denethor to a pig and Faramir to an enigma. The nobility of movie Denethor only exists in Boromir's mind when he chats with Aragorn in Lothlórien.

So, did I enjoy the films at all? Yes, certainly. I just feel they could have been so much better by following Tolkien's very carefully woven plotlines more faithfully, which would have allowed the characters to retain their original attributes rather than devolve into lesser Men and Elves.

Q&A with Verlyn Flieger

Turgon

Verlyn Flieger is a well known Tolkien scholar, with three books on Tolkien to her credit. The first, *Splintered Light: Logos and Language in Tolkien's World*, came out in 1983. Her second, *A Question of Time: J.R.R. Tolkien's Road to Faerie* (1997), won the Mythopoeic Scholarship Award from the Mythopoeic Society, as did her third book, *Tolkien's Legendarium: Essays on the History of Middle-earth* (2000), which she co-edited with Carl F. Hostetter. In 2002 Flieger published not one but two new books. The first is a major revision of her first book on Tolkien, *Splintered Light*, while the second is her first novel, *Pig Tale*. The publisher of the novel, Hyperion, describes it as follows: "Verlyn Flieger weaves elements from Celtic mythology into an unforgettable tale that explores universal truths about the human condition—society's need for scapegoats, the yearning to belong, and love's transcendent power to make the world anew. Thought-provoking, unflinching and original, *Pig Tale* will break your heart, and utterly astonish you." In 2005, Kent State University Press will be publishing her next book on Tolkien, *Interrupted Music: Tolkien's Making of His Mythology*.

Verlyn Flieger teaches Tolkien and mythology at the University of Maryland. Check out her website at: www.mythus.com.

Q. Tell us about the revised edition of *Splintered Light*. What is the central thesis of the book, and how does the new edition differ from the first?

A. I'll answer the last question first. The new edition simply has more information and therefore gives a richer picture. So much more of Tolkien's work has been published than was accessible when my book first came out in 1983—the whole *History of Middle-earth*, twelve volumes detailing the growth of a mythology. In especial, there's more linguistic material available, and I was able to cross-check and in some cases emend things I had written earlier. So I've greatly expanded the linguistic discussion. I've also gone into detail on the influence of the discipline of folklore studies, which was in a state of flux when Tolkien was beginning work on his mythology. The whole subject was in ferment, and there was enormous theoretical disagreement among folklorists. You can find Tolkien's take on the whole controversy in his essay "On Fairy-stories," where he shoots down the current theories and then provides his own. And of course, his own work is the best illustration of what he thought mythology was and what it was for. Re-reading and revising *Splintered Light* after twenty or so years, I had to scrutinize just about every sentence and test every conclusion to keep myself and the book honest.

Now, what is the central theme of the book? That hasn't changed. It's the importance, indeed the centrality, of language to the process of world making that Tolkien calls sub-creation, and the parallel divisions of light, language, and peoples into smaller and more discrete units as the world grows and complicates. The central image of primary light refracted into colors stands for the whole splintering. Things are broken apart, yet out of this great and unexpected beauty is created. Tolkien drew on the work of Owen Barfield, whose *Poetic Diction* explores the fragmentation of meaning, the shift from literal meaning to metaphor, and the effect of that shift on perception.

Q. Can you also describe *A Question of Time* for those of our readership who might not already know about it?

A. That's a bit more complicated. When I visited the Marquette University Archive in 1984, the late and lamented Taum Santoski pointed out to me a note Tolkien had pencilled in the margin of a draft of the Lorien chapter about the difference between time in the outside world and timelessness in Lorien. I'd never noticed any discrepancy, but when I looked back at the published book I saw that Tolkien was, so to speak, playing with time, suggesting that there could be different perceptions of time and different relationships to it. When I mentioned this to Priscilla Tolkien, she put me on to a book her father had read called *An Experiment With Time* by J.W. Dunne that was actually rather popular in England in the thirties. C.S. Lewis knew it. J.B. Priestly based some plays on it, James Hilton mentioned it in several of his novels, and Rumer Godden built a whole novel around it. Dunne's book was about predictive dreams and the ability of the dreaming mind to move backward and forward in time as we conventionally move in space. I found evidence that Tolkien was using Dunne's theory to contrast Elves and Men in his secondary world, and that his treatment of time in *The Lord of the Rings* was very subtly consistent with Dunne's theory. That led me to a consideration of Tolkien in his own time, the 20th century, and how much he was tied to it even as he tried through his fiction to escape it. So the question of time is not only how we relate to time in a metaphysical sense, but how Tolkien related to his own time. Somehow I found a way to tie those two things together, and that's what the book is about.

Q. And while we are at it, give us the scoop on the collection you co-edited with Carl F. Hostetter, *Tolkien's Legendarium*.

A. It began as a Festschrift for Christopher Tolkien on the completion of *The History of Middle-earth*. Carl and I were looking for a way to acknowledge this huge work—twelve volumes and 20 years of unremitting labor—and honor Christopher's contribution to Tolkien studies. Carl suggested a Festschrift, and when we approached contributors they were enthusiastic about the project. Not so publishers. Rayner Unwin had warned us that festschriften were box office poison, so to speak. That is, no publisher would touch one because they were hard to sell. But Greenwood Press told us they would accept the book if we took out the word festschrift. We did and they did, and it's gone through several printings. So without the F-word it wasn't hard to sell. To my knowledge, it's the only collection that focuses on *The Silmarillion* and the larger issues of Tolkien's mythology, so we hope that it makes a useful contribution to Tolkien scholarship. We meant it to cover a broad range of things, so it runs the gamut from general overviews of the mythology to studies of individual stories to highly specific analyses of Tolkien's prosody and the construction and components of his Elven languages.

Q. Your novel, *Pig Tale*, has an almost friendly-looking cover for the young girl's harrowing story found inside. Can you tell us a bit about the novel and its genesis?

A. Is it friendly? I thought she looked a bit bewildered at what she was seeing. It all began with a scene (the one the girl on the cover is looking at) that I saw in my mind's eye—three people, a woman and two men, seated around a candle-lit table with their shadows looming on the wall. I knew their names—Lally Dai, The Skimmer, Dogger John—but I didn't know who they were or why they were there. I had to listen to their conversation to find out. Then my protagonist, Mokie, the girl on the cover, sort of dropped in from a short story I'd been writing, a kind of fairy tale about a misfit girl who minded pigs. After that the story took charge. I don't mean that it wrote itself; it involved a lot of hard work and rewriting. But I did just follow where it led. Your word "harrowing"—I guess it is harrowing, or some of the events in it are harrowing. But I meant it to go through terror and fear and get to some place beyond those. My girl had a hard time. But then, everyone has a hard time. If they're lucky. She also found love, and acceptance, and courage, and friendship. I think those are important.

Q. How long did it take you to write it?

A. In calendar time, about five or six years. In actual time of concentrated work, much shorter—maybe a year or a little more. That's because I let it languish for long periods while I was doing other things. I'd put it away and forget about it, and then get an impulse or an idea or a bit of dialogue and pull it out and work on it for a couple of weeks in my spare time. Writing fiction is a guilty pleasure for me. It's what I do when I know I should be doing other things like grading exams or preparing for class or cleaning house. Instead I play hooky and write stories.

Q. Tell us about your newest Tolkien book, *Interrupted Music*. What is the significance of the title?

A. It comes from the "Ainulindalë," Tolkien's creation story in *The Silmarillion*, in which the godhead, Eru, tries time and again to complete a theme that will be the music of creation. But he is interrupted—time and again—by Morgoth and has to start over. That became my presiding metaphor for a study of Tolkien's starts and stops in the creation of his mythology *as a mythology*—that is, not just as a fantasy to be shelved with science fiction in bookstores, but as a series of texts with the appearance and provenance of actual mythology. Tolkien wanted his mythology to have the stamp of authenticity, and he had to invent ways for what was in fact the product of a single imagination to be accepted as multi-authored stories and poems and annals that were transmitted over a great period of time and eventually put into print. He devised elaborate strategies to further this, fictive narrators like Ælfwine, scribes and redactors like Pengolodh and Rúmil, "editors" like the pseudo-editor of the Prologue to *The Lord of the Rings* and the "Mr. Green" who discovers and edits the Notion Club Papers. They were all part of an elaborate construct designed to make his Silmarillion (not the published volume, but the whole thing) look like real medieval mythic collections. The Red Book of Hergest, The White Book of Rhydderch—these were some of his models. And you can see it in the Red Book of Westmarch, which is supposed to be a compilation of writing by Bilbo and Frodo and Sam. I got interested in tracking all the ways in which he slipped these kinds of verifications into his texts. The sad thing is that he never completed the vision. His "Music" was constantly "Interrupted," by *The Hobbit* and *The Lord of the Rings* and by the pressures of work and family responsibilities, as well as by new ideas on how to go about it. What you see when you dig into it is a remarkable imagination at work on an idea that never fully came to fruition.

Q. Do you have any other Tolkien-related works in progress?

A. At the moment, I'm in a lull. While writing *Interrupted Music*, I got more and more interested in how Tolkien's work relates to the use of myth in the development of nationalism—remember he wanted to dedicate a mythology to England (not Britain)—and how it reflects the darker aspects of the twentieth century—the two World Wars and their psychological aftermath, their effect on art and literature. I don't quite know where I can go with that, now that more and more people—like John Garth in *Tolkien and the Great War*—are already working in that area. Right now I'm interested in positioning Tolkien as a modern author. I think we've been confining him in the medieval category for too long. That's really just one surface of his narrative; it's window dressing in many respects. The movie has done a lot to foster that, with a kind of nonspecific but highly visual medievalism—the women in long, draped dresses with long sleeves, the men in tunics and cloaks. Jackson even has the Black Riders in a kind of generic armor, though the text says clearly that they wore grey robes under their mantles. But Tolkien couldn't escape the 20th century. He was in it and of it, and I think that shows in his fiction. His orcs talk like street thugs and

Saruman talks like a modern politician. Which brings us back to war. Tolkien saw combat in World War I, and if you think about it, all his long fiction, *The Hobbit*, *The Silmarillion*, *The Lord of the Rings*, is about war. *The Silmarillion* is one long war beginning with the return of the Noldor to Middle-earth—huge battles punctuated with uneasy lulls and guerilla warfare. *The Hobbit* starts out as a parodic fairy tale and ends up with The Battle of Five Armies. It's a story about how wars are triggered, how politics makes strange bedfellows, the varying reasons why wars are fought, who seeks to profit, and how lives are sacrificed to somebody's greed. Bilbo's stealing of the cup from Smaug is like the gunshot at Sarajevo; it embroils groups of unrelated peoples (or wolves and goblins) in an escalating conflict. The Master of Lake-town is a war profiteer, a politician making the most of whatever opportunity comes along. Fili and Kili are killed defending Thorin, and Thorin, whose quest to regain the gold started the whole thing, doesn't get what he went for. It's like World War I—four years of slaughter with no advantage to either side, and at the end everything went back to where it was—except people's lives, which were irrevocably changed. And *The Lord of the Rings* is war as past history (the Dead Marshes and the Grey Company), war preparing (Frodo's vision on Amon Hen), war imminent (Eomer's and Faramir's skirmishes on the border), war happening in all its horror (flamethrowers at Helm's Deep and severed heads as ammunition at the Siege of Gondor). And then the predictable aftermath, the degradation of the Shire. Like the War Poets, Siegfried Sassoon, Wilfred Owen, people like that, Tolkien couldn't help writing about war. But he transmuted it into fantasy as a way to deal with what is essentially unbearable.

Q. Any comments on Peter Jackson's films of *The Lord of The Rings*?

A. I didn't like the first film when I saw it, and I don't like the whole thing now that all three films are out. But then, it isn't aimed at me. It's aimed at the generations who've grown up on *Star Wars* and hunger for more and more action and greater and greater special effects. Jackson has turned an extremely sophisticated, complex and subtle—and very long—story into an action movie that I think satisfies the audience for whom he made it. The time constraint that film format enforces made it almost certain that even with three separate movies Jackson couldn't get the fullness of Tolkien's story into film. Three hours at a time of sitting is about the outside limit. After that your bum gets numb. But there must be people who are willing to sit through those four-DVD sets. Of course, that's not all Tolkien. It's mostly Peter Jackson on "How We Made the Movie."

I felt some parts were disastrously miscast—Elrond for example. Not the actor's fault, though if I'd been him I wouldn't have stood for that hairdo. Elijah Wood is just wrong for Frodo—too young, too pretty, too goggle-eyed. And the script gave the character no chance to develop. His moment of growth in the barrow was omitted; his bravery when he turns and faces the Black Riders at the Ford was left out in favor of Arwen as Our Lady of the Ford. Galadriel was terrible, and since Cate Blanchett is a fine actor, she must have been directed to perform in that wooden, zombie-like manner. Sean Bean is the only person who played as if he believed who he was. But he was only in the first movie. His Boromir was a real person, not a type. I found him totally convincing, and his funeral journey down the river and over the falls was the film's finest moment. Truly moving. Although the script sentimentalized and overdid the character's repentance at the end. Boromir is not *that* good. As for un-Tolkienian lines like Gimli's "Nobody tosses a dwarf," and Strider's "Let's hunt some orc," they are beyond comment.

I found Jackson's increased messing with plot and character unnecessary and destructive of the story. Arwen was an unneeded addition to the story and stuck out like a sore thumb. There's no reason to have Faramir go from good to bad, then back to good again. And the silly idea of having Gollum successfully turn Frodo against Sam, so that Sam goes away in tears, should have been stifled at birth. It makes a complete mockery of the friendship, which is one of the strongest motifs in the book, and takes away the last bit of strength the Frodo character was allowed.

The special effects got bigger and bigger as the plot diminished. But that's really all special effects can do. The problem is that they leave no room for imagination. To see an actor run up the side of an elephant as big as a house is visually striking. But not as striking as your own mind imagining Sam's astonishment at seeing an oliphaunt, or your own sense of strangeness at seeing *elephant* spelled *oliphaunt*. Words, now, words can evoke all kinds of images depending on the mind of the particular reader. That is their freedom and their glory. Tolkien said that in a letter, something about how words like "hill" and "tree" and "stone" can evoke for any reader *her* stone or *his* tree and that will be different for every reader. It gives the reader some participation in the text. And an oliphaunt is a subtly different critter from the elephants we're familiar with. But computer-generated effects can only be what they are, and they're stuck with their own specificity. As the translation to a visual medium of the work of a man who loved words, film is bound to fail.

And while we're on the subject of words, I thought it was doing gratuitous violence to Tolkien's concept to take out the phrases in his elven languages that *he* chose to include in his text, which add to the historical background and mythic atmosphere of the story, and then add unnecessary, made-up dialogue by somebody else in which characters like Aragorn and Arwen who have been speaking English (what JRRT called the Common Speech) suddenly slip into Sindarin so Jackson can do subtitles.

I wish I could find things to like about the movie. But I can't. As somebody said (I don't remember who): The scenery was spectacular. But the actors kept getting in front of it.

Q. Where do you see *The Lord of the Rings* now, in the context of 20th-century literature?

A. Very much in the center. Tom Shippey has pointed out that fantasy, far from being the fringe genre it is usually seen as, was in fact a major mode of expression in 20th-century fiction. And Tolkien was at the heart of it. He didn't just legitimize fantasy as a means of expression, he made it a vehicle for some profound commentary—not only on the human condition (though there are few more moving portraits of humanity under stress than Frodo Baggins), but on the 20th century specifically. He saw its malaise, its worship of progress complicated by unease and anxiety about where progress was taking us, its adoration of power tied to impoverishment of the spirit. And he wrote about it. Four British readers' polls and fifty million readers can't be all wrong. It is an important book.

Q. What about the future of Tolkien criticism and scholarship?

A. Well, Tolkien has always had some recognition from those in the academy who understood what he was trying to do. The first generation included people like C.S. Lewis, Patricia Meyer Spacks, Roger Sale, Charles Moorman, Burton Raffel. Then there was a slump, and little critical attention was paid to him. But at the same time, there were students beginning to write dissertations on *The Lord of the Rings*. Those students are now teachers directing other, newer dissertations, and the field is widening. During the second Tolkien at Kalamazoo session at the 2002 International Medieval Congress, Marjorie Burns said "Tolkien studies has come of age." I think she was right, and she spoke for a new generation of readers and scholars who want to give Tolkien his due. Not analyze him into the ground and bury him under theory, but elevate him to the high position he deserves. One indication that this is happening is *Tolkien Studies*, the new hardcover journal devoted entirely to Tolkien. It's jointly edited by Doug Anderson and Mike Drout and me. The first issue is out and is being well received, and the second issue is in the works.

Q&A with Douglas A. Anderson

Turgon

Douglas A. Anderson has done textual work on both *The Hobbit* and *The Lord of the Rings* and has written introductions to various editions of these books published by Houghton Mifflin. His first book was *The Annotated Hobbit*, originally published in 1988. It won the Mythopoeic Scholarship Award from the Mythopoeic Society. A revised and enlarged edition of *The Annotated Hobbit* appeared in 2002. Anderson has been a bookseller in Ithaca, New York, and in northwestern Indiana. He currently lives in southwestern Michigan. His anthology titled *Tales Before Tolkien: The Roots of Modern Fantasy*, was published in August 2003 by Ballantine Books, and its publication was the impetus for this Q&A session.

Q: Tell us about your new book, *Tales Before Tolkien*. Where did the idea for it come from?

A: The idea for the book actually came directly out of my work on the revised edition of *The Annotated Hobbit*. I felt frustrated in only being able to put in small excerpts from some stories that definitely influenced Tolkien, like E. H. Knatchbull-Hugessen's "Puss-cat Mew," into the annotations in *The Annotated Hobbit*. So I started thinking along the lines of what a collection of such stories that influenced Tolkien might be like. After thinking it over for a while, I decided that the best approach would be to highlight some stories that Tolkien definitely knew and which can be seen to have influenced him, and round out the rest of the book with other examples of what fantasy was like before Tolkien came along and made new rules.

After I had thought it out, I approached Ballantine Books. They have published Tolkien in mass-market paperback in the U.S. since the mid-1960s, and they have been a leading publisher of fantasy and science fiction for many years. Plus I think back fondly to the Ballantine Adult Fantasy series (the first series of its kind), which ran from 1969-74 and introduced me to many excellent writers, several of whom appear in my anthology. Ballantine seemed to me a perfect fit as publisher for the book, and happily they felt so too.

Q: So was this an easy book to put together?

A: Well, yes and no. I've read fantasy literature, especially the older writers, for many years. In fact there isn't a single item in the book that I hadn't read at least once before in the last twenty years. Some of them I've read many times. So in one sense it was a pleasure to reread a lot of good stories to consider for inclusion. But the matter of selection itself I found to be a bit more difficult than I had expected. I firmly believe that the concept for a book evolves in the editor/writer's mind almost like an organic thing while you are working on it—it does for me at least! The book takes on a shape of its own, and a life of its own, and you need to listen to that inner voice that nags you when, stubbornly, you're persisting in a wrong direction. All of my books have in the end turned out slightly but significantly different from how I first planned for them to be, and in every case I think it's been for the better.

Q: The book has a gorgeous cover.

A: Yes, that's by John Howe, who we all know worked as one of the conceptual artists for Peter Jackson's movies. It's his early conception of Minas Tirith, and the way he has used light in the sky and on the towers reminds me of Maxfield Parrish. It gives a perfect appearance to the book—kind of a romantic feel of an elegant past, which reflects the content within the book nicely.

Q: Did you select the art for the cover?

A: No, my editor at Ballantine, Betsy Mitchell, chose it, and asked me what I thought. John Howe's illustration of "Smaug over Esgaroth" is one of my favorite illustrations out of those by all of the Tolkien illustrators. So it was Betsy's great idea, which I was more than happy to go along with it.

Q: Any especial favorites in the collection?

A: Three of my favorite writers are represented—writers I've gone to great lengths to read everything they've written. Lord Dunsany wrote the best fantasy fables (among other things) in the English language, while Kenneth Morris wrote superlative original fantasies grounded in various mythologies from around the world—from Celtic to Buddhist, and Taoist to Toltec. And David Lindsay is simply one of my absolute favorite writers. His extremely imaginative book, *A Voyage to Arcturus*, inspired C. S. Lewis's *Out of the Silent Planet* and *Perelandra*. Lindsay wrote only seven novels but no short stories. I'm extremely pleased that I was able to arrange with Lindsay's daughters to print his fairy play for the first time. It's a fun work in itself, though rather different from his novels, which are metaphysical fantasies.

And though I don't especially like extracts, I put in one of my favorite sections, "Golithos the Ogre," from E.A. Wyke-Smith's *The Marvellous Land of Snergs*, which was source for Tolkien's ideas about Hobbits. Golithos is a reformed ogre who no longer eats children but who has become vegetarian.

Q: Any particular novels by these writers that you'd recommend for people to start with?

A: I give several pages of notes on recommended reading, for these and other authors, at the back of my book. For Dunsany there is an omnibus in England called *Time and the Gods*. Unfortunately Kenneth Morris's short stories aren't presently in print. But the volume I edited in 1995, *The Dragon Path: Collected Tales of Kenneth Morris*, is the one to get and can be found fairly easily through the used book sources on the web. For Lindsay, *A Voyage to Arcturus* is probably the one to start with. It's currently available in an edition from the University of Nebraska Press with a truly god-awful, execrable cover. It's the perfect example of why one should never judge a book by its cover alone. There is also a British edition available, with a much better cover. It's part of the Fantasy Masterworks series published in England by Millennium. In fact that whole series, which currently has thirty-some books in print, is excellent. Great books by some of my other favorite writers are available in that series, like *The Emperor of Dreams* by Clark Ashton Smith, and *The Land of Laughs* by Jonathan Carroll.

And of course I have been recommending for years E.A. Wyke-Smith's children's book, *The Marvellous Land of Snergs*. Tolkien called it a source book for Hobbits, and the half-high creatures called Snergs, with names like Gorbo, are very similar to Tolkien's Hobbits.

Q: What authors didn't make it into the book that you would have liked to include?

A: Given the constraints of considering only authors slightly older than Tolkien, I regret that there is nothing in it by E.R. Eddison. He simply wrote no short stories, and an excerpt from one of his novels just wouldn't stand well on its own. So I'd recommend people search out his *Worm Ouroboros*. Tolkien called Eddison "the greatest and most convincing writer of invented worlds that I have read."

And Hope Mirrlees wrote a brilliant book, much admired by Neil Gaiman, called *Lud-in-the-Mist*. It's about a small unimaginative town near the borders of Faerie and its problems with the illegal fairy fruit. But Mirrlees, too, wrote no short stories.

There are a lot of authors just slightly younger than Tolkien whom I would have loved to include. I have quite a thick file of stories that I love that simply wouldn't fit in for reasons of space.

Q: So does that mean we can look forward to another book, *More Tales Before Tolkien*, or maybe even *Tales After Tolkien*?

A: Either would be interesting. But there haven't been any discussions about possible follow-ups. I'm sure the publisher would want to see how this one does before even considering a further volume.

Q: To turn to a specific point in your introduction, you mention that some of the medieval legends of Alexander were the inspiration for Tolkien's Two Trees in Valinor. I've never before seen a source mentioned for the idea of the Two Trees. Can you elaborate?

A: Today we tend of think of the Matter of Britain, including all of the stories of King Arthur, as the greatest body of medieval legendry. But there is as large a tradition of medieval literature about Alexander the Great, much of which is forgotten today. Some of these legends are very fanciful, and in at least one Middle English version Alexander travels to the Far East where he encounter the Trees of the Sun and Moon, which he consults like oracles and they foretell his future.

Tolkien himself is the authority for this comment. An interviewer asked him in 1965 if his Two Trees were in any way a reflection of the World Tree in Old Norse mythology, and Tolkien responded: "No, no, they're not like it; they're much more like the Trees of the Sun and Moon discovered in the Far East, in the great Alexander stories."

Q: The book has been published simultaneously in hardcover and trade paperback, which seems an unusual thing for a publisher to do nowadays. Why was this done?

A: It is unusual, but even when I first had the idea for the book I thought that a dual format was the way to go with it. Having been in the publishing and bookselling industry for twenty years, I felt that the book's natural audience would be in trade paperback. But libraries like hardcovers since they are far more durable than paperbacks, and Tolkien collectors, as well as some other readers, prefer the hardcover format too, so I think in this case it is ideal to have the choice of format. Of course it was the publisher's decision to do the dual format, but we all agreed on its desirability without even discussing it.

Q: What's your next book?

A: Well, I've usually got my fingers in three or four different projects at any given time. I have some edited short story collections by older weird fiction writers coming from specialty presses like Midnight House and Ash-Tree Press. But there is one book for which I've written the introduction that came out in January 2004 that might be of more general interest. It's the first reprinting of a novel from 1825 called *The Rebellion of the Beasts; or, The Ass is Dead! Long Live the Ass!* What it is basically is the same story as Orwell's *Animal Farm*, with the satire directed towards the monarchy. *Animal Farm* is itself a fine book, but *The Rebellion of the Beasts* is more wicked and vicious. The author is believed to be Leigh Hunt, the famous essayist and friend of Byron and Shelley.

And forthcoming is a volume *On Tolkien: Interviews, Reminiscences and Other Essays* that I've co-edited with my friend Marjorie Burns. Plus a number of other things are in the works, including some classic fantasy reissues with Jon Stein of Cold Spring Press. So far we've got settled Hope Mirrlees's *Lud-in-the-Mist*, discussed above, and Kenneth Morris's *Book of the Three Dragons*. With the latter, we're publishing for the first time Morris's final third of the book. The original publisher in 1930 had thought the book was too long, and just lopped off the end!

Q&A with Jane Chance

Turgon

Jane Chance is a professor of English at Rice University in Houston, Texas, where she has taught since 1973. She has taught Tolkien at Rice since 1976 and has published numerous books on medieval literature. Her first book on Tolkien was *Tolkien's Art: A Mythology for England* (1979), which was followed by *The Lord of the Rings: The Mythology of Power* (1992). Revised editions of both books appeared in 2001, published by the University Press of Kentucky, and the rights to translate them into Japanese have been sold (so far, only the translation of *The Lord of the Rings: The Mythology of Power* has appeared). In 2003, a volume of essays that she edited, *Tolkien the Medievalist*, was published by Routledge. This collection has been selected as a finalist for the 2004 Mythopoeic Scholarship Award. In 2004, a further volume of essays appeared from University Press of Kentucky under the title *Tolkien and the Invention of Myth: A Reader*. She and Alfred K. Siewers are currently co-editing a collection on *Tolkien's Modern Middle Ages*. Professor Chance kindly agreed to discuss her Tolkien work with us, and our Q&A session appears below. Her website is located at: www.ruf.rice.edu/~jchance/.

Q: Your *Tolkien's Art* was one of the earliest serious books on Tolkien. Recently republished in a revised edition, it focuses on the way Old English and Middle English literature informed Tolkien's approach to writing as found in his Middle-earth stories and in his other writings, like *Farmer Giles of Ham*, which you present as a burlesque of the medieval heroic ideals. Do you feel that Tolkien's medievalism has been a stumbling block, at least among modernist critics, for the academic acceptance of Tolkien's work?

A: Not at all. I think the resistance to academic acceptance of Tolkien's work comes from ignorance of how seamlessly Tolkien interwove medievalism with his fiction, in large part because the academics resisting are modernists who know little or nothing about the Middle Ages or about Tolkien's own importance as a medieval scholar. The irony here is that Tolkien's very popularity, especially through Peter Jackson's film, has boosted academic student interest in the Middle Ages among those who read Tolkien. So medievalists around the country find themselves offering Tolkien courses to students so interested that waiting lists have to be created. In other words, academic modernists do not understand *The Lord of the Rings*, for the most part, and therefore do not regard it very highly. I'm not even certain that the critics and scholars who scoff at Tolkien—who was designated by the Waterstone/BBC poll as best 20th-century novelist—have even read *The Lord of the Rings*.

Q: Having covered Tolkien's major works in *Tolkien's Art*, you came back to give *The Lord of the Rings* a more extensive treatment in *The Lord of the Rings: The Mythology of Power,* which covers Tolkien's masterpiece from a more contemporary context rather than a medievalist one. Can you comment on the differing approaches and how each adds to our understanding of Tolkien as a writer?

A: Both books argue that Tolkien's writing must be understood through examination of who he was, that is, of his profession—as medievalist—and of his role as an ordinary man buffeted by the wars, intolerance, and misuse of power in the 20th century. *Tolkien's Art* covers all of Tolkien's fiction and his scholarship on medieval literature; *The Lord of the Rings: The Mythology of Power* focuses just on the epic. In *Tolkien's Art* I was particularly interested in examining the genesis of Tolkien's fiction writing in Old English literature, especially in his famous essay on *Beowulf*, "Beowulf: The Monsters and the Critics," which was written about the same time as *The Hobbit*. (Even earlier, he had started the Silmarillion mythology by reworking characters and imagery from Cynewulf's Old English poem *Crist* into his legend of the voyage of Earendil.) In that essay he damns the arrogant scholars who misread *Beowulf*—those who ignore the monsters fought by the hero, which are actually central to the poem, rather than its history, anthropology, philology, etc. The arrogant critic and scholar takes on mythic significance elsewhere in Tolkien's fiction and can be spotted in figures like the wizard Saruman and even the Dark Lord.

In contrast, *The Lord of the Rings: The Mythology of Power* examines the interrelationship of Tolkien's life and modern history with *The Lord of the Rings*. Mostly, I wanted to dispel the modernist anxiety that *The Lord of the Rings* is a work whose ideas might be construed as reactionary, elitist, conservative, fascist, sexist, or racist. Because of Tolkien's experiences of destruction and loss in the two World Wars, his horror over the rise to power of Nazi Germany, and his Christian faith in redemption, he offers instead heroes of Middle-earth in the marginal and unimportant Hobbits, service to the community of the entire world by grubby Strider/Aragorn, king of the west, in his aid of the Hobbits in their peaceful quest to return the Ring to its source, and fulfillment of the prophecy by the female Dernhelm (Éowyn in disguise) that no man will kill the Nazgûl king. My point in *The Lord of the Rings: The Mythology of Power* is that Tolkien celebrates littleness, the marginal, and difference; leadership as based on humility and love; and a rejection of war as a means of solving international disputes.

Q: The book description at Amazon.com for your volume *Tolkien the Medievalist* is rather minimalist. It says: "Interdisciplinary in approach, this book provides a fresh perspective on J.R.R. Tolkien's medievalism. Fifteen essays explore how professor Tolkien responded to a modern age of crisis—historical, academic and personal." Can you tell us more about the volume?

A: The book description should have added that "Eminent scholars as well as new voices in these fifteen essays explore how Professor Tolkien responded to a modern age of crisis—historical, academic, and personal—by adapting his scholarship on medieval literature to his own personal voice and by fictionalizing those works. The four sections reveal the author influenced by his profession, religious faith, and important issues of his time (such as war); by his relationships with other medievalists; by the medieval sources that he read and taught; and even by his own medieval mythologizing."

Q: As a scholar with a particular interest in medieval women writers and in the study of gender, how do you view the role of women in *The Lord of the Rings*?

A: Tolkien allocated women an important role in the epic adventure of the return of the Ring to Mordor. Both Frodo and Bilbo merit their heroic natures and their connection with the greatest Hobbit adventurers of the past through their mothers, Belladonna Took and Primula Brandybuck, a discussion of whom begins the first book. Galadriel, keeper of one of the elven rings, renounces the Ring and her ancient quest for power and therefore helps to save Middle-earth, which wins her race redemption and the return to the West. Éowyn as Dernhelm fulfils the epic prophecy that no man will kill the Nazgûl king and thereby avenges Théoden's fatal wounding; her heroism allows Merry (whom she has sagely brought with her in equal disobedience of the king's orders) to save her from certain death and thus to let her live to marry Faramir, whose life will be similarly saved by Pippin, and thereby together peacefully join the kingdoms of Rohan and Gondor. Aragorn and Arwen marry at the end of the epic narrative, weaving together by their union many elven, Maia, and human families to promote peace on Middle-earth. Aragorn is the descendant of the man Beren and the elf Lúthien, who rescued her lover Beren from death. Arwen is the daughter of Celebrían and Elrond, and granddaughter of Galadriel and Celeborn. The last scene shows us Sam returning to Rosie Cotton and their child, in the last lines of *Return of the King*—they have kept the home fires burning in order for Sam to return. I could go on. I see no disjunction between Tolkien's celebration of women and their influence on Middle-earth.

Q: I understand that you are the main organizer of the Tolkien lectures at the annual Medievalists Conference. Can you elaborate on this?

A: Five years ago I created a scholarly organization called "Tolkien at Kalamazoo" (analogous with "Shakespeare at Kalamazoo" and "Spenser at Kalamazoo") because I felt medievalists needed a scholarly outlet to discuss Tolkien's medievalism—and that because Tolkien as a major author was rarely studied as part of modern literature in English departments around the country he ought to be included as part of medieval literature. I asked for three sessions at the annual International Congress on the Middle Ages the first year (2001), four the second (2002), and five the third (2003); for the fourth, held in May 2004, we requested (and received) five sessions, with a sixth, on teaching Tolkien, cosponsored by the Consortium for the Teaching of the Middle Ages. The fifth meeting, in May 2005, will focus on Un-

Tolkien (unacknowledged influences, insignificant characters, uncanonicity, and so forth). The first sessions received notice in interviews published by the *New York Times* and the *TLS Education Supplement*. At this conference the past three years we have had eighty in the audience. As a result of these sessions, we were asked after the first year to publish a collection on "Tolkien the Medievalist" by Routledge, after the second year, a collection on "Tolkien and the Invention of Myth: A Reader," by University Press of Kentucky, and in anticipation of the fourth, we put together a collection on "Tolkien's Modern Middle Ages" and are close to selecting a press. The website for Tolkien at Kalamazoo is www.Tolkienkzoo.org. We welcome abstracts for scholarly papers to be presented next May. My email is jchance@rice.edu if anyone has questions about the sessions or the conference.

Q: If one thinks of Tolkien as bringing the literary modes of the Middle Ages forward into the twentieth century, how do you view the next wave of post-Tolkien fantasy writers? Are there any you yourself particularly enjoy? Do you see any of these writers as actually extending Tolkien's medievalism rather than merely attempting to copy it?

A: Douglas Anderson or Tom Shippey would be a much better resource for an answer to this question. I don't read contemporary fantasy, alas. Please forgive, but I have my hands full with Tolkien, medieval women writers and gender issues, and medieval literature and mythography!

Q: Are you working on any further Tolkien-related projects?

A: Yes, *Tolkien and the Invention of Myth: A Reader*, just out (2004), is a collection of essays on the ways in which Tolkien's reading of classical and medieval Latin, Old Norse, Old English, and Finnish mythological literature catalyzed aspects of his own mythology in *The Lord of the Rings* and *The Silmarillion*. We use "invention" in the medieval sense of "discovery" and include several important background essays on Tolkien's use of folklore, allegory, religion, philosophy, and philology in his construction of mythology. *Tolkien's Modern Middle Ages*, co-edited with Alfred Siewers, explores the theme of Tolkien's reinvention of the Middle Ages as "imaginary space" in which "alternate pasts" can be "recovered" or "colonized," and therefore "alternate futures" viewed. Tolkien's own fantasies have attracted interest from a wide range in the political spectrum, "from the postmodern counter-culture to conservative Christian traditionalists." I'm also working on essays on "Tolkien and the Other: Race and Gender in Middle-earth" and "Tolkien on Class Difference" for various collections to be published in the future, including the Marquette University collection planned for publication in 2005 after their 2004 conference on Tolkien.

Q: And, finally, as a longtime reader and scholar of Tolkien, what are your views on Peter Jackson's movies of *The Lord of the Rings*?

A: I have already published my specific view on Jackson's *Fellowship* in the journal *Film/Literature Quarterly* (2002) and will discuss gender and women in all three films in a collection on the films edited by Janet Croft to be published by the Mythopoeic Society/Gale Research Group in 2004-5. I think Peter Jackson is to be congratulated for bringing the trilogy to the screen so successfully and by this means drawing attention to Tolkien's stature as a preeminent novelist of the twentieth century. I may quarrel with Jackson's specific deletions from and changes and additions to the epic novel, for which Tolkien, no doubt, would criticize him roundly were he alive to see the films, but I believe Jackson has (thus far, at least) preserved the spirit of Tolkien's master work and powerfully visualized it. The nature of the film medium so differs from that of the novelistic medium that we will from now on need to differentiate between Tolkien's print version and Jackson's film version of *The Lord of the Rings*.

Q&A with Karen Wynn Fonstad

Quickbeam

Karen Wynn Fonstad is the author of *The Atlas of Middle-earth*, first published in 1981.

Q. Greetings, Karen Wynn Fonstad. What was your first experience reading Tolkien?

A. As I mention in the introduction of the *Atlas*, I first learned of *The Lord of the Rings* in 1969-70 when I was a teaching assistant in cartography working on an M.A. in geography at the University of Oklahoma. This was following the period when the "trilogy" was first available in the U.S. in paperback and was popular enough to have "Frodo Lives!" and "Gandalf for President" buttons and graffiti all over. As a grad student focused on my classes, however, I had absolutely NO CLUE about any of this!

One of the students in the class wanted to re-draw the *LotR* map for her term project. When she tried to explain to me what the books were about, I remember being totally puzzled. Hobbits? Dwarves? Huh? Whether she ever did the map, I have no idea. She didn't finish on time, and after that it was the prof's problem...

In the fall of 1971 I was visiting a friend and noticed a set of books on the shelf. Somehow I realized these were the same books the student had told me about. So I borrowed *The Fellowship of the Ring*—ONLY *The Fellowship*. Was that ever a mistake!

I devoured it non-stop, skipping the prologue and poetry, and finished about 3 a.m. I was wide awake and extremely frustrated that I had to wait until morning to go get the rest of the books! I didn't bother borrowing them. I went straight to the bookstore as early as possible and bought the boxed set so I could have "my own, my preciousss..." I still have that set: tattered, underlined, taped, and yellow with age.

I finished the rest of the books at a gulp. From the very beginning I thought, "Now I can see why that student wanted to re-draw the map!" There were so many names, and as I searched the map trying to find them, I didn't know if I were simply missing them or if they weren't there. I became especially frustrated trying to trace the pathways after the Breaking of the Fellowship. When I finished my first reading, I immediately started over (this time with the Prologue and poetry) ... and over ... and over ...

.I read nothing else. It wasn't until June of the next year that I finally read *The Hobbit*. Then I started re-reading *LotR* again. On and on. I quit counting at 30 readings.

Q. Tolkien tells us how much Bilbo loved maps, and that he hung a large map of the "Country Round" inside his home of Bag End, with his favorite paths marked in red ink. Are you and Bilbo kindred spirits?

A. Oh absolutely! As a child on family trips, I would "back-seat drive" by poring over the map and announcing (probably every five minutes) that the next town was (whatever) and its population was (?). My first apartment was decorated with old maps from *National Geographic* mounted on plywood and varnished—with the curtain colors chosen to coordinate with those on the maps!

Q. Did you ever think that someday you'd want to create *The Atlas of Middle-earth?* Was the book born out of wanting to have maps for yourself to enhance your own reading experience?

A. As you can tell from the answer above, the idea of a more detailed, indexed map was actually introduced to me before I ever read the books. I might have thought of the idea on my own, but I have no way of knowing if that would have happened.

The idea of an atlas, however, had never crossed my mind. I simply wanted to do a map for myself. I wasn't very successful doing so. I made a few notes, but not in any consistent way.

Then *The Silmarillion* came out and everything changed. As a die-hard *LotR* fan, I knew of *The Silmarillion*—as a long wished-for unpublished work. Fortunately, my husband had heard me speak of it often enough that when he was at the university bookstore and saw it was available, he immediately bought it and brought it home. That was in early February, 1978.

I dove into reading it instantly, but was only a short way into it when I had the moment that changed my life. It was just that—a MOMENT! I thought : "This is never all going to fit on one map ... If it won't fit on one map, I'll need to make a whole bunch of maps ... If I made a whole bunch of maps, maybe I could make an atlas ... And maybe someone would buy it!"

And that, of course, is just what happened.

Q. How much cartography experience did you have before attempting the *Atlas?*

A. First I must explain that I was originally an art major. That only lasted one semester as an undergraduate, however. The art world was in the midst of 'abstract' art. When my first assignment in Basic Design was to create something artistic using six dots, I knew I was in big trouble! I decided to switch to medical illustration, but that was only available at the M.A. level. Meanwhile I took science courses so I could take anatomy, etc. That is how I ended up with a B.S. in physical therapy. My senior year I was told (by the same person who three years before had said it would be good to have some science background) that I needed a straight commercial art degree. GRRRRR ...

Meanwhile, I had been dating a geography major who had said, "You can draw. Do maps for me." He had handed me the drafting equipment and I was soon doing maps and block diagrams for other students as well. So I graduated in PT, got a job at the university infirmary, and applied for grad school in geography. With only one course in geography, they let me in—benefit of having already built up a reputation. The next year I actually was handed a teaching assistantship in cartography when I hadn't even taken the class yet! Meanwhile, I was making extra spending money doing maps for profs and students alike. My thesis topic was "Guidelines for Preparing Maps for Publication."

Designing a few maps to appear in a dissertation or an article is a very different thing, however, from planning an entire atlas—especially an annotated atlas. When I was preliminarily talking with Houghton Mifflin, however, the editor discovered I had worked on the yearbook staff in high school and as an undergraduate. After asking a few questions he said, "See. You know more than you realize." Laying out the "dummy" for the *Atlas* was a lengthy process that took much thought, but when it was done my husband said, "Now all you have to do is fill in the blanks!"

And that, too, is just what happened.

The *Atlas* has been criticized from the outset for being two-color, for having simple pen-and-ink maps, for having hand lettering—in other words, for not looking like maps from our Primary World. Other reviewers find the style appropriate to Tolkien's world. Having come originally from an art background instead of a cartography background, my style was quite different from that many cartographers would have had. So some might say that the *Atlas* appeared amateur in its style. Part of the choice was based on economics. Even now, when the full-color process is far more economical than it was twenty-plus years ago, it would be difficult to keep small printings from becoming prohibitively expensive.

Similarly, when the 1991 revised edition was produced, only about one-third of the book could be changed and keep the cost moderate. Over the years between the 1981 and 1991 editions , I became much more bold in my approach (having completed four other fantasy atlases). Unfortunately, many of the changes that I would like to have made, including a different lettering style and more elaborate drafting style, were not feasible cost-wise.

Q. Can you describe the process of how you approached the Tolkien Estate? What manner of materials were made available to you?

A. I did not approach the Tolkien estate. I contacted an acquaintance who, as a prof, had done some academic publishing. He gave me his editor's name and phone number. The editor very helpfully told me to go straight to the publisher who held the rights (Houghton Mifflin). He said, "Don't write them. They get hundreds of proposals every week and it will just sit on somebody's desk. CALL THEM."

This, by the way, was within DAYS of my husband's having brought home *The Silmarillion.* Having had my "Eureka!" moment when I first started reading it, I had made notes as I read through it of which maps would be needed to cover its material. As many times as I had read *LotR* and *The Hobbit* by then, I didn't even need to open them to list the important topics to cover for them. I did go through the Appendices more carefully than ever before to see what topics to include from them. So by the time I called my friend's editor, I already had an outline in hand.

It took a lot of nerve, but not much time, to find out where to call. Heart pounding, I asked to talk with someone in the division that handled Tolkien-related projects. When I reached someone in the right department and briefly explained what I had in mind, she said, "Oh! You need to talk with Anne Barrett. She is semi-retired and is only here a few times a week, but she is here now." Anne, it turned out, was the only person on the staff who had personally worked with the Professor before his death. She had actually lived in England one summer to assist him in handling some of his work!

When Anne came on and I had briefly repeated what I was proposing, she said, "We get a lot of ideas for projects on Tolkien and most of them are pure garbage—but I think this one will work!" She went on to say that the head of the Tolkien division (Austin Olney) was flying to London two days later for meetings with the British publisher and family estate on proposed projects. In 1978 there were no fax machines and no overnight shipping, so Anne hand-copied my outline as I dictated it over the phone. Mr. Olney took it with him when he went and came back with permission to pursue the *Atlas*. When people ask me advice on how to get started, I have no clue what to tell them. My experience was comparable to an ingenue arriving in Hollywood and being offered a screen test upon arriving at the airport!

Houghton Mifflin very kindly provided me with every Tolkien-related book they had published, and they have continued to do so with many additions over the years. They also contacted Christopher Tolkien on my behalf with several questions I thought he might be able to answer—most about Valinor. As he was working on *Unfinished Tales* at the time, and the *History of M-e* books were only a thought for the future, he replied, but without any additional information. When the *Atlas* was released, however, he was very complimentary.

Q. Were you able to access the original manuscripts and maps stored at Marquette University?

A. The same acquaintance who had given me his editor's name was a Milwaukee native and knew of the Tolkien Collection at Marquette. Houghton Mifflin sent a note verifying that I was working on a legitimate project and Marquette granted permission for me to have access to anything in the collection I needed. That was quite an experience! I had to chuckle over the chapters scribbled inside blue books—exactly the same kind of examination books I had used at school! But what an incredible feeling ... touching those same pages that had been held by the Master of Middle-earth!

I groaned mentally trying to read his writing, but it was that problem that led me to a wonderful discovery. The archives staff had sent me a list of drawings that were scattered through the manuscripts. One was obviously of the citadel of Minas Tirith, but the writing was so poor that I couldn't read what one of the buildings was called. The sketch appeared in the typewritten version, so I switched to the handwritten copy of the same chapter, and there I made the discovery—another sketch that was NOT on the list. There was no need for it to have a title. I knew instantly what it was...the entire city of Minas Tirith! It showed no buildings, but clearly indicated the shape of the Hill of Guard, the placement of each of the walls and the gates, and the main road winding from the Great Gate to the Citadel.

There were many other sketches as well, and all were extremely helpful, but finding the previously unknown drawing of the White City remains one of my best memories.

Q. What was the single most difficult aspect of putting together the *Atlas?*

A. Doing the "base map." The first step in researching and drawing any map is to find or produce a "base map"—literally the base on which any added information is overlaid. The map of Middle-earth in *The Lord of the Rings* was the obvious starting point, with the map of Beleriand tacked on. I couldn't simply start doodling in my drawing style instead of Tolkien's, however.

First, I had to decide on what size to draw the map so that all the regional maps would be at the same scale and would fit on the 'spread' (usually 150 percent of a double page size) without having to be redrafted. Then, every single clue had to be listed and analyzed to fit as well as possible. I started with a detailed tracing of any journeys—not only distances, but clues such as streams, woods, hill slopes, rock types, elevation—literally anything that might help reveal where and how features should appear on the maps. Only then could I begin drawing.

Using a piece of equipment that is the cartographer's equivalent to an overhead projector, I enlarged Tolkien's maps to the size I needed and carefully traced off every detail. These I transferred to translucent drafting film. The mega-map measured about seven by 10 feet. I actually taped it to my kitchen floor and used the width of the maple floorboards to draw the index lines: 50 miles per board width! At that point I could finally start drawing.

One other challenge was cramming this huge map down to the size I would need for the various half-page maps. There were no PCs then. Enlarging-reducing copy machines were not even available yet! Using the same equipment as that mentioned above, but with the lens reversed for reduction, I painstakingly recopied the map section by section. The maximum piece that could fit on the machine was about 14' square. Remember that seven by 10-foot mega-map? That is a LOT of sections. It took me ten hours!

Once the basic research and the base map were ready, I was able to produce about one page per day of rough draft; then after finishing the rough copies I could produce about two pages per day of the final inked copies. Nevertheless, the whole process took nearly three years.

Q. Were you thinking about how other *LotR* fans would scrutinize your work as you assembled the book?

A. Not at all. I could have been on a desert island. I was aware of fanzines and had jotted down items of interest from a few articles in the ones at Marquette, but an initial decision was to base my work strictly on that of Tolkien, uninfluenced by others' interpretations. I must quickly add that an absolutely invaluable resource was Robert Foster's *Complete Guide to Middle-earth.*

In contrast, some maps in the revised edition were modified based on comments that readers had sent me. In almost every case I regretted the changes I made based on someone else's complaints. I was never comfortable with them. Besides, I was reacting to one person's suggestion, when hundreds of others might have disagreed had they had the opportunity.

One prime example was the battle of Helm's Deep. Originally I had Gandalf and Erkenbrand's riders arrive from the east—in spite of the comment that the cliffs near the Deeping Wall were too steep for the Orcs to climb. In the revised edition, based on someone's comment that Gandalf would have been in shadow if he had been coming from the east, rather than lit by the sun in his face, I changed the arrival to one from the west. I didn't like doing so, however. The higher peaks would have been west of the Coomb, and that didn't seem a logical way to arrive. I was delighted when the film of *The Two Towers* solved this dilemma by: (1) showing a lower place in the eastern cliff—just as I had on the original map, and (2) having Gandalf's own light make him appear fiercely bright, even with the sun behind him.

I'm afraid I am rather thin-skinned. One reason I have kept a fairly low profile all these years is because I agonize over negative comments far out of proportion to the positive ones I read. There ARE places that I realize I have missed or misinterpreted a clue. Far more often, though, there are simply multiple interpretations possible, as in the Battle of Helm's Deep. It angers me to have my interpretations referred to as 'wrong' when they are simply different from those of the critic.

Q. Did you ever realize that your *Atlas* appeared on the scene as a seminal reference for Tolkien fans, one that is now a classic? It allows for a remarkable exploration of the world.

A. I have been pleasantly surprised over the 23 years since its first publication that it has been continuously in print. I credit that to the popularity of the books themselves, though, rather than to my *Atlas*. I was told by a librarian when it was first published that she thought the *Atlas* would be a sleeper that was likely to last a long time. She certainly has been proven right.

I was absolutely astounded, however, that the current printing (with the Alan Lee cover) when released in April, 2001, sold outstandingly even before the first film was released. I have continued to be astounded with surges of sales as each new film has come out. The *Atlas* has been in the top 100 on Amazon.com in the U.S. for three years running in December and January and actually reached No. 7 on Amazon.com in Canada at one point!

Q. Considering what Tolkien said about leaving the Primary World and entering the Secondary World, which became one of the main aspects of *LotR* that fans love, I think your *Atlas* vastly helps that immersing process for the reader.

A. When the *Atlas* was first released, I told the interviewer from the local television channel that in many ways Tolkien's world had become more real to me than my own! One of the delightful things that I have discovered over the years is that I have many kindred spirits in this feeling. A Baton Rouge newspaper review in 1981 began: "At long last the final argument comes to light to put to the lie to all those disbelievers who remain unconvinced of the existence of Middle-earth and the ancient civilizations that once lived there. Doubts have often been raised concerning the authenticity of the original Tolkien manuscripts, and many of these doubts centered upon the paucity of adequate geographical data upon which to build the whole foundation." The reviewer, N. Kent Goldsmith, ended the review: "A must for the true believer." Ah, how Tolkien's world calls us to make it our own ...

Q. I once asked my readership to create a fanciful "travelogue" of faraway places in Middle-earth they would like to travel. See this story: http://greenbooks.theonering.net/quickbeam/files/070100.html. Some readers wanted to travel beyond the edges of the maps. Does this surprise you?

A. It would surprise me if they didn't! It is part of being human. It is why our Primary World was explored ... why we look out to the stars with wonder and curiosity. Tolkien says it best in his *LotR* foreword, "The book is too short."

Q. Where would you most like to spend time, while travelling in Middle-earth?

A. Before answering this question, I want to comment on something that has nothing to do with it—your spelling of "travelling." The editor assigned to work with me on the original edition wanted me to spell it 'traveling' instead. If it had only affected the text, I probably wouldn't have paid much attention, but she wanted me to change the spelling on the "Bag End to Rivendell" pathway map in *The Hobbit* section that compared Bilbo's and Frodo's journeys. The change would have required relettering and respacing a line that ran across a whole double-page spread: "Frodo and Friends—28 travelling days, average of 17.5 miles daily on foot." I argued that the *Atlas* spelling should agree with that in the books. Fortunately, Anne Barrett backed me up by saying, "Of course it has to agree with the Professor!"

Now, regarding your real question. Ah, to live in the Shire! The best of both worlds is to be an armchair explorer—"I sit beside my fire and think .." are wonderful words. They become ever more comfortable as life goes on. On the other hand, in our Primary World and in Tolkien's Secondary World, one has to go out the door for adventures...and adventures enrich one's life immensely! If I could have instant transportation and invisibility to avoid detection, there is nowhere I would NOT want to go—even to the deepest pits of Barad-dûr!

Q. Why do you think this *LotR* phenomenon continues unabated after 50 years?

A. The tales are timeless as they take place in a Secondary World. They will not become dated. They require no knowledge of current events or phrases. Further, they are laced with many cosmic themes: Good versus Evil, the power of hope, of friendship, and of sacrifice. The stories and the place are strong enough to keep people reading and re-reading them—and passing that legacy on. I read *LotR* to my son when he was in fourth grade. He read *The Silmarillion* in ninth grade and has closely followed all *LotR*-related things since. He once thanked me for having read him Tolkien instead of Dr. Seuss! (He got that too, just younger.) I am far from being unique in this, and when thousands of people love something, that love spreads to those around them. The films have added hundreds of thousands more to the mix. On a bonus feature for *RotK*, John Rhys-Davies said, "I think we have made a trilogy that will live as long as there is film." I believe that may well be true with all of Tolkien. Wouldn't it be wonderful to pop ahead a thousand years and check?!

Dr. Brad Birzer and *Tolkien's Sanctifying Myth*

Anwyn

"[Myths are] lies and therefore worthless, even though breathed through silver," [said Lewis.]

"*No,*" said Tolkien. "*They are not lies.*"

—As recorded by Humphrey Carpenter in *The Inklings*

Since the very publication of *The Lord of the Rings*, theories have abounded on the deeper significance or meaning that Tolkien intended his story to have. The atomic bomb, WWII at large, psychoanalytic journeys through adolescence, Frodo as Christ, Gandalf as Christ, Aragorn as Christ, etc. rampage ad nauseam, and the argument of Tolkien himself that he "despised allegory" becomes tired and cannot carry the fight alone. A shift in perspective is warranted, one that has a basis in other Professorial remarks: that *The Lord of the Rings* is decidedly a work saturated with, though not intoxicated by, Christianity; that though no one figure in the story is meant to represent or can be interpreted to resemble Christ, still the most prominent characters embody severally the highest virtues known to moral man; that death itself is a Christian reward for godly persons and heroic deeds; that modernism can be successfully shunned by one living in the modern world; that humans reach their highest potential when fulfilling God's purpose; and that all myths contain fragments of a larger, objective truth.

Dr. Brad Birzer's book, *Tolkien's Sanctifying Myth*, contains all these points and many more, richly supported by primary sources and the observations of those surrounding J.R. R. Tolkien during his life.

As a Catholic, like Professor Tolkien, Dr. Birzer is deeply sympathetic to Tolkien's struggles with modernism, both in the world around him and inside the organized church. Birzer gently lays out the different facets of Tolkien's belief system and clearly shows how each affected the writing of *The Lord of the Rings* and its appended works. For those of us who have long tried to reconcile the Christianity of *The Lord of the Rings* with Tolkien's clear desire that the work not be looked upon as a fable or a representation, Birzer's book is the fresh air we have been looking for—everything set out clearly and with sound reasoning supporting the thesis that Tolkien's paramount desire was to use myth to inform the greater truth.

I had the pleasure of a recent conversation with Dr. Birzer, in which he shared some of the motivations and circumstances that brought about his writing. A history professor at Hillsdale College in Michigan, Dr. Birzer observed that his position in a small liberal arts school gives him a considerable amount of freedom in his academic life. Because his administration puts the emphasis on teaching rather than on publishing, he is able to pursue projects that, like *Sanctifying Myth*, are more literary in nature than historical, but it is obvious that his historical studies prepared him for the painstaking research required by *Myth*. "If I were at a state school I'd have to publish in history," he explains. "My approach to Tolkien is 'liberal artish'–not social science-based." He says that he attempted to come at Tolkien as objectively as possible–not an easy feat after having been a Tolkien reader for 25 years. When asked to elaborate upon the liberal arts perspective, he offers, "I really tried to ask a couple of basic questions: What is the human person? What is the relationship of the person to God, to society—those are the fundamental questions of liberal arts, so that's how I approached it."

His method has resulted in some keen observations about Tolkien as well as a seamless drawing together of many views already published elsewhere, largely by other Christian scholars. "I tried really hard to ask questions without expecting a certain answer," he observes. "Now having said that, I really tried to put my mind into the mindset of what an English Roman Catholic would have thought, between two world wars. There are so few English Roman Catholics, and [Tolkien] would have been aware of all of them. I looked for who was writing what in the '20s, '30s, and found a number of parallels [between published works and Tolkien's thinking]." In particular, Birzer cites the works of Christopher Dawson, a friend of Tolkien's friend Havard whom

Tolkien met on a few occasions. Birzer makes it clear that though Dawson was something of a recluse and did not really attend meetings of Tolkien's friends in the form of the Inklings, Tolkien was very aware of Dawson's philosophic Catholicism.

The largest gem mined out of the wealth of information Birzer drew upon is identified in the title of his book. He expounds upon Tolkien's desire to sanctify myth and through myth, reality. Birzer describes once again, in case any of us have missed it over the years, the flaming acrimony leveled at Tolkien by rabid modernists, to whom anything not dealing with "those fundamental human concerns through which societies ultimately define themselves–religion, philosophy, politics, and the conduct of sexual relationships" is simply trash. Those words were taken from a review by one Andrew Rissik, writing for the *London Guardian* and quoted by Dr. Birzer. But what Birzer brings to the forefront is Tolkien's belief that societies shouldn't define themselves by those things, and that indeed, the sanctification Tolkien so earnestly desired begins with putting those elements in their proper places and dealing instead with the virtues so eloquently described by Tolkien in the pages of *The Lord of the Rings*—heroism, sacrifice, treatment of one's friends, treatment of one's enemies, and understanding of the higher purpose to which one is called. I'm quite sure that Tolkien would squirm in his chair or spin in his grave at talk of societies defining themselves by their sexual relationships, though unfortunately it is a fact of modern life.

Life under the anti-modernist Catholic umbrella is not all harmony and sunshine, however. Dr. Birzer does not mask the natural friction between Tolkien's ardent Catholicism and the Protestantism of one of his closest friends, C.S. Lewis. While he reiterates what has been pointed out by others, that Lewis was personally biased against Catholicism while maintaining a broader view in his outside writings, he also makes clear the less well known idea that Tolkien had his share of prejudices against Protestantism. Birzer gives us the startling viewpoint that Tolkien blamed Protestants for causing the Enlightenment and thus modernism, by rejecting the authority of the Pope during the Reformation. Appended to this idea is the notion that a lack of uniform Christianity results in a much higher sense of nationalism, and thus potential for national conflict. In defense of this perspective, Dr. Birzer, in our conversation, painted for me a picture of the medieval world that Tolkien so embraced. "[Tolkien's] understanding of Catholicism and the Middle Ages–you have Latin that all the scholars speak, you have certain literature, the Bible, papal encyclicals and council papers, then national cultures—ethnic cultures. English (of Chaucer), French, Hungarians, etc. But in terms of larger overview, they are tied together. A scholar leaving Hungary could go to Oxford and speak Latin."

So the umbrella of Catholicism and scholarly Latin was more important than the existing nationalism, even though ethnic differences continued to be upheld. Dr. Birzer referred to "Christiana res publica. Politically decentralized but culturally unified—higher culture, not lower folk culture."

It is clear that Tolkien longed for this kind of disparate national entity–Aragorn's hands-off approach to the Shire once he became king makes that point beyond doubt—but that he still wished for that protective umbrella of Catholicism and Latin for all. Our modern "multicultural" craze tends to bear out the peacemaking possibilities of Tolkien's wish—with the lack of submission to a higher authority comes a search for a guiding principle, and when people make nationalism and heritage their ultimate calling, we see firsthand today the results. Nation against nation, citizen of one continental descent against citizen of another. It was this kind of conflict Tolkien was anxious to alleviate with his sanctifying force.

Dr. Birzer makes a terrific case for what he sees as Tolkien's ultimate objective: the sanctification of the whole world and his small part in it through sub-creation of truthful myth. But does Dr. Birzer, or did Tolkien, see any hope of achievement of these lofty goals? I reminded him of the fate of Christians who speak up publicly and the common rallying cry of the modernist: You can't push your morality on others. He answered at length.

"Let me put it this way—I think this is how Tolkien would have answered that. Essentially, people who are doing things in politics, that's great. But every aspect of society needs to be sanctified. It doesn't matter if it's a book, or a video game, or a family. It doesn't demand moral rigor in the sense of pushing morality on others. Tolkien would be distraught at that; that's the tool of the enemy. Tolkien was open and wanting to come at people on their own terms. But I also think nothing is going to change politically for any long period of time before culture has been changed. Culture is the beginning of all things. Not until the culture has been changed will anything else be changed—economics, politics, etc. Tolkien showed this through Sam: Always use your gifts for the greater good. Of course we're fallen, but use your gifts and follow the cardinal virtues—prudence, temperance, justice, fortitude, faith, hope and charity. Of course, we don't do that–it's God working through us. Frodo and Sam have to leave their community to save it, and go into hell with the Ring, but they do it.

"The mystery is how we do what we're supposed to do, regardless of the outcome or why. You never know how anything you do—anything you do—will affect anything, even a thousand years from now, even someone who just happens to see you, what they will pass on to their children. Tolkien said each one of us is an allegory of God, an allegory of Christ. We have eternal life; we're given this gift of pilgrimage here. Tolkien was very clear: We do our part and let God take care of the rest. We can't change the world. That's what Sauron and Melkor tried to do; they wanted to see what they could do, and of course it's not about them.

"I was born in September of 1967. Why then? Why not a hundred years ago? Why not a hundred years from now? Each one of us has a purpose. [The apostle] Paul talks about this. We are altogether small beings that form the body of Christ. And to me that's what the Fellowship is about. A small group of small people, with disparate gifts—and it failed sometimes! Sometimes it failed miserably! Boromir failed, and was redeemed by his sacrifice."

Dr. Birzer is clear that Tolkien's characters were ultimately all about the love required to attain higher purpose. And like our own Quickbeam, he knows the secret truth about Samwise Gamgee—"He is the hero of the story," Birzer says.

"If we can't be loving, we can't be anything. Every one in the Fellowship was loving. Gandalf willing to sacrifice himself—an act of love. Frodo, same thing. Sam, same thing. Aragorn confronting Sauron was loving. I think we do our duty, see what happens, and not be too impatient.

"It may take a thousand years before the culture's redeemed. If we push it, we only cause problems. We can only lead by example. That's how the early church was formed. They didn't push it. They died in the arenas over and over again."

But does he see any realistic hope for the sanctification of civilization? Or, hearkening back to a time when a large majority of the western population was Catholic, re-sanctification? What about the inevitable fall of society?

"Tolkien did address this. He, like all of us, on some days was optimistic and some days pessimistic. There's no doubt that we're getting closer and closer together and we're being homogenized. It's good and bad. It's bad in that we often take the lowest common denominator in order to agree with each other."

And apparently good in that a story like Tolkien's can be easily passed around the entire world and free discussion can take place in every corner of the globe about whether Balrogs have wings and how Tolkien's Christianity affects the character of, say, Boromir. Ultimately, if humans are getting closer and closer together, then their myths are more widely known to one another—and if each myth holds a fragment of truth, eventually society may put it all together. After all, Tolkien knew, as most 20th-century writers apparently do not, that "the fantastic may tell us more about reality than scientific fact." Dr. Birzer definitely thinks so. He reminded me that fact and reality are not necessarily the same thing.

"We have] blinders over our eyes so that we only see things in a certain age. Never in the Middle Ages would anybody blink an eye if somebody said they saw somebody come down with a halo. We limit ourselves by only trying to figure out what we can see, smell, touch. There's a deeper reality. To Tolkien, myth was truth."

The Films (continued)

So You're *Still* Watching Jackson?

Anwyn

I basely stole the title for this introduction from Tehanu, who prefaced the first *People's Guide to J.R.R. Tolkien* with "So You're *Still* Reading Tolkien?" It seems appropriate, for the man who took one of the most beloved books of the 20th century and created three of the most beloved films of the 21st seems to have become an icon in the realm of Tolkien fandom and study, one who bids fair to have his work last as long in the public consciousness as Tolkien's itself.

Upon one point there is no doubt: Jackson's work generates strong reactions, just as Tolkien's has and continues to do. In many cases it is as Richard Gere's character commented about opera in *Pretty Woman:* "If you love it, you will always love it. If you don't, you may learn to appreciate it, but it will never become part of your soul." I know many folks who love Tolkien's *The Lord of the Rings*. I know many more who tolerate it, for whom it is not part of their souls. And in ever-growing numbers are those who love Jackson's *The Lord of the Rings*, those who merely tolerate it, and those who despise it as being a desecration of the work of Tolkien they hold so dear. Dramatic reactions indeed.

What is in these films that prompts this strength of reaction in people? Partly, obviously, it is the life given to the story, the breath given to the characters, the visualization given to the landscape that previously lived only in our imaginations, in ours and in Tolkien's, that draws us and holds us to Jackson's vision. Partly, probably, it is hearing the magic of Tolkien's language spoken aloud, wherever the filmmakers retained it. Partly, surely, it is the magic of modern filmmaking, beautiful set dressing, and fantastic effects. But there must be more. Those alone are not enough to make these films become "part of your soul."

We at Green Books and TheOneRing.net have written independently over the years about the effects of Jackson's work, before the films were made, as they were rolling out, and at their conclusion. By and large, our reactions go like this: Quickbeam unabashedly adores Jackson's work; Turgon just as unabashedly despises it. Tehanu likes it and likes to plumb to the depths for the ins and outs and whys and wherefores; Ostadan likes to analyze as well, ultimately deciding that the films are worthy. And Anwyn is a wee bit of a fence sitter, my friends. Back and forth, do I love these movies or hate them? Or something in between? It's a terrible dichotomy to be a pretty heavy-handed purist and then to find myself riveted to the screen for three-plus hours, mouth hanging open and eyes wide at many points, and to leave the theater a bit dazed, finding it very difficult to evaluate what I have just seen.

But before I was able to see *The Return of the King* in the theater, I finally realized one little thing that focused my perspective for me. I went to my line party in December and helped put on an exciting costume contest, though I couldn't stay for the film because I had my three-month-old son with me. And I finally saw firsthand what many people have been emailing to us since *The Fellowship of the Ring* unspoiled: These films touch people. They become part of their souls, apparently very much in the way that Tolkien's story has. Whether this happens for me personally is rather irrelevant at this point. The fact that it happens for many means that Jackson very possibly has succeeded at something Tolkien would approve of, however he may have winced at some of Jackson's representations. Ralph Bakshi and Rankin and Bass have their names in the lore of Tolkien's world, but generally with some snide comment appended. Not so Jackson. He succeeded beyond their wildest dreams, and his work will live on as the films that, in addition to bringing to life the most beloved book of the century, set the new benchmark for all fantasy films to come, resurrecting the genre and helping to make it respectable.

In the following pages, we offer our perspectives on how Jackson and his team managed it. Agree or disagree, like them or hate them, love them or tolerate them, whether these films are in your soul or not, Jackson's work is the new gold standard, and he can hope that Tolkien would not *entirely* disapprove.

The Return of the King Film Review

Quickbeam

My Rating: 10 out of 10

Turn on the waterworks. Bring a whole box of Kleenex. *RotK* is the glorious emotional crescendo to the *Lord of the Rings* films, and it will surely bring you to tears. Generations of Tolkien fans know the story—replete with tragedy, soaring heroism, and the bittersweet partings of their favorite characters. Filmgoers who have not read Tolkien's masterwork will recognize this film as Peter Jackson's masterwork—and rightly so.

Personally, I feel *RotK* is in greater concordance with Tolkien than the prior films. We don't have main characters shifted far from their printed origins (remember Faramir), nor do the hobbits get dragged off to Osgiliath again, so the core fans should be very pleased with this adaptation. The more PJ adheres to the book, the higher his film soars. Granted, his team has done a smashing job putting together all three, but this one is special. The director, showing remarkable control over such a huge narrative, knocks the ball out of the park. He and co-screenwriters Philippa Boyens and Fran Walsh have captured the most delicate of emotions previously found only in Tolkien's original, and in this aspect above all others their work should be lauded to the top of the highest mountain. *RotK* is a singular triumph.

We have been visiting these characters for years now, and they are familiar to us from repeated viewings on DVD. Just as they have been on a long journey of endurance, so too has the audience been on a similar journey, eager for the largest and most complex story arc in film history to come to a sweeping close. PJ masterfully weaves his film with threads of heart-stopping fury and tender grace, just as Tolkien did 50 years ago. I have learned over time to recognize his directing style, feeling the rhythms of carefully connected scenes as PJ moved the story forward. This film, however, is a magnificent finale—and like an orchestra conductor with an army of musicians, he gives every phrase of this mythic symphony just the right flourish.

We have seen so much wonderful imagery from the team at WETA, working under Richard Taylor and Tania Rodger, the digital folks under Jim Rygiel, and of course the glorious production design by Oscar winner Grant Major, among others. Bless them and keep them! Not a single frame of film unspools without visual wonder. A special tip of the hat to Alex Funke and Andrew Lesnie for photographing Middle-earth on the large and small scales. You will not find colors or compositions as fine as these. Of course, New Zealand itself is still the star of the show. You've seen the majesty of its savage landscapes—you have felt the Tookish part in you waking up just a bit the more you watch. I promise you'll want to go there yourself someday, seeking your own intrepid adventure. Call up Vic James at Red Carpet Tours this instant. Trust me on this.

To my mind, Howard Shore's music is a brilliant match for the luminous images. This is his finest showing. Here are beauties that pierce like swords, to borrow a phrase from C.S. Lewis, and Shore clearly understands how emotional connections are made between ear and heart. He deserves our acknowledgment and shall have it in spades. "The Lighting of the Beacons" is a magical euphoria of hope rekindled (yup, that's the point where my eyes first welled up), while the plaintive song "Into the West" allows the angelic Annie Lennox to sing as she has never sung. She carries a melody where sorrow begets strength—where time stands still at the Grey Havens.

At the end of the day, the heart of this whole endeavor is the story. Music, costumes, and shiny clean CGI never once upstage the epic story—not once. PJ knows what he is doing, and so do the actors. Now we come to the rich blood flowing through the film's veins; the most nuanced acting of the entire trilogy is here, for these performances carry us through the agony of the heroes' many sacrifices. When we realize what has happened to our wee hobbits during the great War of the Ring, from the verdant Shire to the terrifying Plateau of Gorgoroth—well, it's too late for us. We are also there right alongside them. The screenwriters have wisely focused the central narrative on Frodo and

Sam. Remember that teaser poster image with a ragged, collapsed Frodo being held by Samwise in Mordor? Well, there you have it. That is the soul of *RotK* right on that poster. Their struggle against hopelessness is the perfect thematic course to take. All other characters reflect the same struggle in their individual scenes. It all seems to fit so well.

I am in awe at how I responded to this remarkable film. I expected going in that some deeper feelings would surface, but I was not prepared for how completely it would all wash over me.

Several moments of *RotK* are worth special mention:

Pippin Took finds himself taking center stage in a lot of scenes. I told Billy Boyd at the press junket in Wellington that his performance was brilliant. "You were fantastic. You owned every scene you were in," I said. And I meant it truthfully. Pippin has a terrifying encounter with Sauron via the Palantir, and when Gandalf interrogates him afterward the look on Pippin's face shows layers of terror, guilt, yet also the burning curiosity to look inside the stone just one more time, though he knows it would bring ruin. And much later, where he sings for Denethor in the Citadel of Minas Tirith, the audience I sat with was clearly moved by his intimate voice. It's such a fantastic portrayal of our youngest, most naïve hobbit. But naïve no more. Well done, Billy... well done.

Sean Astin totally rocks. Severity and agony are not the kinds of things we expect to see on Samwise's gentle face. But with the character being pushed to the final throw by Gollum's treachery and the horrors of Mordor, we see everything gentle in him change. Behold the performance of the year. Sean is just stunning here—he throws himself into the work with such passion. After the Ring is unmade and the two wounded hobbits are awaiting their death on the slopes of Mt. Doom, lava rushing past them, Sam suddenly admits his desire to marry Rosie Cotton. He wants to use his final breath to claim his own emotional ground for himself... a final, miserable regret. After such a long time of ignoring his own needs and emotions in his selfless attendance of Mr. Frodo, it is a shock to hear him openly say this. There is such crushing heartbreak in this utterance. It is the most visceral and honest performance I've yet seen throughout Sean's career.

Frodo is lost to the Ring. Thus Elijah Wood takes us to a place of pain and emptiness. We see the struggle in his soul shown more on the outside—and it works. Elijah hasn't given us this kind of performance before. He is incredibly skillful at balancing very difficult lines of dialogue that might otherwise sound stilted. And one of the finest shots ever put on film completely belongs to him. After Gwaihir and his brethren gather up the hobbits from the outcropping, we see the churning lava far below Frodo as his body gently sways in the wind. Frodo is finally free of his burden, with both agony and ecstasy written across his face. I will never forget Elijah's amazing performance.

Viggo Mortensen faces his destiny when Lord Elrond brings to him the reforged sword Andúril. His challenge is to command the Army of the Dead, making the final declaration that he is the King, the true heir of Isildur. Viggo has a shining light in his eyes when he realizes that Arwen has given up everything for him, that the world of Men will indeed succumb to Sauron, and that he must prove himself now, or never. Setting aside his doubts, he truly embraces his birthright. You can hear it in his voice. Although we don't get to see the Houses of the Healing sequence (drat!) where the "hands of a healer" dialogue offers more kingly proof of the true heir, we still have a most compelling line that Aragorn delivers to the hobbits at a key moment: "My friends, you bow down to no one." It is such a magnificent change in him (and far better dialogue than "Let's hunt some Orc").

If you can't get enough of Sméagol/Gollum, then sit back and enjoy another award-deserving performance from Andy Serkis. The opening scenes are all about Sméagol and Déagol, with the two cousins first encountering the Ring. Here we see his full transformation in lurid detail, from a river-folk Hobbit to a horrid creature crawling under the mountains. It is so very sad. And disgusting. And necessary to understanding the psyche of one person being pulled apart by Sauron's will. We are suddenly afraid of what is happening to Frodo as he carries the Ring. It is a completely brutal opening, and it sets the tone for the rest of the film—the stakes are higher and the reality of the Ring's evil more acute.

My favorite moment? Oh come now, that's just not possible. Especially when you have a film with such a cornucopia of brilliant moments. I love the personal victory of Miranda Otto on the Pelennor Fields—Théoden's death—the ugly look on Denethor's face when he says aloud to his surviving son that he would have preferred that Faramir died instead of Boromir—the cunning strategy of Gandalf as he takes charge of the city of Minas Tirith—and the shrill horror of Shelob as she poisons poor Frodo, seemingly to his death. It's really something to see.

If there is any complaint I would make, it seems unfortunate to even mention it. There is a very tight funnel of time between the events after the Battle of the Pelennor Fields and the time that Frodo and Sam make their final ascent to Mount Doom. It almost seems that the two hobbits aren't really spending that many days crawling across the volcanic plateau. At this point, I sensed a bit too much editorial trimming (similar problem we had with *TTT*, but this is just a nit-picky thing). With all my thoughts toward the upcoming Extended Edition DVD, I'm sure we'll see the missing bits put back in. But to wait that long is just a pain. Sigh.

The final parting at the Grey Havens… well, I'm not even going to talk about it. Best you see it for yourselves. The perfect balance of emotions. The perfect ending of the journey. The end of a very long piece of cinema history.

It is immensely satisfying to watch my most beloved book come to life so vibrantly on the big screen. Indeed, part of me wishes it could go on forever.

In most movie theatres around the world, workers have to clean stale popcorn off the floor when an audience leaves. But after *RotK*, they'll be collecting many a wet Kleenex instead, filled with many tears. And what greater praise can a filmmaker receive than to know his audience has been moved with such power?

The Return of the King Film Review

Tehanu

As with all the *LotR* films it took a number of viewings before I could finally settle into that comfortable, happy state of being able to remember enough to think about what I'd seen. I think we forget that the movie critics that we read in the first days of a film's release don't have that luxury. I would have hated to make a judgement on any of these films after seeing it only once.

Plenty has been written about the film's epic qualities and the exhilarating tour-de-force that it is. I hardly need to comment on the acting—if Sean Astin and Elijah Wood seemed outstanding, they also had more screen time in which to work. Everyone else seemed equally in command of whatever they were given, whether it was the subtlest facial gestures or the most dramatic whole-body action. It has been a hallmark of these movies that they are unafraid to move between different genres, so that at one moment we're watching an comic-book action flick, next a horror movie, and then a subtle, understated piece of inward drama that might belong to a great art house movie. They are all well done; how the movie succeeds with the viewers depends on their willingness to adapt to all these different styles in the same story. For me it makes for a very rich experience.

I'm going to write now about the things that struck me either with pain or delight. I'll also state my position on the purism/revisionist continuum, because that debate has never wholly died out. To purists, the movie is automatically bad wherever it departs from the books, and to revisionists, the film is a separate entity which has different parameters for telling the same story; divergence from the text is interesting and at times enriching. I'd have to say I'm one of the latter.

Often we treat Middle-earth as if it were a real place and as if the events that Tolkien wrote about really happened. That being so, I take the pretence further and say: With any event that happens, public or personal, there will be as many interpretations of the story as there are observers. You see it all the time in journalism (try reading five newspapers from five different countries about the same world event, if you doubt me!), and you meet it all the time in real life. After spending a month agonizing that the man of your dreams walked out of a party just as you were getting to know him, because of some stupid remark of yours, another person who was at the party reveals that he left because his pager went and he was on call. A third person says no, that wasn't a work pager, that was his wife. No, that wasn't his wife, that's his business partner, actually he's gay, says another. And so on and so on. You were right there and saw his departure with your own eyes, and you thought you caused it, but was your "story" the true one?

Tolkien's world and Tolkien's story are big enough that I can easily pretend, just for the fun of it, that all those things he wrote did really happen. He told it the way he heard it (or found it in that pit of hearsay, inaccurate recollection, skimpy research and biased observation no doubt riddled with family politics called *The Red Book of Westmarch*). Peter Jackson, Fran Walsh and Philippa Boyens tell a different story of the same events. What fun, I get to hear a whole different interpretation of it all! I love the newness and surprise. After all, nobody's taken away the original story I always knew. Every time I return to the written page, it surprises me and moves me with its power and beauty. But so does the film—in different ways and for different reasons.

I love the way *The Return of the King* is paced and the way the stories are separated out, then tied together closer and closer as the film progresses. There's a nice symmetry. The prologue is one storyline only (Sméagol's), and emotionally it's as much of a downward plunge as Gandalf's physical plunge at the beginning of *The Two Towers*. Then we pick up the story of the Fellowship, who quickly roll up into two stories: Frodo and Sam in Ithilien, and (reunited almost immediately at Isengard) the rest of the Fellowship. And then it all unravels again into a big hank of parallel stories and you have four or five lines to follow, but this time the connections between the stories are tighter. At times it's wonderfully done, like Pippin's heart-wrenching song that carries us between the great hall at Minas Tirith and the field outside Osgiliath where Faramir's men are charging to their death, or the sequence of beacons that carry Gondor's call to Rohan. At other times the action cuts across as the characters in one story wonder what is happening to the rest of the Fellowship. Sometimes the Eye itself is the link, for we follow its gaze from one event to another.

And then towards the end, the stories have narrowed down again to just two, but the cutting between the hobbits' story in Mordor and the Army of the West outside it sets up a counterpoint of two different kinds of tension that works very well in my opinion. And then the ending, one storyline at last.

Much has been said about the many "endings" of the film. To me the endings feel quite right. Like the rhythm of a slowing heartbeat, the story jumps forward in "pulses"—the awakening after Mt. Doom, the coronation, the Shire homecoming, the reflective, rueful moment between the hobbits back at the Green Dragon, Frodo's spoken coda about how he feels adrift in the Shire, the leavetaking at the Grey Havens, and finally Sam's return home. It feels like deep breaths moving towards sleep. Like your last waking moments before you drop off. Memories of the day flash past; then you drift off and jolt awake to another thought, then another, then finally you don't wake again. For such a long epic, this seems appropriate. Almost as if a long story was winding to a close, but you yourself were coming adrift from it, so the action has leapt forwards and the tone changed while you were away. In the first two movies we were pulled away from the final scene by the camera rising, dragging us away from the hobbits and out of Middle-earth. Here we seem to sink slowly to rest. Some people can't cope with that as a storytelling device. Their loss, I reckon.

By this the third movie we're becoming more aware of the way things are likely to be included in the extended editions to come, so even at first viewing I passed over some of the scene changes I didn't like with a sigh, thinking "Oh well, I bet they'll add something here and it'll all make more sense in the extended DVD comes out." Hard to say what a Tolkien newbie would make of it all, though. When Gandalf and the others ride up to Isengard, look at it for a moment, then decide to go away again, a voice in my head kept piping up with that line from *Monty Python and the Holy Grail*, "On second thoughts, let's *not* go to Camelot. 'Tis a silly place!" I know that of all things, the filmmakers did not want *LotR* to remind anyone of *Monty Python and the Holy Grail*, so that's a shame. The scene before the Black Gates was the same. Gallop up, issue a challenge, and run off when the gate opens. When I watch that scene, that Monty Python voice in my head has popped up again more than once: "Run away!!!" Behind the gate we see pretty much the wall of orcs and trolls we all expected to see anyway, but no Mouth of Sauron. There's a similar sense of deflation during the defense of Minas Tirith, when Gandalf rallies the troops to withstand the assault on the gates. "You are soldiers of Gondor! No matter what comes through that gate you will stand your ground!" My heart was in my mouth as the gate opened, the first time I saw that, for I expected to see the Witch-king waiting to confront Gandalf. But no, to my disappointment there were just more orcs and trolls. For all those scenes there's room to insert some pretty juicy drama—Saruman's demise, in particular. I'm one of those warped Gríma fanciers, and so I'm hungry to see any amount of Shakespearean tragedy played out between him and Christopher Lee. Dish it out, I say! Tear up the floorboards!

I really, really looked forward to Éowyn's scene with the Witch-king, and it was very good. She was exactly as I imagined in the book. And as Merry saw her, "...so fair, so desperate!" Beautifully done by Miranda Otto. Well fought, and the way the Witch-king crumpled up was creepy and effective. If I have a complaint, it's that the scene didn't pause to let us savor the emotion for a moment before leaping straight to the boys' heroics—Legolas's fancy stuntwork against the Mûmakil and so on. Fun, that, but I wanted to spend some more time letting Éowyn's extraordinary deed sink in before rushing to the next corner of the battle.

I liked the way Éowyn and Merry in the movie relate to each other. In the book Merry doesn't realize he's sharing Dernhelm's horse with a woman. The innocent wee lad! In the film, I treasure his look of glee when she scoops him up—"Whee, you mean I'm going to sit on Éowyn's lap for three days?" It means we lose that Macbeth-like moment of shock when Dernhelm reveals herself to the Witch-king, who says, "No living man may hinder me!" (A misleading prophecy like "No man of woman born shall harm Macbeth...") I'm not sure audiences really got the full shock value of that. But then we see all the more clearly Merry's progress from thinking that this battle is going to be a bit of a lark, to the terrified realization of what war really is.

There were so many good moments with the Rohirrim. I was deeply moved by the charge of the riders of Rohan, but then I knew I would be. For some people horses are just a pathetic forerunner of the motorbikes and cars we've replaced them with, but the filmmakers knew how to film their power and courage. Horses can't act, really. Their excitement, terror, fierceness, and the trust with which they fling themselves towards whatever end their riders command—those are not feigned. The camera running on tracks beside them caught the glory of those moments beautifully. There is a verse from the Bible which goes, in part:

> Hast thou given the horse strength?
> Hast thou clothed his neck with thunder?
> Canst thou make him afraid as a grasshopper?
> The glory of his nostrils is terrible.
> He paweth in the valley and rejoiceth in his strength:
> He goeth to meet the armed men;
> He mocketh at fear and is not affrighted,
> Neither turneth he back from the sword.
> The quiver rattleth against him,
> The glittering spear and the shield—
> He swalloweth the ground with fierceness and rage,
> Neither believeth he that it is the sound of the trumpet—
> He sayeth among the trumpets, "Ha! Ha!"
> And he smelleth the battle far off,
> The thunder of the captains, and the shouting.
>
> —*Job 39*

This is one of the earliest poems I can remember reading and understanding, and something deep inside me had always dreamed of seeing it the flesh. The filmic Charge of the Rohirrim was as close to it as I could ever have hoped.

I loved the fact that so much of Tolkien's speech was used as Théoden urged his troops to battle. "Oaths ye have taken—now fulfill them!" and "Arise now, riders of Théoden!" and so on. The horns of Rohan were fantastic too—such a wild, stirring sound. (If ever there's one prop I'd want to have from the movies, it'd be one of the horns!) Then the riders chanting "Death! Death!" That is in the books too, though at a later point, when Éomer finds Éowyn unconscious on the battlefield.

I'd have loved to have seen more of Éomer—Karl Urban is such a fine actor. But I could see the storylines would have gotten further complicated with the crowning of *another* king on the battlefield and the further deeds of Éomer as he fought his way towards Aragorn.

In the book, Théoden speaks his final words to Merry, not Éowyn, before dying. The films have made more of the father/daughter relationship between Théoden and Éowyn than the book did. (It is a father/daughter *kind* of relationship, although Éowyn is not Théoden's daughter but his "sister-daughter.") Given the closeness we've seen between them, it has more impact to give Éowyn and Théoden that final farewell scene together. All through the film there are examples like that where speeches from the books are reassigned from one character to another—so the story gets told, but the net of relationships is cast slightly differently.

The emphasis for Merry has been his relationship with Pippin. The film dwells on his anguish at parting from Pippin, and so instead of moving the focus to a scene between him and Théoden, the film leaves him alone to be found by Pippin on the battlefield. I like the way the camera draws back from them as Pippin says "I'm going to look after you." The way he's solicitously tucking Merry's cloak around him is a wonderful gesture—both futile and pathetic, yet staunchly optimistic given the piles of dead and dying lying around on all sides. It sums up their relationship and hobbit nature so well.

I thought the film paid tribute to Tolkien's sources in a subtle way when Théoden caught sight of the Mûmakil. What Gimli expresses a lot more crudely later on ("Impossible odds, certain chance of death, what are we waiting for?") Théoden expresses with one look. Yes, he's never seen anything so terrifying before, but they are worthy foes for a hero. Tolkien's translation of the Old English poem *The Battle of Maldon* has the hero, faced with impossible odds, say,

Heart shall be bolder, harder be purpose,
More proud the spirit as our power lessens.

That was the spirit of those ancient warrior people—preferring to die in glory rather than live in defeat. You see Théoden's eyes narrow with the realization that the odds are hopeless but the fight will be worthy to live long in the memory of the bards.

I loved the moments when the film told the story in the way that *only* film can. For instance the very beginning, when we witness Sméagol's transformation into Gollum. Yes, it's a chance for the SFX department to show off, but it's more than that. The images of Sméagol's dissolution and enslavement to the Ring are potent and drive home the point as well as any amount of dialogue could. Another one is the lighting of the beacons—this is startlingly moving. It's just a moment in the book—Pippin sees them lit and Gandalf names them, all on their desperate ride to Gondor on Shadowfax. In the film that moment is transposed to a later point in the story. How the camera luxuriates in the power of the visual symbol! Hope and light are kindled and passed on, over the tops of the tall mountains in the gorgeous dawn and luminous star-studded night of the beautiful Middle-earth that they hope to save.

The moment when Pippin sings as Denethor eats, grim and wasted, in the deathly formality of his hall, and Faramir rides into the host of orcs in front of Osgiliath—how unexpected it is to hear Bilbo's walking song in this context, recast as a lament. I thought that was a stroke of genius (and what a good voice Billy Boyd had for it too). I had never seen that yearning in it before. By simply removing the lines in it about "bed," the harmless-looking lines "Through shadow to the edge of night" and "Away shall fade," become loaded with tragedy in the context of the visual elements of the doomed assault.

That reminds me of two things—one a false note that happens as Faramir is leaving. There's a beautifully played scene between David Wenham and John Noble as Faramir asks him, "Do you wish that I had died instead of Boromir?" and Denethor replies, "Yes. I do wish that." And Faramir volunteers for a suicide mission. As he's riding out of Minas Tirith in front of the assembled crowd, Gandalf asks him to change his mind, for his father loves him "and will remember it before the end." This irks me—the absolutely stupidest time to get somebody to change their mind by announcing their personal situation is when they're actively leading a group who is sworn to follow them and are in front of a large crowd who also has come to see them carry out their duty. Faramir's not likely to stop, say "Oh, you're right!" and order everyone home. Maybe sometimes Gandalf is more like an unwelcome prophet who won't shut up than a subtle counselor who can bend others to his will. But in moments like those the film teeters uncomfortably between art house and comic-book cinema. At the same time, however, that scene did something quite beautiful as it played on the faces of the people of Minas Tirith. Some of the frames looked as though they'd been composed by the Old Masters. I kept thinking "I've seen that face, that look, that pose, those colors, somewhere before. In a Rubens or a Rembrandt or is it Da Vinci?" The closest I've found is Vermeer's "Girl with a Pearl Earring," but that is not exactly it. I'm also reminded of the many paintings by the Old Masters of The Entombment of Christ or Mary at the Cross.

Which, if we're going in for religious imagery, reminds me of something I loved about the ending (or one of the endings). After that moment where the Eagles pick Frodo and Sam up (all hail to WETA's digital artists for showing those grasping talons reaching down with such tender delicacy), we see Frodo flying through the air as though pillowed on the clouds themselves, for all the world like one of those old paintings of the saints as they're drawn up to heaven. Their bodies are so lax and rays of light come through the clouds to surround them in glory. And while we're on the subject, after Sam finds Frodo unconscious outside Shelob's lair, I'm reminded of Michelangelo's marble Pietá, where Mary is cradling the body of Jesus. I'm sure it's not accidental in a film that talks about making and mourning the ultimate sacrifice. Sam cradles Frodo's body as a mother would cradle the body of her child. If you think that's too far a stretch, consider the words of the closing song, "Into the West." Who is sleeping safe in whose arms, and is it really just sleep they're talking about? All those ideas seem linked to me, and I enjoyed finding tributes and echoes in the film of great art from the past.

Backing up to the Steward of Gondor and his family: Once again, it's not the Denethor of the book. Rather, we only see his greatness and nobility remembered in the way his sons still, in their different ways, love and respect him. His greatness is reflected in Boromir's wish to do right by him, spoken aloud at Lothlórien in *FotR*. By the time the film catches up with him he's more far gone in madness than in the book. There is still authority in his look, but the stifling formality of his court is at odds with his slovenly behavior. It's a question whether he eats like a slob because he is too powerful to be criticized, or because his grief has put him beyond caring what anyone thinks. I'd say the latter.

He still radiates a quite terrifying power. I find the scenes between him and Faramir very believable. They are consistent with themselves, if not with the book. The way Denethor wields his authority makes an interesting contrast with Aragorn, who is so reluctant to hold power. Yes, people will follow Aragorn's lead without hesitation. But he is never that eager to lead them, understanding the weight of the life-and-death decisions a king makes. Denethor has forgotten that, and I think the film is making a subtle point about leadership and the rightful use of power. Viggo's Aragorn will make a greater leader. He looks like he's trying to be the Tao Te Ching's idea of a leader:

> *To have without possessing,*
> *Do without claiming,*
> *Lead without controlling:*
> *This is mysterious power.*

I have met people who don't question their right to rule everyone around them. So have you. You might work for one. What a lot of grief they spread around the world.

We don't see a lot of Arwen in the film. She does well with what she does have—her moment of foresight and her insistence that Elrond reforge Narsil. As an aside, there's a nice moment there for the internet fans because Figwit the "Elf Escort" even got a line. I feel a bit like a midwife to Figwit, the Elf character totally invented by the makers of the "Figwit Lives" website. I thought their championing of a totally unknown extra that we saw for a split second on *FotR* was funny and imaginative. I kept plugging their spoof Figwit news on TheOneRing.net until he became a cult phenomenon. We appreciated Peter Jackson's people for noticing and putting him back in!

However, back to Arwen: I hated the cheap device of having Elrond tell Aragorn that her life depended on his success. That notion of him doing everything for love seems so "Hollywood," somehow. It's such a warm pink fluffy idea, totally at odds with the gravity of the situation. I'm not saying "Down with love!" It's just that when I think of interesting, brave, heroic things people do—rescues, battles, explorations, scientific endeavors—they seem more often motivated by a sense of duty, doing the right thing, and the love of adventure. It didn't make Aragorn "more human" to have him go through all that "for love." How often do you read in the paper about some heroic rescue where the people involved don't even know each other? They risk their life because it's the right thing to do for another human being. Selfless, and completely human. In Tolkien's world that sense of civic duty, of standing by people, of defending them to the death, was a primary virtue. I think it cheapened Aragorn to make it seem like he needed any more incentive than that. I think everyone understood that all kinds of loving would be extinguished if Sauron won, anyway.

I do wonder if Elrond was just beating up a scare by telling Arwen that her life was leaving her and she was dying. As soon as she decided to become mortal she would be aging and dying, in Elf terms. We all are—for humans, good health is simply the art of dying as slowly as possible. So she has a mere 120 more years to live—an eyeblink of time for an Elf, but nothing to panic about from our point of view. Is Elrond telling the whole truth here, any more than when he tells Arwen that in her future he sees only death?

I'm pretty happy that the film tries to show that Arwen has a struggle that is not a contest of arms, but instead is about finding the courage to face mortality. Three years ago I wrote in on of my "Tehanu's Notes" on TheOneRing.net:

> If Tolkien had written Arwen's story she wouldn't have *done* any more than she does in *The Lord of the Rings,* but we might have known whether she pricked her finger sewing the banner for Aragorn, and looked at the blood, and considered for the first time that it would one day be finite—a symbol of physical pains that might not heal once she chose mortality.
>
> I imagine Arwen's Quest for the courage to gamble a few decades of mortal love against the immortality (and all she might there meet!) would move us through such symbolic moments.

As far as I'm concerned, the films have found a satisfying way of showing her Quest, what I once called a Yin quest of inward searching.

I'm not going to talk much about the conflict between Frodo and Sam—in terms of the movie, it feels psychologically plausible, and it's moving and dramatic. It rejoins with Tolkien's version of the story at the point where Sam fights Shelob without making a difference to the plot from that point on. It's worth remembering that in the book, in the Tower of Cirith Ungol, when Sam goes to hand the Ring back to Frodo, Tolkien makes Frodo call Sam a thief. For a moment, Frodo sees Sam as a foul, greedy, leering orc pawing at him to get the Ring off him. "This is what the Ring can do to you," Tolkien is saying. It's not implausible to have them act that way at the point which they do in the film, on the stairs of Cirith Ungol. Adding Gollum's connivance makes the most of an emotional triangle that had great story potential, and the film played it for all it was worth.

Now to the endings. All along I've liked the way the Eye has become more and more clearly outlined throughout the films—it was another visible symbol of Sauron's growing control. By this third film it's able to turn and focus like a real eye, and its gaze rakes the landscape like an inquisitor's lantern. (Not that I think, myself, that it was ever something you could see with your physical eye, but how else could a film show the presence of that prying, spying, all-seeing will?) What did let it down at the last moment was the way the eye strained downward at the crumbling foundations of the Dark Tower, boggling with disbelief until Sauron was destroyed. It looked funny. The last thing I wanted to feel right then was amusement—it ridiculed Sauron, made him seem less than the great evil I imagined. A bit of an idiot, in fact. It's debatable whether it makes Sauron more or less plausible to give him human emotions and reactions, though. I'd have preferred to see the last gasp of Sauron's power as it was described in the book—a huge shadowy shape rising into the sky, lightening-crowned, seeming to reach out with one last stretch of a threatening hand, only to be blown away by the wind, its impotence made manifest. That seemed intensely cinematic to me. Why should the filmmakers draw back from trying to create such an apocalyptic gesture? I don't know. Not lack of courage, for sure.

For those who can't stomach grand gestures and high drama, the film offers the endgame on Mt. Doom. That moment when Sam regrets all that might have been is possibly my favorite moment in the movie. "Rosie Cotton dancing...she had ribbons in her hair...if ever I was to have married someone, it would have been her... It would have been her." It undoes me every time.

Just before that a lot of important things happen, though. Maybe having Gollum fight an invisible Frodo just wasn't visually interesting enough (it looked *odd*—and I don't know how it could *not* look odd) but I still would have been happy enough to see Gollum fall off the cliff by himself. Instead Frodo pushes him. Or close to—Frodo doesn't intend to fall himself, but his final assault is what pushes them both over. Is that making things too simple? An added crime in my opinion was the fact that Sam, reaching for Frodo's hand, says "Don't let go!" and I have a terrible flashback to the movie *Titanic*. Two things redeem it, though—one is the symmetry between that gesture and its reverse, at the end of *FotR*, where Frodo reaches down to save Sam from drowning. The second is something very subtle but I hope deliberate. As Gollum falls into the molten lava, he doesn't instantly vaporize. The Ring is protecting him and unnaturally prolonging his life *even then!* But soon enough the lava consumes him. Then the Ring floats on the lava, heating up until the letters begin to glow. But it's still not melting. It doesn't melt until the moment when Frodo makes a choice. You can call that choice what you like—accepting that Sam's love has a claim on him, choosing life, choosing hope, choosing to resist death. The moment he reaches up to allow Sam to save his life, the Ring is destroyed. As though that tiny act of individual love and faith were Sauron's undoing.

Peter Jackson's *The Return of the King*: Humanity, Horror, Haste, Heroism

Anwyn

A common criticism against J.R.R. Tolkien is that his characters lack human realism. The complaint is that they are too black or white, too high or low, too noble or common, too Good Guy or Orc, as it were. Ironically, Peter Jackson's rendering of those same characters draws criticism for their very humanism. For starters, they're filthy. Viggo Mortensen's stringy, oily hair, the hobbits' dirty fingernails, everybody's general all-around grime … yuck! Then there's their audacity in having human failings: they doubt and question their leaders, make jokes at inappropriate times, treat badly those around them. Well, how clean would you be if you spent about a year living outdoors with no tent and walking hundreds of miles, fighting battles along the way?

Peter Jackson's *The Return of the King* is far and away the best of his three *Lord of the Rings* films, though I can't decide if that's because it's really that much better or if it's because I'm three times more inured to his way of doing things. These films seem to cast a spell on me quite apart from my assessment of the value of each departure from Tolkien. It's partly the effect of the New Zealand landscape, partly the great casting, and partly—yes, it's time to admit it—Jackson's success in bringing so many different elements of Tolkien's *The Lord of the Rings* to life before my very eyes.

Once again Jackson uses to good effect his trick of showing us things Tolkien mentioned but did not elaborate upon. In *The Two Towers* it was Théodred's funeral; in *Fellowship* it was Boromir's death; here it's the flaming of the beacons of Gondor. All three scenes are more than stirring; they're grand in the best tradition of heroic fiction. Too bad he couldn't resist the physical comedy (and silly plot feature) of having Pippin sneak up to light them.

Once again Jackson's love of heroic battle (read: massive action scenes, no pun intended) serves him well; the Riders of Rohan drawn up on the edge of the Pelennor, their call to battle, their king saluting their spears with his sword as he exhorts them to valor were moving to the point of tears. Too bad he and his ham-fisted dialogue-writing cohorts came too damn close to ruining Éowyn's big moment with ridiculously dumbed-down dialogue.

Once again we are reminded that Jackson is first and foremost a maker of horror movies. In many places his love of gore is appropriate—Shelob? Shudder! But in many others it's just gratuitous yuck. There are only so many latex orcs with slime dripping from them that we can look at. Was it just me, or did the lead baddie on the Pelennor resemble Sloth from Sean Astin's childhood triumph, *The Goonies*?

However, Jackson's less savory tricks also make their return. Once again he trots out that tired favorite, making us think people are dead or dying, to little sense and less use. This time Arwen Undómiel is his primary target. Excuse me; Arwen? Could I be less impressed with that selection? The readers scoffed; the viewers should have. The irony here is that he went out of his way to make her a strong character in her *Fellowship* incarnation. To turn her around into a wimpy little girl back home, dying of ... what exactly? She seemed to return to full health pretty quickly after Aragorn attained the kingship. Further irony is that the impact of the only two "Ack! [S]He's dead! ...no, wait, [S]he's alive" threads that Tolkien himself ever wrote—those of Frodo under Shelob's lair and Éowyn under the fell beast's shadow—are lost in the pile that Jackson has already presented.

And speaking of Éowyn, Jackson lost a perfect opportunity to really put one over on folks who hadn't read Tolkien; raise your hand if you've heard of *Dernhelm*. Where was he? It would have been an amusing inside joke for the readers and a nice filmic surprise for the viewers if he had made an appearance. Oh well. Too subtle for stupid 21st-century moviegoers, I guess.

The story of *The Return of the King* is, in the last analysis, more compact and lends itself better than the previous two to film—especially the kind of film Jackson most prefers to unspool: action. With at least three enormous battles, death and maybe-death scenes left and right, the story flowed along at a much more consistent rate than either *Fellowship* or *Towers*. However, the pacing still left a lot to be desired. Haste seemed to be the hallmark, haste to get through the word-heavy passages of dialogue between friends and foes so that we could get right back to the slime-dripping orcs. After watching the storybook Academy Awards sweep and seeing *RotK* pick up two highly undeserved Oscars—Best Adapted Screenplay and Best Song—I just have to wonder: are Jackson and company really that unaware of how heavy-handed and inane a lot of their dialogue is? They took a book with the most emphasis on beautiful language of any in the 20th century and reduced it to chop. This complaint is not exclusive to *RotK*, of course; I guess I was hoping they would somehow manage to salvage more of the language than they ended up doing. Silly me.

For the record, I have no problem with the dropping of the Scouring of the Shire. Before I even saw the movie, I knew it could not end with another battle after the climax (the Ring's destruction). It just wouldn't make for good viewing. What I *do* have a problem with is the alteration of the characters of Sam and Frodo to such a degree that Frodo would order Sam to leave his side and that Sam would actually do it. On the very border of Mordor, no less! What a crock! Jackson et. al. have made some rather sweeping character changes in the past (see also Faramir), but this really took the lembas.

For the record, I have no problem with the dropping of Saruman's death scene. I can certainly live without what would have been, after all, just another gratuitous change from Tolkien's story and moreover would have had no good place since they were dropping the Scouring. What I do have a problem with are the dead warriors. Over and over we're reminded that Jackson is a horror/action movie maker. The dead just went into Minas Tirith and swarmed over all the baddies in about thirty seconds? I'm thinking that if the orcs and trolls had actually made that much of a breakthrough into Minas Tirith, there would have been nobody left inside to save.

But all told, *Return of the King* put me under a spell the other two had come close but not quite achieved. The last third or so, including the army's approach to the Black Gate and Gollum's fight with Frodo at the lip of the Cracks of Doom, were as masterful as anything we've seen so far, including Gandalf's death in Moria. Sam and Frodo, both before and after the deed was done, were heartbreaking—as they are meant to be. The humanity in them—grimy faces, dirty fingernails and all—shines clearly. Tolkien's characters not human? Bah, I say. Jackson showed us all of their humanity and more. Bravo. Bravo, I say.

But did he really have to make Rosie Cotton a barmaid?

Peter Jackson's *The Return of the King*

Ostadan

Tolkien's *The Lord of the Rings* has always been a book that requires the sort of literary belief described by J.R.R. Tolkien in "On Fairy-stories": the belief in "secondary reality." Those who love the work are just those people who are willing to believe in the world that Tolkien created, to experience it from the inside; those who are indifferent or hostile to it seem to be just those people for whom the magical art of "sub-creation" somehow fails, whether because they insist on (what they call) realistic worlds, or are put off by the prose, or the pacing. Whatever the reason, the art has failed for these people, and if they cannot manage to suspend (or stifle) their disbelief, the reading of Tolkien's tale does indeed become intolerable.

Peter Jackson's interpretations of Tolkien's work similarly demand that the viewers believe, for a few hours, that they are watching a true story: that Frodo and Sam, Sauron and Gandalf are all real individuals whose tale is unfolding before our eyes. If the magic works, we are carried along in the story, responding in turn with wonder, fear, anger, excitement, and joy. But when the spell is broken, or fails to take effect in the first place, we can see only actors, scenery, scripted lines, costumes, props, and (nowadays) digital artistry. And no matter how impressively executed these are, they are no match for the "real thing." It seems that those who are fans of Tolkien's books are those most likely to experience this effect when we first see all three of Jackson's films of *The Lord of the Rings*. On that first viewing, we are more likely to be asking questions like, "Is he going to show Bombadil? How will he portray the Balrog? Why does Galadriel light up like that? Is that how

I picture Gollum? Why are they in Osgiliath?" and so on. Each time we ask these questions, we are no longer watching Middle-earth; we are watching a movie in a theatre. The second time around, when we know what is coming, it is a more relaxed experience, and we can sit back and experience it as it is intended: we can watch Jackson's version of Middle-earth from the "inside" and experience its magic in full measure.

For me, this dichotomy was far more pronounced in *The Lord of the Rings: The Return of the King* than in the previous two outings. I cannot explain why this was the case, save that it seems to have been a reflection of my own mood at the time of my first viewing, watching with a more critical eye than before. Perhaps I was trying to watch the *artistry* of the film (and hence, always had at least one eye firmly fixed in our Primary World), rather than simply experiencing the work on its own terms. And in that frame of mind, the film was a disappointment. While I could name several scenes that I thought were well executed and admired the technical aspects of the film, I had a list of complaints: it was too long; the prologue with Sméagol and Déagol added little to the film; the battle scenes seemed repetitive and more exhausting than exhilerating; the Army of the Dead was too overpowering and undermined the presence of Aragorn, Gimli, and Legolas; Frodo's awakening in Minas Tirith was more like the ending to the 1939 *The Wizard of Oz* than the joyous scenes I had hoped for; and the final parting at the Grey Havens left me cold, impatient as I was to get out of the theatre. Note that little of this was from a so-called "purist" standpoint; I simply found the storytelling to be inferior to the previous films.

My estimable collagues Quickbeam and Asfaloth read my opinion and strongly suggested that I give the film another chance, reminding me that the previous two films had also improved on the second viewing, and suggesting (correctly, I now think) that I had not allowed myself to experience the movie as an entertainment rather than simply as a piece of cinematic art. So at their urging, I saw the film again—perhaps not incidentally, in a much better equipped and comfortable theatre than where I first had seen it. And when the film was over, with a lump in my throat, I asked Quickbeam, "So, I don't get it: what was that disappointing film I saw the first time?" Because the film I saw the second time was an *entirely* different experience from the first time I saw it, although every frame was the same. Where the lighting of the beacons of Gondor (possibly the best non-book-canon scene from all three films) was "very well executed" the first time, it was quite literally breathtaking on the second viewing; where the muster of the Rohirrim out of Dunharrow struck me as "quite impressive" the first time, it made my breath catch the second time. And though Gandalf's "Do not weep: for not all tears are an evil" parting line first did get a nod of approval for being accurate to the book, on the second viewing it had me at the verge of tears.

In a way, I got to see the movies from both points of view: one akin to that of the staunch purist who judges the movie from the harshest critical standpoint, and the other that of the movie fan who is able to simply get into the film without the distractions of over-analytical judgment. Even from the former viewpoint, there is much to admire (though, of course, not love) in the present film. Nobody can fault the sheer craftsmanship of the film—the detailed costumes and props; the magnificent sets; the unprecedented CGI imagery of the battle of the Pelennor; and Howard Shore's score. Gollum is still a milestone of CGI characterization. Shelob's attack on Frodo is an astonishing piece of work; even the "critical Ostadan" was pulled in enough by its apparent realism to think, "Yes, of course, that's *exactly* the way a giant spider wraps her prey in webbing." The sheer logistical audacity in staging the Ride of the Rohirrim exceeds anything that Cecil B. DeMille could ever have hoped to accomplish in his wildest dreams. On the second viewing, the dramatic moments became more apparent: Sean Astin's performance as Sam hits all the right notes for that character ("I can't carry it for you, but I can carry you and it as well."—sniff!—that's our Sam!); the aforementioned scene of the lighting of the beacons is one of the most powerful scenes in epic cinema; Arwen's vision of Elessar and Eldarion is a beautiful and touching moment; Aragorn's confrontation with the King of the Dead is a striking moment (no pun intended) as Aragorn claims his place as Elendil's heir. Indeed, it is hard to avoid the temptation here to simply catalog the many "favorite" moments (some from the book, some not) in this film. But one surprise worth mentioning separately here is the unexpectedly meaty role for Billy Boyd as Pippin, who rose to the challenges of the role very nicely indeed.

Some of my objections to the film do remain, even after the second viewing. I think it is too long; or rather, a film this long is taxing to those with long legs or small bladders and requires an intermission, just as the long films of the past had (Kubrick's *2001: A Space Odyssey* has an intermission, and it ran only 139 minutes, cut back from 156 minutes, according to IMDb). This uninterrupted length accounts, I think, for the peculiar situation where the denouement simultaneously appears to be drawn out—many have spoken of the multiple false finishes—and yet very sketchy compared to the book. It is not that the ending is long; it is that the viewers are physically tired by this point and are a bit too eager to be on their way. I also think that the flashback prologue (which a non-reader friend of mine simply found confusing) does not carry its weight in contribution to the whole film. It would be outstanding as a bonus stand-alone item on the DVD, but delays the start of the film as it stands.

There were also some bits that were jarring enough to take me back, temporarily, to the Primary World, even on the second viewing. I did not particularly mind Frodo dismissing Sam, though it is a change from the book; but it strained my belief when Sam—who was willing to drown to accompany Frodo—consents to this and turns for home, leaving Frodo alone with the hobbitcidal Gollum. I was expecting him to secretly follow and was shocked when he did not. And why should finding the lembas make him change his mind? Didn't he already know Gollum was a traitor? The character of Denethor was also jarring. Partly because he lacked the grandeur (albeit wounded) of his book counterpart, but also because it was difficult to see him as anything but an obstruction. Indeed, it seems a pity that one of the moments that draws audience applause and laughter is when Gandalf behaves in a most un-Gandalfic manner and pummels the Lord of Gondor into submission. Jackson took the step, controversial to some, of making the book characters more conflicted and complex for the film. Yet the book Denethor is already the most conflicted and complex character that we find in the books, and Jackson chose to simplify him to a crabbed madman. A pity.

The movie badly misses the Houses of Healing (presumed to be restored in the extended DVD). As it stands, the seemingly important characters of Éowyn and Faramir get no closure, except for a cameo-like appearance at Aragorn's coronation (I do hope that when the scenes are restored, we will see Faramir immediately recognize Aragorn as his king when he awakens. The contrast with Denethor would mitigate the problems with the Denethor portrayal somewhat). And it would have been good to see more of Merry; for three years we have seen him swear fealty to Théoden in the trailers, but we must wait still longer to see that scene in its proper context. Also presumed to be on the extended DVD is the Mouth of Sauron. The present version of the scene, with Aragorn riding up to the Morannon, only to ride away when it opens, borders on unintentional humor.

But these criticisms—critical for those who remain in the Primary World and can merely tally the virtues and defects of the film they are watching—are minor for those who allow themselves to be caught up in Jackson and Tolkien's magic and become part of Middle-earth for a few hours. For them, Jackson has created a towering work of imagination, encompassing those elements of Fantasy, Escape, Recovery, and Consolation that Tolkien wrote of in his seminal essay "On Fairy-stories:"

> It is the mark of a good fairy-story, of the higher or more complete kind, that however wild its events, however fantastic or terrible the adventures, it can give to child or man that hears it, when the "turn" comes, a catch of the breath, a beat and lifting of the heart, near to (or indeed accompanied by) tears, as keen as that given by any form of literary art, and having a peculiar quality.

Jackson has turned Tolkien's masterpiece into what will likely be his own life achievement, a monumental work that will endure and bestow upon its viewers those pleasures peculiar to the fairy-story for generations to come.

(And thanks, Quickbeam and Asfaloth, for helping me back into Jackson's world.)

Note:

I have referred here to Tolkien's seminal essay, "On Fairy-stories." While this essay, first published in 1947, is sometimes difficult reading, it represents a kind of manifesto of Tolkien's philosophies about fantasy and its importance in the human psyche. It can be found in *The Tolkien Reader*, a volume that should be of interest to all serious Tolkien fans.

Aragorn in Lincoln Green

Ostadan

It is likely that Tolkien's fans toyed with the notion of a film adaptation of *The Lord of the Rings* practically from the time it was first published and its readers began to talk about the book with their friends. As early as 1960, an article by Dr. Arthur Weir in the general science fiction fanzine *Triode* considered whether such a film could be made satisfactorily and offered some ideas on such matters as scenery and casting, realizing that such a project would require "unlimited money." One particularly interesting suggestion was the casting of Alec Guinness in the role of Gandalf; this was more than a dozen years before George Lucas cast him in the rather Gandalf-like role of Obi-Wan Kenobi in *Star Wars*!

Incidentally, one envies the Tolkien fans of those days; the professor himself favored the article with a letter of comment:

> I was very pleased to hear of the pleasure my book has given you. I think I agree with you in the matter of making a film out of the story. There have been some serious negotiations with regard to this, but my experience with scripts and "story-line" has warned me that only an overwhelming financial reward could possibly compensate an author for the horrors of the conversion of such a tale into film. Even when the pictorial part is very good. Fortunately, my publishers and I retain a legal hold in this matter and nothing can be done without our approval in detail.

Both the original article and the commentary were reprinted in the third issue of the first Tolkien fanzine, *I Palantir* (1964).

Even in the days when a movie seemed impractical, and even for those to whom the very idea is unpalatable, the "casting game" of selecting a suitable actor for the roles of characters in *The Lord of the*

Rings has always been beguiling and popular. It is not hard to see why this is so: by proposing a particular actor for a role, we communicate to the other participants in the discussion something about how we think about that character. For example, if we are talking about Tom Bombadil, someone who imagines Brian Blessed (Augustus in *I, Claudius*) very well may see Bombadil's exuberance and sense of power as his chief visible characteristics; someone who prefers Robin Williams sees more of Bombadil's humorous or whimsical side. In effect, then, the pantheon of well known actors becomes a kind of vocabulary for talking about the characters. The casting game is less about the actors or practicalities of filmmaking than it is just another way to discuss Tolkien's characterizations.

Mention might also be made of the darkly humorous "contrarian" form of the game, in which a grotesquely inappropriate suggestion, typically a big-name Hollywood actor, is made for a role, such as Sylvester Stallone for Frodo. In this form, generally the goal is more a wry commentary on Hollywood casting practices than anything having to do with Tolkien *per se*.

Of course, any movie—like any illustration—fixes a particular image to the subject matter. For many people who have seen Peter Jackson's film, Sir Ian McKellan's portrayal of Gandalf is truly definitive; when they read the book, they will visualize Gandalf as he appeared on the screen, rather than creating a wizard from the furnishings of their own imagination. In a note to his essay "On Fairy-stories," Tolkien said that illustrations do little good to fantasy for this reason. Literature speaks mind to mind, he said, and when a reader is told that a character climbed a hill, the reader will furnish his own picture from all the hills he has seen, and especially from The Hill that was for him the first embodiment of that word. Or, returning to show business for another expression of the same notion, "The pictures are better on radio." On the other hand, it may be noted that Tolkien himself produced numerous illustrations of scenes (and occasionally characters) in *The Silmarillion* and *The Hobbit* as well as *The Lord of the Rings*, including art intended as dust-jackets for *The Lord of the Rings*, which would have been quite definitive in their own way. One can only suppose that Tolkien, like the rest of us, was sometimes contradictory, and his own artistic compulsion to create illustrations was indeed at odds with his philosophy on fairy-stories.

Of course, some people are more visual in their imaginations than others. Some readers of *The Lord of the Rings* visualize a fairly detailed movie in their minds when they first read the story, while others are more vague and sketchy in their visualization of characters, locales, and objects. Tolkien was himself fairly vague in his descriptions much of the time—perhaps because he indeed wished to avoid fixing too specific an image in the readers' minds—which is why artists' portrayals of Middle-earth over the past 50 years have been so diverse. I personally am in the less visual group. I have never had particularly strong or detailed visions of the characters, and so much of the casting in the film was entirely acceptable to me. In some cases, though, I was surprised to find that I had more of an opinion on the matter than I had realized. Isn't Denethor taller and thinner (think Raymond Massey, if you are of a suitable age)? I had a vague idea that Merry was stouter than Pippin, probably due to some idiosyncratic response to the "shapes" of their printed names. Legolas isn't blond-haired—um, or is he?

But the character whose casting was must strikingly (and surprisingly) at odds with whatever vague idea I had was Viggo Mortensen as Aragorn. Let it be said here that I am more than satisfied with Mr. Mortensen's work in the film, and came to accept him as Aragorn well before the closing credits for *Fellowship* rolled. But my initial reaction to him in the pre-film publicity was, "That's not *my* Aragorn!" I soon realized that my response was unusual; while some people may have quibbled a bit with his age or his grooming, most found Mortensen entirely acceptable, perhaps even "perfect" from the outset. And so naturally, I tried, for the first time, to pin down just how I *was* visualizing Aragorn, and what was wrong with the Aragorn I was seeing in the picture.

A little bit of introspection gave me the answer. My version of Aragorn was shaped, in large part at least, by another legendary hero. This hero, like Aragorn, came from humble beginnings and became a ruler and a commander in a war. He was tall and physically strong, but his initial appearance was not of a handsome man; he "looked fouler and felt fairer," according to the legends. He reunited a land that was divided North and South. And his picture is seen on almost a daily basis by every American. Ladies and gentlemen, I bring you Ostadan's own peculiar movie version of *The Lord of the Rings*, in which Aragorn is portrayed by none other than … Abraham Lincoln.

This may sound, at first, to be a rather far-fetched comparison, especially for those readers outside the United States who might only know Lincoln's name in a general sort of way as a famous American president who signed the Emancipation Proclamation. How could such a person be compared to an epic hero like Aragorn? Lincoln was, after all, a historic figure, and even more mundanely, a lawyer and a politician. Surely no rational person could model his image of the Heir of Elendil on someone who ran in an American election!

But, in a larger sense, Lincoln is an example of how historic figures can become quite literally legendary. In discussing the origins of fairy-stories, Tolkien discusses one story, told in the thirteenth century, of Bertha Broadfoot, the mother of Charlemagne, which is substantially the same as the German folk tale *The Goosegirl*, and compares the standard analysis that "this tale became attached to her" to what he considers the more accurate statement that it was she who had become attached to the already existing story. In effect, he says, she was tossed into the ever-simmering Cauldron of Story (in which familiar elements of legend are bubbling), and after cooking for a suitable length of time, emerged with a distinct legend. Tolkien points to other more formidable examples of historical figures who have been boiled well in this Pot, such as Arthur, who "once historical ... emerged as a King of Faerie."

Much the same kind of thing, though of lesser magnitude, has happened to historical American figures. John Chapman, American frontiersman, is cooked in the Cauldron of Story to emerge as Johnny Appleseed. Congressman David Crockett becomes Davy Crockett, who could "run faster, jump higher, squat lower, dive deeper, stay under longer, and come out drier than any man in the whole country." And Abraham Lincoln, cooking for but a few score of years in the Cauldron, has taken on some aspects of legend, for now his image is seen in schoolrooms (and on currency) even as his statue sits looming like a colossus (or one of the Argonath) over the National Mall in Washington, D.C. Some readers will remember the positively reverential scene in the 1950s film *The Day the Earth Stood Still* when the alien visitor Klaatu is taken to see the Lincoln Memorial. "Those are great words," Klaatu says with the deepest respect, and he asks his young guide, "Where can I find a great man like that?" Like a character from a folk tale, Lincoln was the son of a woodcutter and had a stepmother; like Aragorn, Lincoln is the Hidden King (or our best approximation), the Heir of Washington, the Great Emancipator, the Restorer of the Union, the Commander-in-Chief; unlike him, he is eventually the Slain God—an odd echo of Baldur in Norse mythology. Even in his own time, his seamstress Lizzie Keckley said of his death, "No common mortal had died. The Moses of my people had fallen in the hour of triumph."

Perhaps in some distant future, when the historical details of our age have been obscured by time, folklorists will argue over how the legend of Aragorn of Gondor had influenced the tale of Lincoln of Gettysburg, or how the aristocratic Mary Todd relates to the still more aristocratic Arwen Evenstar. It is tempting to think of fanciful versions of the legends of that time: Aragorn delivering a speech dedicating a portion of the Pelennor as a military cemetary, or Lincoln leading the ghosts of Revolutionary War Tories (including the shade of Benedict Arnold) on the battlefields of Virginia. But as the folklorists of the age try to untangle the legends, perhaps they will have among them someone like Tolkien who understands the complex reciprocal relationship in human thought between history and legend.

The One Ring (dot net)

The One Ring (dot net)

Anwyn

"Great site! Thank you!"

"Thanks! Keep it up!"

"Hello, I love your site. Can you answer this question for me ... ? Thanks a lot!"

Thank you. This is the simple phrase that glues www.TheOneRing.net to the Tolkien fans of the world, to the Jackson productions, and—most importantly—those same fans to those same Jackson productions.

Readers of the site thank us for being here, for sharing our resources, our time, and our thoughts on *The Lord of the Rings* with them, and for connecting them to New Zealand and the world of Peter Jackson's *The Lord of the Rings*. We thank them for listening, for checking the site daily, and for supporting our efforts so graciously and diligently. And we thank Peter Jackson's production team for being more accessible to its fans than any other film experience in history, and we like to think they thank us for providing the kind of worldwide publicity fervor that you can't buy nowadays—but can generate with the right web resources.

Working with TheOneRing.net is a unique experience shared by many staff members from all parts of the globe. Occasionally, even now, after more than ten years of access to this new-fangled web thing, I still am stunned at how much can be accomplished at a lightning-fast rate of speed, and I wonder how business functioned before the internet. Thus it is that images and data could speed from New Zealand to a server based in the U.S. and thus throughout the world—the original foundations of TheOneRing.net's success.

Sometimes that success comes with a price. A group of volunteers, both amateur and professional, don't get this far without being able to work in the real world as well as on the internet. Connecting with people—face to face—"earning our stripes" with Peter Jackson's crew until we became a trusted fan resource for them as well as for the eager readers of every scrap of news from the set, and keeping the vast electronic storehouse of data organized and flowing take time and effort. For many of our dedicated staff, TheOneRing.net is a second job, and it does take almost as many hours per day as their "first jobs." Others squeeze in TORn duties as they can, sometimes with guilt at not being able to give more time. "Real life" and TORn are demanding and competing taskmasters at times. And of course, you can't have an organization this big without inevitable personality clashes, hurt feelings, and politicking.

But on the other hand, the rewards too are great. Those "first jobs" I mentioned? Some of us now have our dream jobs due to the work we've done for TORn. Some of us have become engaged and married to persons we met through the site. (Many fans have met and become involved this way as well!) For others of us, TORn is a rock-solid constant through years of life turmoil—a place to which we can turn for solace, for unwavering support and friendship, and a sense that we are doing something of historic importance in bringing eager fans closer to their objects than ever before and adding our bit to the 20th-century legend that is J.R.R.T.'s *The Lord of the Rings*.

One personal way in which we have facilitated that contact is through our amazing Oscar parties. For each of Peter Jackson's films, TheOneRing.net has thrown a lavish bash on Oscar night for hundreds of fans who wanted nothing more than to dress up and cheer each time *The Lord of the Rings* was announced from Oscar's stage, either as a nominee or as a celebrated winner. But we managed to bring them even more. Actors and crew members from the productions who recognized and appreciated what we were trying to do both for them and for fans returned our support by appearing at these terrific parties—appearing, and speaking, and hamming it up, and thanking the fans, who hung on their every word while TORn staff watched, listened, appreciated, and thanked them in return. These gallant celebs let us mere mortals hold their Oscar statuettes, for crying out loud! We held three mutual admiration society meetings that set Hollywood talking and will not be forgotten, three parties that together are unique in the annals of

Tinseltown—stars choosing to party not with their own, but with their own fans.

But now that the last Oscar has been given and the sets are long wrapped, what will TORn do? Already we are branching out into coverage of other fantasy films, other Peter Jackson efforts, and we will be going strong as long as readers want us. We are blessed with a large base of support and will continue, in the best tradition of the internet.

In the following section, Quickbeam, Tehanu, and the Green Books staff will take you into the past for a nostalgic look at the historic Oscar parties, into the future for a look at TORn's new directions, and all over the present with a selection of the most thoughtful Questions and Answers Green Books has produced. But wherever TORn may go in the future, we will be able to continue our success because we, Peter Jackson, and our readership across the globe know the meaning of those two little words: Thank you. Thank you, dear readers, for your continued interest. We at TORn love what we do, and we thank you for making it possible.

Oscar, My Precious

Quickbeam

It was a special time. It was our chance to fashion a unique and uplifting event for our friends—for the Ringers out there who felt just as we did. It was also an opporunity to show our well polished appreciation of a certain Kiwi director. Fuzzy feelings and bright-eyed ambitions to please filled our heads when we first started planning the "One Party to Rule Them All." An Oscar Party of special magnificence.

Little did we know what we were in for.

It seems so many years ago. Sheesh, it was early 2002. I recall the way it began:

We were a friendly group getting more familiar with each other around the time of the 59th Annual Golden Globe Awards. We had a little gathering of hobbit fanciers at the famous Cat 'n' Fiddle Pub down on Sunset Boulevard in the heart of Hollywood. There were nearly two dozen of us, eating and laughing at the exact filming location of Rick's Café Américain from *Casablanca*. 'Twas a night of good cheer and merriment. A team of talented individuals started talking: Catherine had studio-level experience throwing parties, and Carlene had some stunning marketing strategies. Chris had the website where millions of willing fans would hear about it. Cathy knew the ins and outs of fan conventions. So did Josh. Then there was me, Cliff, the actor/writer who arrogantly assumed that working as master of ceremonies for a Fan Party would be easy as snatching fireworks from a wizard's cart. Again, little did I know… But the six of us united under one banner, under One Party, calling ourselves "The Five Cs and J." Combined as a group, we were just crazy enough to do it. We were alive with possibilities. We all asked: Can we do something bigger and better?

Ah, yes we could.

TORn was going strong, posting news and spy reports daily. New Line Cinema was keeping a watchful eye on us. The production team in New Zealand loved the attention, I daresay. We were familiar enough with the movie stars themselves, and I was quite proud of the TORn Digital segments where I had been in their faces interviewing them on every red carpet in town. And production folks from Peter Jackson on down were aware of us. We decided to use this familiarity to see if these artistic folks would like to crash our Oscar bash. So we spread the word around town and to the stars' publicists!

Joining forces with Premiere Events, a company that engineers parties and catering, was our next step. We chose the Hollywood Athletic Club for two good reasons: (a) it was close to the Kodak Theatre where the Academy Awards ceremony was held, and (b) it was a Hollywood landmark full of old ghosts. Carlene was constantly creeped out by John Barrymore's shade down in the "Pool Room." How delicious! The Party Planners were going full steam ahead. We had energy to burn, and perhaps because we were all volunteers, a palpable vigor kept us going. Hard to explain what it was. To this day I am left with affectionate memories. I must have been having fun while I was doing it. We believed we could create something unique. Without an example or easy path laid out before us, confidence was basically all we had to go on. There was absolutely no precedent for this. So forward we went...

It was a struggle. There's no better word for it. We struggled to arrange a party for hundreds of people, the myriad details of which included getting a DJ, assembling a corps of volunteers, creating signs and decorations, inviting the press (who didn't have a clue), getting security and audio/video support, preparing TONS of food, stripping and dyeing my hair bright green, signing agreements with sponsors, and also creating a careful system of raffle ticket drawings and silent auctions to help TORn raise some money. A site like ours doesn't grow on trees (or even Huorns)—our servers and ISP bills were significant, and we trusted the fans would turn out in good numbers on Oscar Sunday to help us. They certainly did.

Being surrounded by happy people is an elixir, let me tell you. It was euphoria by osmosis. We were simply in hobbit heaven just to be amongst other fans, enjoying the plentiful food and cheering throughout the Oscar telecast. Our evening was already gold, but then after the ceremony, the REAL gold actually showed up. Huzzah!

PJ dropped in with his partner Fran Walsh on his arm. Producer Barrie Osborne appeared with executive producer Mark Ordesky, Sir Ian McKellen, and screenwriter Philippa Boyens. Everyone was so happy to see them. When the Oscar statues starting coming up the stairs, *en masse*, the magical energy blew the roof off the H.A.C. Our hopes of extracting a special evening for the fans had been met to perfection. Howard Shore waved and greeted everyone, holding his award. The WETA team headed by Richard Taylor sauntered in, causing a raucous round of applause. He waved his two Oscars aloft as the cameras flashed wildly. Dan Hennah, Jim Rygiel, Randall William Cook, Mark Stetson, and several others were there too. Mr. Shore agreed to let me hold his statue (my first Oscar "encounter"). You cannot imagine the weight.

I'm sure we damaged the hearing of our V.I.P. guests that night. The screaming and applauding and hollering wouldn't stop until PJ took the microphone and acknowledged the Ringers who supported his film. He had lost Best Director and Best Picture that night, but no matter. The Partygoers showered him with an affection more valuable.

Two more films were yet to arrive. Doubtless, we knew, more nominations, more Parties were in store. The "One Party's" success caused endless buzz online, which set the stakes higher, of course. We had to plan everything bigger, grander, and more expensive for the "Two Towers: One Party." I envisioned an elaborate new hair color—a flaming array of orange, yellow, and red that emulated the poor Ent who was set alight and later ducks his "head branches" into the Isen's flood waters.

On Sunday, 23 March 2003, the bewildering mix of Hollywood glamor and Ringer fanaticism came together again at the H.A.C. for our second event. Over 1000 guests attended, more than twice the previous year, taking over two floors of the building. Surely the ghosts deemed it wise to make way for the Elven Ladies in varying states of costume. We all felt the stress. Headaches were abundant, but a legion of volunteers came forward from our TORn staff. They came from all over the world to work the night away—and special credit is due to they who so mightily conjured another brilliant party out of nothing but love of the Ringer community.

The night took my breath away. I've never seen people so enthusiastic. We only won two technical awards, but our fervor would continue unabated. I stood on the stage and addressed the audience after *Chicago* was announced as Best Picture, declaring "We may have lost this one, kids, but we are so gonna win next year!!" Judging from the crowd's wild ovation, the point was conceded by all. More stars showed up that night, but PJ was stuck down in Wellington, working tirelessly. Barrie Osborne patched a cell phone call through our speaker system, and thus PJ's endearing Kiwi accent was heard by all the guests. We could barely make out a word of what the director said, but he certainly heard us whooping and applauding!

After two glorious years, how could we top ourselves? What more could we do? The same equation was probably in PJ's mind while finishing his film, as everyone felt *The Return of the King* was the final, best chance for a perfect synergy between art and accolades. Ringers are optimistic by definition. Industry pundits were also predicting a grand slam. The future carried the fragrant smell of success.

"The Return of the One Party" was moved to a new location at the American Legion Hall, barely two blocks from the Kodak. We prepared for many months ahead of time, asking Alyse and Peter from "LiningUp.net" to join forces in our endeavor. Tickets went on sale in early December 2003, with shocking results. We sold out for over 800 guests in less than ten minutes! The flood of requests crashed the PayPal financial network for a time. You heard me right, a bunch of Ringers took down PayPal nationwide. Every one of them knew in their hearts this final Oscar Party was THE place to be. By now, all the creative people behind *LotR* were also revved up for it. Songs will be sung about this night, I kept telling myself.

Yes. It was everything we wanted it to be. It was leviathan.

Now as I reflect back, dozens of colorful memories play for dominance: the giant spider in the hall... the equipment control room where Matthew struggled valiantly with webcam malfunctions... the vast proscenium in the Great Hall... the army of security guys (one of them an experienced cage fighter who could stop a tank with his bare hands)... the hair color? Well, that year I didn't color anything. Instead, I surprised the audience with several costume changes including Elrond (in a vastly overdecorated Liberace robe), Aragorn, and ultimately a full drag outfit as Éowyn, Shieldmaiden of Rohan. Before an audience of 2000 people I pulled off my helmet, revealing a wild spray of blonde locks, shouting, "I AM NO MAN!" Now that's what I call comedy.

Throughout the night, the swirling euphoria increased with every award *RotK* took home. The buildup was palpable—the crowd's nascent delight heading towards an explosion. When PJ was given the Best Director award, we fired the confetti cannons into the Hall. What shouting! What delirium! Even though I was downstairs changing costumes, I felt the very stone walls rumble around me. The crowd rose to their feet with each announcemet. The defining moment was Steven Spielberg opening the Best Picture envelope, with a gentle smile, and saying four perfect little words: "It's a clean sweep!" The skies were sundered. Ragnarok in Asgard. Hell frozen over. A fantasy film had just won the Oscar. The mighty powers of Hollywood confirmed what we already knew. A trilogy total of seventeen Academy Awards and three billion dollars later, the massive imagination of J.R.R. Tolkien was now, miraculously, the biggest full sweep in Oscar history.

That night we had heroes in our midst. I feel the comparison to heroism is deserved. The way fans respond to PJ, Fran, Richard and all the actors is abundantly clear. It is the core reason why these Parties were conceived. These events were the perfect outlet for us to celebrate our "artistic heroes" and show how proud we were of their accomplishment. Bringing the Oscar winners onto the stage, a terrific waving of gold statues across the horizon, was especially moving for me. What my fellow Ringers were getting out of this matched everything that the filmmakers got in return. The genuine power of acknowledgment was alive in every molecule of every person. This was the true grit of fandom.

Peter stood before the crowd, and after settling them down a bit, showed incredible grace by placing the focus on his audience. We were there in tuxedoes and sequined gowns to support him—or so we thought. Truth be told, PJ kept coming to these events in order to show his love for us. He reminded everyone that we Ringers were the reason the films got made. Without us, his endeavors would have been futile. He reinforced the cardinal rule of all artistic expression: that artistry is a gift idealized for those who openly receive it.

Again, there was no precedent for this! The winners didn't go to the chi-chi Vanity Fair Party. They didn't obey their publicists, who desire maximum photo opportunities at the expense of all else. PJ and his team even stood up the official New Line event until after they hit our Party. Fans and filmmakers had NEVER come together in such a setting. Can you imagine any other director appearing at a fancy wingding held by his core audience? Throughout the history of cinema, no creative powers have ever come down from on high to mingle with their fans like that. Nothing even comes close. The singularity of the evening was not lost on us.

The press later carried headlines of how a bunch of Ringers caused a major burp in the evening (from an industry point of view). Several people at the New Line party were uncomfortably sweating until well after 1:00 a.m., when PJ's glorious parade of Oscars finally appeared at their location. By then he had done what was most important for him. Having an Oscar in your hand is without question an honor, I don't dispute that, but the real honor, the honor that carries more weight than gold, is that ephemeral moment in time when people say: "Thank you. We love your work. We are so thrilled to share this with you."

The small group of us who put all this together were not interested in stealing New Line's thunder. We were not even making enough money off the Parties to pay for TORn's server. None of that really mattered. We just wanted to celebrate for the sake of Tolkien's fans, most of whom are also Peter's fans now. If we succeeded, and I feel we certainly did, it was on the belief that creativity is best rewarded, not with awards, but with the fundamental connection between artist and audience.

Where to from Here?

Tehanu

So the long-awaited third movie is out, and the Oscars they so richly deserved have been awarded, and we feel like we've shared in the joy of that. It is a double delight to see the Oscar winners recognized for their talent and to see the fantasy genre we love so much taken seriously at last. We feel thankful that they used their great talents with honesty and clarity of purpose that allowed their own merits to shine forth at the same time as they served Tolkien's story so beautifully.

I acknowledge the achievement of *LotR*'s Oscar winners, but I think a lot of you reading this would agree that some of the actors deserved to be nominated as well. The fact that the actors themselves won nothing shows that there is one last barrier for fantasy movies to overcome. That is the critics' belief that the actors' performances are less worthy of consideration because the moral dilemmas and emotions they experience in a fantasy film are less valid than what actors portray in a "real life" drama.

At the Oscars party in February, the four of us who founded TheOneRing.net had a moment to stand up on stage and address the people who'd come. Everyone there represented all of you who have followed the making of the *Lord of the Rings* films as though the process were a great adventure we all shared in. And we did share in it. Peter Jackson and Barrie Osborne and the others confirmed that when they spoke to the crowd at the party. To them as well, the fans were more than bystanders. Fans were invited to accompany them in the adventure, and we felt that we did. I think we were, on the whole, as generous with our praise as they were generous in sharing the experience.

The internet has been the window through which we were invited to follow the progress of the movies. I've always understood what a dilemma this must have been. On the one hand, the filmmakers needed to keep the secrets of their trade, especially where it concerned some of the ground-breaking technology they were developing. Also, as storytellers, I think they wanted to keep surprises in store for everyone so that even the most diligent movie spy would see the movies for the first time and be jolted by novelties and unforeseen visions. What storyteller would give up the thrill of springing surprises on their audience? But on the other hand, it was a secret too good not to share, if the right audience could be found to share it with. An audience that could appreciate what they were doing. (Or at least, one that could debate knowledgeably about what they heard concerning the film.) Web sites like ours gave them that audience, and it seems that as time went on they came to trust us (or all of you collectively) as a sounding board.

Since the party—well, since before that, when the third movie came out—many fans have been feeling a little flat. Bereft, actually, of anything to look forward to apart from the release of the extended edition of *RotK* later this year. We've been looking forward to the movies for so long that we've gotten used to having that sense of anticipation. People ask themselves (and they ask me, by e-mail) "Is anything ever going to take its place?"

Well, what is it you want? As I looked out at that Oscars party crowd that night, I tried to explain what I thought in response to the question at the back of everyone's minds even then: Where to from here? Seeing the people gathered in front of me, I thought: Here is a crowd of people who love adventure and excitement and creativity and imagination. They would not love *The Lord of the Rings* if they did not respect those things. These people are willing to follow those feelings enough to travel here, to Los Angeles, to be at this party. Many more would have come if they could; if we'd held the party somewhere more remote, they still would have come. The hundreds of international visitors who came to the Return of the Ringers party in New Zealand prove that. So: You "Ringers" are people who can dream, and some of you take steps to make that dream come true.

But that is just the least tremor of the earthquake that these films were. For many people, the books and the movies turned their lives around in ways they could never have foreseen. They started out simply following their attraction to *The Lord of the Rings* and what it represented for them. But soon their feelings led them towards new friends, new pastimes, new talents, new jobs, new countries, a new life entirely. This is not something we intended to happen; nor did the filmmakers intend it to happen. I don't know if this is something you *can* plan for. Certainly at TORn we felt like we rode the wave wherever it would take us. We were canny to take advantage of opportunities that arose, but I can't say we ever had a plan as such. What I remember most about starting out was that we moved forward in whatever direction seemed most interesting and ended up going much farther than we'd ever imagined.

I remember when I'd race home after work or get up early in the morning to open my e-mail, and every time it was like walking the beach after a storm tide—the internet would have cast up all kinds of unforeseen treasures. If I was bored, I'd write another article or pursue another line of enquiry with the film, and another wave of bright, shiny treasure e-mails would wash up the next day. The best ones, from our point of view, were the ones that started "Hi, some film people dropped these off at the place where I work—I think they might be stills from *LotR*. Want to post them on TORn?" *Would we ever!* Or, "Hey I found this hidden on the official web site. Not public yet. Check out these designs!" That sort of thing could make our day. And that of a lot more people besides, once we'd shared via the web.

I'm pretty distant from the corporate or commercial world, so I only later realized how New Line borg-level functionaries might have felt about us prying around and occasionally sticking what we thought was a playful spanner in the works. This mostly seemed to affect people lower down the corporate ladder. We didn't consider how our hobby could mess them up. We were thinking more about the feelings of people at the top, whose main concern was whether what we did hurt the films. But if somebody lower down in the food chain had the job of managing a carefully planned million-dollar advertising campaign, for instance, then our ability to seize spoiler images and disseminate them on the web ahead of schedule fouled things up for them. I can see they'd be justified in feeling upset about it.

To be fair, to them we probably seemed chaotic and unpredictable, and they may have imagined that we were capable of a great deal of damage. I suppose we might have been, if we'd hated what Peter Jackson and his crew were doing, but we were so impressed with their way of going about things from the very first that we had faith in them all the way along.

Luckily for everyone, TORn was about more than just spy reports about the movies. As nice as it was to receive those spymails, I enjoyed just as much the constant stream of mail from people who wanted to discuss Tolkien. People who offered points of view, who debated and explained, and who brought their life experience to bear on their understanding of the books. Best of all was the diversity—there were Tolkien fans of all ages and backgrounds from so many parts of the world. As time went on I began to sense a community growing across the distances. I could read between the lines and trace how, for some people, the act of entering this community enlarged their lives and in some cases freed them from a burden of dullness, isolation and entrapment. There can be nothing that has given me more satisfaction.

Still, the question remains: What to look forward to now that the movies are as good as done? Well, what have you learned from them? Not the story of the Ring; you knew that already. What is the lesson in the story of the making of the movies? That's the story of *you* getting involved in the excitement, the guesswork, the speculation, the ideas, the process of seeing them come into the light. The story of *you* spending time thinking about Middle-earth and your delight in discovering that other people care about it as much as you do. *This story* is the point, and it is what the great mythographer Joseph Campbell called "following your bliss."

We've spent five years watching something that was fun. We enjoyed it whole-heartedly and without self-interest. We didn't question whether it had any point. It just *was*, and we were childlike in our acceptance of it. Because our guard was down, it enriched our lives almost before we were aware of its effect on us. Now the challenge is to ask ourselves what it is that we love to do the way the filmmakers loved to do their work. It's time to notice the silly drawings we used to do, but put aside when we grew up. Time to remember the dreams we had of learning to weave a medieval tapestry, or the idea for that perfect adventure game—and let those ideas come out and play. Play hard. We've watched PJ's people do it, working long hours into the night, day after day, month after month, fired up by a vision. We know Tolkien did it, with every spare moment and spare scrap of paper he had. And remember: for many years his life appeared as something completely boring and unproductive to the casual observer. He published little, and outside of his philological work he appeared absorbed in his family. The only hint of difference was the regularity with which he met his like-minded friends at the Eagle and Child pub. There they would drink and argue and read out their latest writing to each other, sometimes with no real hope of a wider audience. But Tolkien in his own private mind remained committed to the elaboration of his fantasy world.

But this all sounds as if all it takes to create great art is to try hard. It sounds like all you need to do to become a writer or artist yourself is to work at it, and if you're not succeeding it's because you're not trying hard enough. I don't believe that myself however, and I'm not saying that Tolkien's example should drive you to transform yourself into a writer, least of all a writer of fantasy. It *might* do that for you, but on the other hand your talent might be something quite different, something you've used all along but not given due honor. You could have a talent for living a life of comfort and balance, like a hobbit. A talent for fellowship, for loyalty, and for peacemaking among friends and family. You could be Elf-like in your determination to bring grace and quality to everything you do or make, even if it's just the way you set up your workspace or the way you make tea. (Values that the Japanese have understood for a long time, if their tea ceremony is anything to go by.)

There are lots of gifts that, even if practised with consummate skill, leave no lasting physical monument that one can point to with a flourish. Maybe nobody will write an entry in *Who's Who* about you to say "Her household was warmly accepting, and all visitors seemed to show their best nature for as long as they were there," or "He took in savage strays and they became loyal and gentle creatures after a short time," or "She raised five children who had the courage to overcome tremendous obstacles." Talents like that generally go unsung, but they are worth no less for all that.

Meanwhile, every journey begins with the first step, as Frodo (and even more so Sam) discovered when they set out from Bag End, hardly knowing anything of the road ahead. If your dream is to build a hobbit hole, then you don't have to have a piece of land and a degree in engineering by tomorrow. You can at least talk to other people who are doing it for a few years first. To ride elf-fashion, without saddle or bridle? Well, you could start by getting lessons to ride normally. Practise the hospitality of a hobbit, throw memorable dinner parties, and nobody will care that your house doesn't look like a Gondorian palace. Follow your curiosity, find something that interests you and throw yourself into it wholeheartedly! You never know where the Road will take you, once you step out that door.

Q&A

Q1: Why is Rohan also called the Riddermark?

A: "Rohan" is a Sindarin name and is the name for that land used by the people of Gondor and by the Elves. As the index entry in *LotR* explains (rather tersely), it is a modernization or adaptation of the name "Riddena-mearc", meaning "Land of the Knights"—the name of Rohan used by the people of Rohan themselves in their own language (represented as Old English). Usually just "the Mark."

—Ostadan

Q2: How is it possible that Barahir's ring survived the Fall of Númenor, so that Aragorn can happily wear it in the Third Age? If it was indeed passed down in the line of Elros, it should have been in the King's possession and with him; it should have been lost under the wave. How did it come to Elendil, the lord of Andúnië? I tried to look it up in *Unfinished Tales*, but I found no explanation. It is great that Aragorn wears that ring—it connects with the story of Beren and Lúthien and also it gives an impression of his ancestry coming from the deeps of time, yet still I am curious whether Tolkien solved or noticed this problem anywhere.

A: The Ring of Barahir was given to Barahir, father of Beren, by Felagund of Nargothrond as a token of his oath of abiding friendship, as told in the tale of the Ruin of Beleriand in *The Silmarillion*. In the tale of Beren and Lúthien, we learn how the captain of the Orcs that slew Barahir cut his hand from his wrist with the ring still on it, and how Beren slew the captain and took the hand and ring. The ring passed to Beren's heirs and so became an heirloom of the house of Elros Tar-Minyatur, the first king of Númenor.

In *Unfinished Tales*, a note to the Description of Númenor tells us that "Only the Ring of Barahir father of Beren One-hand survived the Downfall; for it was given by Tar-Elendil to his daughter Silmariën and was preserved in the House of the Lords of Andúnië, of whom the last was Elendil the Faithful who fled from the wrack of Númenor to Middle-earth."

If Tolkien had not written this note, something like it would probably be an inevitable inference anyway.

—Ostadan

Q3: At the end of the chapter *Mount Doom*, Sméagol takes the Ring from Frodo and falls into the Cracks of Doom. However, what would have happened to Sméagol if the Ring had been destroyed by some other means, and he survived? Bearing in mind that he is over five hundred years old, would he have continued living, like Bilbo did, or died there and then?

also

Q3: Bilbo possessed the Ring for about 70 years. According to *LotR*, he aged little while in possession of it. Once he gave up the Ring, he aged rather quickly over the next 30 years. On the other hand, Gollum, a Hobbit-like creature, had the Ring for about 500 years. He aged little while he possessed it. However, during the 100 years more or less after he lost it, he remained quite vigorous and does not appear to have aged much more. Why?

A: Keep in mind that the "sudden" aging of Bilbo is largely a movie invention. While it is true that according to Tolkien, the Ring slowed the effects of his aging, Tolkien does not say that Bilbo suddenly became white-haired and decrepit after he lost the Ring. I'm sure his aging *tended* back to normal speed, but there's no saying that he didn't live many years longer in Valinor.

As for Gollum, Bilbo clearly lived on after the destruction of the Ring. I have no reason to think that Gollum would just up and die. Moreover, Gollum had, as you have pointed out, around 500 years for the Ring to act to slow his aging. It is likely that he would tend back to "normal" aging even slower than Bilbo, and no reason why he wouldn't have lived on for quite a time after the Ring was destroyed.

—Anwyn

Q4: There is something about the name Nazgûl that I wondered about. I am quite interested in the Black Speech, where the word "Nazgûl" means **Ringwraith(s)**. However, if you take the word apart you get "nazg" and "ûl". "Nazg" means **ring** and "ûl" has no meaning (although "ul" means **them**). The word **wraith** in the Black Speech is "gûl", so shouldn't it be "Nazggûl" instead of "Nazgûl"? Or is it meant to be written with only one G?

A: Tolkien does indeed write that Ring-wraith is a translation of "*Nazgûl*, from *nazg* 'ring' and *gûl*, any one of the major invisible servants of Sauron dominated entirely by his will" (in the Guide to Names). Remembering that Tolkien always writes his languages phonetically, we must conclude that in Black Speech the sound of a double-G is reduced to a single one and not pronounced separately. This is similar to English; only when speaking very carefully do we pronounce a pair like "bag-grabber" with two distinct Gs. It is certainly no more unexpected than other phonological changes, such as Sindarin "caran" + "ras" becoming "caradhras".

Remember, this is Tolkien's invention. He is *always* right (even when he changes his mind)!

—Ostadan

Q5: What happened with the remaining Dwarves in the North after the passing of the Elves in early the Fourth Age? Is there any mention of them in and after the Fourth Age? This might be trivial, but even as Gimli is allowed to join the boats to the West, would any other Dwarf think of the same idea?

A: In Appendix A, we are told that: "Gimli brought south a part of the Dwarf-folk of Erebor, and he became Lord of the Glittering Caves. He and his people did great works in Gondor and Rohan. For Minas Tirith they forged gates of mithril and steel to replace those broken by the Witch-king." To this we may add material that was written for Appendix A, but omitted (perhaps for space or due to haste in collation): "And the line of Dáin prospered, and the wealth and renown of the kingship was renewed, until there arose again for the last time an heir of that House that bore the name of Durin, and he returned to Moria; and there was light again in deep places, and the ringing of hammers and the harping of harps, until the world grew old and the Dwarves failed and the days of Durin's race were ended." Although the passage was omitted, "Durin VII and Last" appears in the genealogy in Appendix A.

Tolkien makes it clear in the note that ends Appendix A about Gimli accompanying Legolas over the sea that this was a unique circumstance. The Dwarves are "a race apart," and they do not pass over the Sea.

—Ostadan

Q6: Why are Gandalf, Elrond, and everyone else so afraid of Sauron getting the One Ring back? Sauron wielded the Ring once before and the Last Alliance overpowered him and took the Ring from his hand, so why can't they just do it again if he regains the Ring? If they can do it once, they can do it twice, right?

A: Much of your supposition is discussed in "The Shadow of the Past," if indirectly. It would not be simple in any way to contest and overthrow Sauron if he indeed regained the One Ring. When the Elves and Men allied themselves at the end of the Second Age, it took a whopping eleven years of fighting and siege against Barad-dûr before they accomplished anything. Gandalf explains that "the strength of the Elves to resist him was greater long ago; and not all Men were estranged from them." The Dark Lord's power was considerably greater at the close of the Third Age; and you must also imagine the Elves as a waning power—fewer and less involved with the worries of Middle-earth. Alas, at that time there were no great Men of Westernesse to join their cause should they need to confront the Shadow once more. The focus of Sauron's will would be *greatly increased* with the return of the Ring to his hand (also he would categorically control the other Rings, undoing the works created with them). So with weaker Elves and Men and an exponentially stronger Sauron with his happy little Ring back—with his regained ability to control the thoughts and will of all others, and his massive armies, I would say "no," no one could stop him. Almost makes you respect Frodo in a whole new way for taking on such a mind-boggling responsibility.

—Quickbeam

Q7: Hi, I had a question on the traveling on the seas to Valinor and Tol Eressëa for the Elves. I know that **The Straight Road** has always been open to the Elves after the Valar pardoned them after the War of the Jewels. But once an Elf sailed to Aman, could they go back to

Middle-earth? I know it sounds ridiculous, because after going to Valinor, who would want to go back? But maybe to visit someone they missed who did not come with them to the Undying Lands, they would. I don't remember any mention of this in *The Silmarillion*.

A: When Tolkien considered the matter of the identification of Glorfindel of Rivendell with Glorfindel of Gondolin (in notes published in *The Peoples of Middle-earth*, *The History of Middle-earth* Volume XII), he wrote, "When did Glorfindel return to Middle-earth? This must probably have occurred *before* the end of the Second Age, and the 'Change of the World' and the Drowning of Númenor, after which no living embodied creature, 'humane' or of lesser kinds, could return from the Blessed Realm which had been 'removed from the Circles of the World'. This was according to a general ordinance proceeding from Eru Himself; and though, until the end of the Third Age, when Eru decreed that the Dominion of Men must begin, Manwë could be supposed to have received the permission of Eru to make an exception in his case... this is improbable and would make Glorfindel of greater power and importance than seems fitting."

It's always nice when we can find a direct answer written by Tolkien himself.

—Ostadan

Q8: In *RotK* it is told that after the death of the Witch-king, both Merry and Éowyn suffered a bizarre deadening in the arm (Merry in the arm with which he stabbed the Witch-king's foot, and Éowyn in the arm she used to behead him). They also suffered some illness, as well, which I assume was due to the Witch-king's "Black Breath." My question is this: Why did Isildur not suffer similar symptoms after he cut the Ring from Sauron's hand? It would stand to reason that if Merry and Éowyn suffered this strange numbness after wounding a servant of Sauron, wounding Sauron himself would have a similar, if not more perilous, effect.

A: A good question, for which there is no certain answer. It may be that the nature of the Nazgûl—mortals held in this world unnaturally by the power of the Nine Rings—is quite different, and affects mortal flesh differently, from Sauron, a self-incarnated Maia. It might also be significant that (unlike the situation portrayed in the Jackson movie), Sauron was already subdued and defeated by the time Isildur struck the Ring from his hand. As an incarnated being—like Gandalf—Sauron's physical body was subject to destruction and death (as in the fall of Númenor). Recall Elrond's narrative: he says that Sauron was overthrown before Isildur cut the Ring from him. It seems to be the case that Sauron's body was already unconscious or even dead when Isildur cut the Ring from it (else the order in the sentence would have been different). Finally, it may be that the mere possession of the Ring itself, although Isildur never found the strength to master it, conferred some immunity to whatever effect Isildur might otherwise have suffered. But Tolkien never addressed this directly, leaving us free to speculate until we tire of the game.

—Ostadan

Q9: I was wondering about your thoughts on Old Man Willow. Do you think he could be some kind of "twisted" Ent (like the Orcs are "twisted" elves), or should we just throw him onto the obscure pile with Tom Bombadil and Goldberry?

A: No, Old Man Willow was not some kind of tortured, de-evolved Ent. Rather, I always figured the Willow might be a Huorn, like the kind we see outside Helm's Deep. Or maybe he was a tree that became more *Entish*. The dialogue that Treebeard has with Merry and Pippin seems to support the idea that some trees do indeed go bad. Treebeard says that sometimes trees have bad hearts, and Merry inquires about the Old Forest. Treebeard agrees that these trees have this kind of life of their own and seems to refer to the power of Angmar from the distant past. I surmise that without a population of older and competent Ents (doing their job as tree-herds) then the Old Forest might very well have become a place of lingering malice from the time of the Witch-king. Thus, maybe, Old Man Willow could have been become more mobile, more "Ent-like"—showing how wicked and rotten his heart had truly become. This is of course speculation.

—Quickbeam

Q10: What exactly is the significance of the "white jewel" that Arwen gives Frodo at the end of *The Return of the King*? Does it hold some sort of magic power, or is it just some token of sentimental value?

A: The *real deal* with this white gem, in the books, has a specific emotional color. We have no idea what the real white gem looked like. We only know that Frodo received it, hung from a silver chain, with Arwen telling him that it would bring him help in times of darkness and trouble. This gift seems to possess an inherent calming, pacific effect. She thinks it will be needed, and she is right. Nowhere does Tolkien say it could heal Frodo, but as he clutches it in the very last chapter of *RotK*, perhaps he is reminded of the healing and peace he felt in the House of Elrond. Perhaps it bestowed on Frodo the gentle grace of Arwen herself. I do not assume, however, that this gem had such great powers as we see in other Elvish artifacts (like the Phial for instance).

—Quickbeam

Q11: Towards the end of *RotK* Frodo vows to never use a sword again. True to his word, he never does, even though he wears one. This holds true even when he and his friends return to the Shire, see the devastation and are attacked by the ruffians. Why does Frodo choose not to defend himself, his friends or the Shire that he loves so dearly? Also—after Frodo, Sam, Merry and Pippin return to the Shire, why does it seem like everyone ignores Frodo's good deeds? Tolkien points out how Merry and Pippin are thought of more highly and how Frodo falls to the wayside. After everything Frodo and Sam have done, you'd think the hobbits would be more appreciative.

A: The first of your questions is the more difficult. It's easy to say that Frodo knew that Merry and Pippin and Sam would take care of what needed to be done, but on the other hand, he cautioned them about killing, even of the ruffians, and it's difficult to say whether or not he would have drawn his sword if he had come back alone and had to rally the Shire-hobbits to defend themselves. I can only answer that he felt he'd been through enough violence and bloodshed that he decided not to contribute directly to more of it—even while he may have acknowledged the necessity for it. It is the more curious given Tolkien's attitude towards pacifism—he felt that some things were worth fighting for and that anybody who would sell peace and freedom to avoid war was weak and poor indeed. On the other hand, he saw horrors in the trenches of World War I that may have led him to select this position for Frodo.

As for your second question, Frodo deliberately keeps more to the background. He tells Sam that it is often that way, that some must fight to save a thing so that others may keep it, and he knows he will not stay in the Shire forever. Merry and Pippin and even Sam appreciated the limelight a little more, and the crowds always flock to those who respond to their adulation. Moreover, Merry and Pippin were the captains of the great battle that threw the ruffians out of the Shire. They were visibly heroes, while Frodo's deeds had been done on a mountain far from the sight or minds of the Hobbits.

—Anwyn

Q12: Since the Black Riders were invisible, why did they wear cloaks that made them visible? Wouldn't being invisible be a great advantage when it came to hunting down the hobbits?

A: The Black Riders could not see very well, and therefore probably had trouble even finding their way across country. As for finding one Hobbit in a warren of them, even one bearing the Ring, it was out of the question unless they asked people where they would find *Baggins*. In order to ask, they had to be visible.

Besides, their very appearance struck terror into the hearts of those they dealt with, and nobody dared mess with them except Aragorn. They had nothing to fear from being visible.

—Anwyn

Q13: Once Elros had chosen to become mortal that choice was irrevocable, and all of his descendents were likewise mortal. Why, then, was Arwen given the same choice, when Elrond had already chosen to become an Elf? Shouldn't she be bound to Elfdom just as assuredly as any of Elros's descendents were bound to mortality?

A: Tolkien gives a good explanation for this in his published *Letters*, specifically, Letter No. 153. He says that Elros chose to be human, thus mortal even though long-lived, so all his descendents are also mortal. But Elrond chose to be among the Elves, and his children still have to make their own choices.

So it seems that because of the renewed Elvish blood-line from Celebrían's side of the family, the children of Elrond face the same choice as their father once did. But I have heard people debating this point before, without agreement. There are many things in the mythology, certainly, where Tolkien makes his own rules, his own way, and the reader has to accept them on his terms. This issue of who gets to choose immortality and why cannot always be ascribed to a system of "genetic logic"—and we shouldn't try too hard to determine which Elf gets the "recessive XY gene of immortality" (which many people are indeed trying to figure out, I'm afraid). Remember what Gandalf said: He who breaks a thing...

—Quickbeam

Q14: What exactly were the "Dwarf Masks" mentioned several times in *The Silmarillion*? It seems that they gave their wearers some kind of power to face danger more steadily and gave them the ability to face the Dragons. Turin wore one for a time in his travels. Where did Tolkien get this idea from? I know that in Polynesia and the South Pacific there were many cultures that made "War Masks", but I have to wonder if there might be a European connection here. These masks are such fascinating artifacts, yet they are barely mentioned.

A: The dwarf masks to which you refer are mentioned primarily in the account "Of the Fifth Battle:" "...It was their custom moreover to wear great masks in battle hideous to look upon; and those stood them in good stead against the dragons." There are two interesting points about this passage. First, it was introduced after the writing of *Lord of the Rings*; in the pre-*LotR* version (found in *The Lost Road*, Volume V of *The History of Middle-earth*), the Dwarves did not participate, "for we favor neither side—until one hath the mastery." As he used this manuscript as the basis for the post-*LotR* version, he wrote, "Not true of Dwarvish attitude."

In the later version, the passage first read "...great masks or visors...", but the last two words were crossed out. The Dragon-helm of Hador was evidently of similar design, as you point out; from the "Narn i Hîn Húrin:" "It was wrought by Telchar, the smith of Nogrod... It had a visor (after the manner of those that the dwarves used in their forges for the shielding of their eyes), and the face of one that wore it struck fear into the hearts of all beholders."

There are apparently two important features to these helms or masks: the fearsome face, and the visor that protects the wearer's vision. In one of the scraps of writing related to the "Narn" in *Unfinished Tales*, we read that that "Turin dared not look straight into his [Glaurung's] eyes, but had kept the visor of his helmet down, shielding his face, and in his parley had looked no higher than Glaurung's feet." When he raises the visor, Glaurung is able to work his spell upon Turin.

I personally think of these masks as resembling ornate versions of modern welders' masks (as they serve similar functions); I cannot guess Tolkien's inspiration for them. As usual, though, he may have had a variety of different things in the back of his mind, including welders' masks and the masks of classical Greek theatre. In researching this answer, I found an interesting web page with an essay on "Arms and Armour in J.R.R. Tolkien's Middle-earth," which includes photographs of one person's idea of how these masks looked.

—Ostadan

Q15: What exactly is it that haunts the Dead Marshes? Supposedly, they are the ghosts of the warriors that died in the battle of Dagorlad, but wouldn't their spirits all go to their respective afterlives? Even if they were somehow trapped there because of the manner of their deaths, I doubt they would be trying to lure people into the water, so is there something evil that takes on their form to do this?

A: I do not find where Tolkien explains this with many particulars. Here is what we know: within the Dead Marshes could be found the Mere of Dead Faces, which was the actual name of the pools wherein you'd see the flickering corpse-lights. A ghastly place indeed, but not wholly anachronistic with other "haunted" places in Middle-earth. Remember the Paths of the Dead? That location was haunted by the Oathbreakers. But our main concern here is whether the Mere of Dead Faces is actually an abode of spirits that should have left Arda and gone to their respective "homes." After these Men, Elves, and Orcs died during the War of the Last Alliance, I too would assume that their spirits went to the various places meant for them: the Halls of Mandos (for the Elves) and beyond the Circles of the World (for the Men), but who knows about the Orcs? Samwise suggests that there is some unknown necromantic work of Sauron occurring here, which is entirely possible. Unfortunately, I cannot say with certainty why the Dead Marshes were inhabited by these spirits. They weren't trying to lure anyone into the waters (that happens in the movie, not the book) mind you, they were just part of the "tableaux." But Tolkien has shown specific events that could, although rarely, determine that a spirit would stay bound to the world of Arda, even though the flesh was long gone. The existence of the Nazgûl is another example. So it is clear that within these stories, Tolkien gives instances of terrible extremes that prevent the spirit from leaving the physical plane at the point of death, but often the details and parameters of this notion are left unclear.

Then, on the other hand, you have the Barrow-wights. I previously wrote a great deal about them, and they illustrate another possibility. The Barrow-wights were malignant, demonic spirits that had descended upon the bodies within the barrows, animating the corpses (while the corpses themselves retained some vestigial memory of their previous lives). So following this example you might consider that the dead soldiers within the Marshes were only empty shells—that the spirits of the fallen had indeed gone to their afterlives, yet somehow the corpses had since been infested with some evil will or other unknown entities.

—Quickbeam

Q16: I've been working on the hypothetical situation: What if Saruman hadn't gone bad? With the massive industrial capabilities of Isengard, and the power of five Istari (Saruman didn't lead Alatar and Pallando into the East), just think what damage the Captains of the West could have achieved with that!! What are your opinions on this matter? Also—slightly related to the above question, could the forces of good have spawned Orcs and made them fight for the good guys? I know they'd see it as immoral, and Tolkien hated mass-production and industrialization, but it would still be a cool idea, don't you think?

A: You answer your own question when you say Tolkien hated mass production and industrialism. As such, Saruman's evil was predicated at least partially on his having wheels and machines to begin with—i.e., if he'd have stayed good, he wouldn't have had those things, so he couldn't have used them for good. As for Orcs, no, they are a very specific form of evil, and the "good guys" would never have mass-produced beings and forced them to do anything—free will is the entire essence of the "good side." In addition, I don't think there's any question of Orcs being "spawned" and mass-produced in the same way that Peter Jackson depicted it—"spawn" simply means having a large number of offspring, and is also slang for foul or vile offspring. We suppose that Orcs propagate in the normal mammalian manner.

—Anwyn

Q17: When Gandalf and Pippin are riding Shadowfax from Rohan to Minas Tirith, Gandalf seems able to make out the watch fires on the various hills and towers along the northern side of the White Mountains, naming many, in fact. But if Middle-earth is curved, as is our

Earth, this would seem impossible. I live at the very foot of the Rocky Mountains and must travel a mere 30-40 miles out on the plains before even the tops of our 14,000-foot-plus peaks disappear over the horizon; the journey from the heart of Rohan to Gondor is many hundred miles. Far-sighting ability by Gandalf? Flat earth? I would note, also, that Legolas apparently has an ability to perceive things over the curve of the horizons.

A: "See! The beacons of Gondor are alight, calling for aid. War is kindled. See, there is the fire on Amon Dîn, and flame on Eilenach; and there they go speeding west: Nardol, Erelas, Min-Rimmon, Calenhad, and the Halifirien on the borders of Rohan." So Gandalf declares to Pippin as they ride eastward through Anórien. Yes, indeed, at this later point in the history of Arda the world was round and had been since the Fall of Númenor. In Karen Wynn Fonstad's *Atlas of Middle-earth*, she has an opening chapter about the challenges of mapping a round world that Tolkien himself mapped out as if it were flat. She stuck to Tolkien's mapping methods, even though her experience as a cartographer demanded otherwise, for ease of the reader. It's all very interesting, but let's get back to the physics of your question. I estimate (from looking at Fonstad's maps of Gondor) that the road Gandalf traveled that night was, at furthest, about 10 miles distant from the foothills where these beacons sat. We do *not* know the elevation of these beacon-towers, however. I'm inclined to think they were set quite high up, for practical reasons. According to the website "Howstuffworks.com" a 100 foot-tall ship sailing on the ocean 15 miles away from the viewer standing on the shore is not visible because of the curvature of the earth. So if you assume these Gondorian beacon-towers were built at an elevation close to 1,000 feet (which is safe to assume; after all, the Hollywood Sign in Los Angeles rests on Mt. Lee at approximately 1,600 feet above sea level, and I can see the Sign from ANYWHERE in the metropolitan Los Angeles area—and these wee little Hollywood Hills can hardly compare to the greater elevations of the Ered Nimrais!) then it would be very easy for Gandalf to see the fires along the road. Perhaps the trick here is looking at exactly what Gandalf said. He named all of them, but maybe they were only looking at two, the two closest to them at that point being Amon Dîn and Eilenach. It seems that the phrase "and there they go speeding west..." is Gandalf only reciting the many more that went further west behind them, once already passed in the night.

Now about Legolas having far-seeing eyes. Let's try the same approach, again assuming the curvature of Arda is exactly the same as the curvature of our world today. In "The Riders of Rohan," Legolas says he can see the hobbits' captors about 12 leagues away. At the point where he was standing, rather high up on the Emyn Muil, above the East Wall of Rohan, he could see many things across a distance of twelve leagues (36 statute miles). If the Three Hunters were at least 250 feet up when they looked out west, then it fits my calculations fine. It's possible they stood at a higher elevation. There is nothing Tolkien says that indicates Elf-vision could defy normal physics; it was just easier for Legolas to make out some details. Easy for an Elf, a bit of a challenge for a Man, yet Aragorn can see them also! There does not seem to be any concrete, inarguable examples of Tolkien violating the basic rules of vision across the horizon, at least that I can find.

—Quickbeam

Q18: When Saruman sent Radagast the Brown to seek out Gandalf, during their conversation he referred to the name "Shire" as uncouth. Do we know why? Was it equal to some taboo in the common tongue? Do we know what the word "Shire" means?

A: While the word "uncouth" in modern English means "crude," "rustic," or "unrefined," it also can mean "unknown" or "unfamiliar," which is its earlier meaning. The word "cuth" was the Old English past participle of "cunnan," meaning "to know." Of course, Tolkien would have been very familiar with the older meaning of this word. The word "shire" is an ordinary English word for a county or territorial division. In the United States, it occurs only as part of names like Devonshire, derived from England. It is worth observing that Radagast did not recognize this strange name as a word in the Common Speech—he takes it to be a proper name like "Rohan," and Gandalf corrects him by replying, "*The* Shire." In this, Radagast is not unlike modern Americans, at least, whose only acquaintance with the word is through Tolkien's writings. It is not uncommon, for example, for visitors to an American "Renaissance Faire" to hear the actors referring to their "shire" and conclude that this is some fanciful reference to hobbits!

—Ostadan

Q19: In *The Two Towers* film there is a scene where Aragorn is dead of old age (in the future) where Arwen seems as young as ever. But if she had become mortal, shouldn't she have aged, too? Then also I thought that in the book, when Elladan and Elrohir stay in Middle-earth, there isn't much ado about them becoming mortal etc. as was with Arwen. It seems like they were only delaying their departure for a while. But then why would Arwen have to become mortal if SHE stayed and married Aragorn? I had thought that she would become mortal only because she decided not to leave Middle-earth when her father did. Couldn't she decide to stay until Aragorn died and then go to Valinor (as Aragorn himself proposed to her), possibly with Legolas and Gimli? How exactly are things with the mortality/immortality choice?

A: 1) On the question of Arwen aging, I don't think there's any reason to suppose that she would show outward signs of mortality just because she had agreed to "die from the world" after the manner of Men. After all, Aragorn is over 80 years old at the time of the events in *Lord of the Rings*, and he clearly does not look it. If he, a human descended from the kings of Númenor, can appear younger than he is, then certainly the daughter of Elrond may, mortal or not.

2) On the question of why she wouldn't have just stayed with Aragorn until he died and then gone over-Sea, she could have, if she'd been willing to abandon the possibility of spending eternity with him. Aragorn tells her that as mortals they are not bound forever to the Circles of the World, as are Elves, and that beyond those circles (beyond death) is "more than memory," meaning they both believe their spirits will be together in some more tangible way than just memory, which is all Arwen would have left if Aragorn died and she returned to her people.

—Anwyn

Q20: In the Tale of Aragorn and Arwen it is mentioned that after many hard and tiring journeys, Aragorn wished to return to Rivendell for some time to rest, and on the way he passed by Lothlórien. Now it is also given that he was admitted into the Hidden Land by the Lady Galadriel. She clothed him in silver and grey and she sent him to Arwen. It was at that point that Arwen's choice was made and her doom appointed. Now Elrond was always against a union between Aragorn and Arwen because he probably knew how difficult it would be for Arwen to face the Doom of Men. Galadriel was Arwen's grandmother, but she helped Aragorn win Arwen's favour. Galadriel must have known all along that if Arwen chose Aragorn, she would give up immortal life. Why did Galadriel help them? I really don't get it!

A: It frequently happens that other people are more clear-sighted on the subject of daughters' marriages than their fathers. Galadriel had her mirror and she had far sight; it has always been a theory of mine that Aragorn was able to do his duty partly because he knew what his reward would be in the end, and perhaps Galadriel realized that for events to take their proper course, Aragorn and especially Arwen needed to be free to make their own decisions, as perhaps Elrond would not have wanted them to be. Women are painted as quite self-sacrificing in many stories, and Galadriel could have sacrificed her wish to retain Arwen among her own people for what she saw as the higher good for the world. We don't really know for sure.

—Anwyn

Q21: I was just wondering, did Elves and Men have surnames? I know of Legolas Greenleaf and Arwen Undómiel, but was this usual practice or a rarity? Were surnames more like titles, like Galadriel, Lady of Light? Are there any other examples of surnames?

A: Hobbits (and their Big Folk neighbors in Bree-land) appear to be the only people who use the modern Western practice of a personal name and a family surname. Other characters may not even recognize this practice, preferring to address the Hobbits with such patronymics as "Frodo son of Drogo." The other names we see that appear to be surnames are more appositives. The word "Greenleaf" simply translates "Legolas;" one might as well say "Legolas, the Greenleaf," as we sometimes see Elessar, the Elfstone. We see this kind of apposition in other usages such as "Théoden King" (not Mr. and Mrs. King's little boy Théoden).

Elvish names are more complicated, as Tolkien wrote in an essay on the customs of the Eldar that appears in Volume X of *The History of Middle-earth*, *Morgoth's Ring*; this note is summarized in *Unfinished Tales* in the notes on Galadriel's and Celeborn's names. When a child was born, its father gave it its first name. Other names were added later. Each child among the Noldor (but not the other Eldar, perhaps) could choose his or her own name once he or she had mastered their language fully, around their tenth year. This name did not necessarily have meaning in the Elvish language. These chosen names were not secret, but were treated as a private possession, used only by intimates.

Additional names might be given by a child's mother in a moment of insight or foresight, "indicating some dominant feature of its nature as perceived by her, or some foresight of its special fate." These mother names were also regarded as true names, and might be private or public. Tolkien gives as an example the eldest son of Finwë, whom his father first named Finwion, later modified when his talent was revealed to Curufinwë. "But the name of insight which his mother Míriel gave him in the hour of his birth was Feanáro 'Spirit of Fire'; and by this name he became known to all and he is so called in all the histories. (It is said that he also took this name as his chosen name, in honour of his mother, whom he never saw.)"

Other names are "given" names, not "true" names; in effect, they are nicknames, as in one example Tolkien gives, "Mormacil (that is Blacksword)". The example in the question, Arwen Undómiel, the Evenstar of her people, is almost certainly another such "given" name, not a mother-name of insight. The closest we get to a family surname is Aragorn's self identification in his letter to Sam (in the Epilogue found in *Sauron Defeated, History of Middle-earth* Volume VIII) Elessar Telcontar (Elfstone, Strider), in which the name Telcontar, that is Strider, is the name of Aragorn's house—but even then, it is not known whether Eldarion styled himself as "Eldarion Telcontar" or "Eldarion son of Elessar Telcontar" or "Eldarion Elessarion of the House of Telcontar (as in "Gildor Inglorion of the House of Finrod"—Inglorion simply means "Son of Inglor"). The name "Galadriel" is said to be one such "given" name, given to her by Celeborn, and so her favorite name.

—Ostadan

Q22: I have always wondered about Gandalf's rescue from Celebdil by Gwaihir after he returned to life following his fight with the Balrog. In the text of *LotR*, Gandalf asks the great Eagle to bear him to Lothlórien, and Gwaihir responds that that is the command of Galadriel, who sent the Eagle to look for him. My first question is, how could Galadriel know (a) that Gandalf was alive and needed rescuing, and (b) that he could be found on that peak or indeed anywhere accessible to an Eagle? All that Galadriel is told (as far as we know) by the Fellowship is that Gandalf "fell" while saving the others. By all indications, it seems that everyone assumed that Gandalf was dead, including the Fellowship and Galadriel and Celeborn. It seems difficult to assume that Galadriel could "sense" or divine anything to the contrary, as she admits that she "cannot see [Gandalf] from afar… a grey mist is about him, and the ways of his feet and his mind are hidden from [her]." Even if she had no knowledge that he was alive and just wanted to recover his body, it seems odd to send an Eagle to do so, since by all accounts he fell into the earth, deep under the mountain, and certainly a place inaccessible to an Eagle.

My second question is, even assuming she receives some indication that he is alive, why does she not alert the Fellowship to this possibility? In appendix B of *LotR*, it indicates that Gandalf returns to life on February 14. The Fellowship leaves Lórien on February 16. Gandalf is borne by Gwaihir to Lórien on February 17, only one day after the Fellowship departs! Surely Galadriel had dispatched the Eagle to search for Gandalf prior to the Fellowship's departure. Why then did she not at least inform them of this? It seems inconceivable that Galadriel had some knowledge or inclination that Gandalf still lived yet had not relayed this information to the Fellowship.

A: Seemingly difficult questions at first, but not necessarily if we remember the natures of both Galadriel and Gandalf. 1) Gandalf was not human, and Galadriel knew this. Tolkien tells us that Círdan knew what the Istari really were and that he communicated his knowledge to Elrond and Galadriel. The very fact that she could not see him "from afar," which implies that he was not a good subject for the Mirror, indicates that he is something high and set apart, and Galadriel would have made her deductions accordingly. That being said, she would assume that he could not be killed easily, and though she would have no real way of knowing for sure that he was alive, she would have decided that a search for him would not do any harm. Regardless of where he was, an Eagle was the swiftest means of search—Elves on foot would have availed nothing; they could not get back into Moria, and Galadriel would probably not have sent them to try. 2) Whatever Galadriel may have suspected about Gandalf's whereabouts, she knew nothing would be gained by raising the hopes of the Company, hopes that she could not begin to guarantee would be answered. She had no way of knowing what Gwaihir would find, how long he would be gone, what he would tell her when he came back. For all she knew, the Company had lost Gandalf for the duration, whether he was actually dead or alive, and she clearly felt it best that they be able to mourn him as though he were dead and not get their hearts set on false hopes.

—Anwyn

Q23: I've read *LotR* a few times and I've always been intrigued by one thing. In *The Fellowship of the Ring*, chapter "Lothlórien," Tolkien says "When he had gone and passed again to the outer world, still Frodo the wanderer from the Shire would walk there, upon the grass among the elanor and niphredil in fair Lothlórien." Did he mean simply in a clear, vivid memory or does he mean something else? For a while I thought it referred to Lórien the gardens of Irmo in the Blessed Realm, but I don't think that it is ever referred to as "Lothlórien" as the passage in *The Fellowship of the Ring* specifies.

A: There's always a danger of taking things too literally in Tolkien. Here I think we'd be well advised to postulate a sort of netherworld in between literalism and imagination. Given the peculiar qualities of Lothlórien, I think it's safe to say that the land would retain a memory of his passage, that the souls of the people who come there are imprinted, so to speak. Remember that wonderful passage about Aragorn on the hill of Cerin Amroth, or rather at the foot of it—that he spoke words to somebody Frodo could not see. These words are to Arwen, and we know that their troth was plighted on that hill. It seems that he could probably almost see her spirit walking there still, just as on the day when they became betrothed. And undoubtedly, as you say, Frodo himself would retain a very vivid memory of walking in Lórien—so it is kind of a mutual imprint, the land upon Frodo and Frodo upon the land. The land would remember him always walking there, no matter what happened to him in the future, just as he would always remember walking there.

—Anwyn

Q24: In *The History of Middle-earth XII: The Peoples of Middle-earth*, Christopher Tolkien says he has recently identified the previously announced "illegible" reverse side of his father's Essay on the Istari. Within this Tolkien gives the names Morinehtar and Rómestámo in relation to the Ithryn Luin. Have we got here the real names of the Blue Wizards? And if so, why has no "fuss" been made about it, and why do people still refer to the Ithryn Luin as Alatar and Pallando?

A: Probably simply because *Unfinished Tales* came out in 1980, when we learned of Alatar and Pallando, whereas *Peoples of Middle-earth* came out in 1996. And old habits die hard. But we don't really have any reason to give primacy to either set of names, unlike with Gandalf, whom we almost always refer to as Gandalf, while he had many other names as well (Olórin, Mithrandir, Incánus, etc.), since we really don't know much of the history of the Blue Wizards.

—Turgon

I would also add that the names Morinehtar and Rómestámo are, unlike Alatar and Pallando, translated for us (Darkness-Slayer and East-Helper), and so give the impression of being functions or titles, especially in context. So Alatar and Pallando, whose interpretations are less obvious (they seem to be related to roots for "wide" and "far") "feel more like names." One can even imagine, had Tolkien developed their stories more, that both names could appear in apposition, as, for example, "Alatar Morinehtar," Alatar the Darkness-slayer; or the latter names might be their Middle-earth "aliases," as "Mithrandir" is an alias for Olórin (but who would give them these aliases? The Elves knew nothing of them). All this, of course, is entirely hypothetical speculation, supported by nothing in Tolkien's writings other than his style of naming.

—Ostadan

Q25: I don't have the exact figures at hand, but I remember reading in *Unfinished Tales* that when Eorl led the Rohirrim to the aid of Gondor, he had some 7,000 cavalry and some hundreds of horse archers. Similarly, when Théoden rides to the battle of the Pelennor, he has some 7,000 cavalry. Now, assuming there were losses to both armies before they left for Gondor, it seems to me that the basic population of Rohan needed to field a 7,000-man-plus army is given as too low. Most societies base a military on about three to five percent of the population, to keep the economy viable in times of war. However, Tolkien repeatedly uses quotes such as "every able-bodied man"...etc. This implies a far higher percentage of the total population was called upon for war. If every one of those 7,000 men were married with two children, it would set Rohan's total population at 28,000-plus. And logically, not all of these men would be married with two children. So how could Rohan be sustained? It's similar to Gondor in its decline. There is a point below which the population is simply not viable to sustain the civilization, and it appears to me that Rohan, at least, could not have existed the way Tolkien described it.

A: I am not sure I fully agree with your conclusion. Looking at the back-story of Rohan (some of which is in Appendix A), I fail to see what could be construed as "faulty history building." The Rohirrim were descended from Men who once lived in the far north (the éothéod), and though we don't have specific numbers from Tolkien, when they first arrived in the area that would become Rohan they were probably in very large numbers. Tolkien explains that the éothéod were numerous during their time "near the sources of Anduin," thus they had to push outward to other lands as their population expanded. But things certainly changed, and at the end of the Third Age they were indeed MUCH fewer.

There is a section in Karen Wynn Fonstad's *Atlas of Middle-earth* where she shows population density all across Middle-earth in three different Ages. She states: "Middle-earth's population at the end of the Third Age was extremely sparse. The Elves had continued to sail west … The Dwarves had been driven from their homes … The realms of Arnor had been virtually depopulated by war and plague." And of the Rohirrim she writes: "Their greatest concentrations were near Edoras and in the Westfold Vale. The Wold was used mainly for pasturage." Tolkien himself considered the problem of Rohan's depopulation. He implies in Appendix A that after the Fell Winter of T.A. 2758 that Rohan was lucky it did not suffer more loss of life, for that would have resulted in exactly what you have suggested: the failure of the civilization. Tolkien states: "The Rohirrim were grievously reduced by war and dearth and loss of cattle and horses; and it was well that no great danger threatened them again for many years, for it was not until the time of King Folcwine that they recovered their former strength." So Tolkien had considered this issue, and he ultimately reasoned there was indeed enough of a population in Rohan to support the nation and its culture.

—Quickbeam

Q26: Why didn't Gollum ever go look for Bilbo in the Shire? Why go to Mordor / Mirkwood, etc. but not where he knew Bilbo was?

A: Gandalf tells us that Gollum tried to. That he set out west, but never made it. And of course he goes on to state that Gollum wound up in Mordor. Why Mordor? Would YOU go to Mordor voluntarily for no apparent reason? Of course not. The key lies in his comment that something else pulled Gollum off the trail. The mark of the Ring was on him, and the growing power of Sauron drew Gollum down to give whatever information could be had. In addition to being drawn by

Sauron, Gollum probably thought he could find help in getting the Ring back and making Bilbo pay for having taken it. Alas!

—Anwyn

Q27: If Gandalf and Sauron are both Maiar, then they are both on the same level of power, right? So why couldn't they match each other power for power? Why is Sauron always considered more powerful than Gandalf and the rest of the Istari? Was there some restriction set by the Valar? Also if Sauron did manage to get the One Ring and rule Middle-earth, could there be a chance that he could overthrow them?

A: Let's examine your basic premise. "If Gandalf and Sauron are both Maiar, then they are both on the same level of power, right?" "If Arnold Schwarzenegger and I are both humans, then we have the same physical strength, right?" "If George Bush and Saddam Hussein are both presidents of nations, then they must have the same level of power, right?" You see my point. Gandalf (Olórin) and Sauron are both Maiar, but Maiar have different levels of power—and those levels of power can change, as in the case of Saruman and Sauron, whose power is dissipated beyond recollection at the end of the book.

But your specific question is about why Gandalf, even enhanced as Gandalf the White, could not match Sauron's power directly. Tolkien wrote (Letter #156), "He is still under the obligation of concealing his power and of teaching rather than forcing or dominating wills, but where the physical powers of the Enemy are too great for the good will of the opposers to be effective he can act in emergency as an 'angel'—no more violently than the release of St. Peter from prison. He seldom does so, operating through others..." [followed by the citations of Gandalf's direct actions in rescuing Faramir and forbidding the Witch-king from entering Minas Tirith]. As to *why* the Istari were so constrained, we need only look at Saruman, who attempted to match Sauron's force and "beat him at his own game"—the result that he just became a Sauron wannabe, as we say in this latter age.

Aman had been removed from the rounded world not by the Valar, but by Ilúvatar Himself. It seems unlikely that Sauron or any forces at his command could even reach Aman uninvited, let alone overcome the Valar.

—Ostadan

Q28: In *RotK*, Tolkien describes Elladan and Elrohir, sons of Elrond, as having stars on their brows. I thought the fact that Aragorn was seen with a star on his brow had something to do with the Elessar. Is it instead some sort of connection to Eärendil and the Silmaril he bore?

A: The star on Aragorn's brow is, as the text says, the Star of Elendil, also known as the Elendilmir. Its history is described in some detail in *Unfinished Tales* in the chapter "The Disaster of the Gladden Fields." It was an heirloom of the North-Kingdom and the symbol of the kingship of Arnor. Tom Bombadil foreshadows Aragorn's appearance when he tells the hobbits about the wars with Angmar.

The Elessar is a different stone entirely, a green stone mounted in an eagle brooch, given by Galadriel as a bridal token to Aragorn on behalf of her granddaughter Arwen (roughly corresponding to the "evenstar" jewelry that Liv Tyler gives Viggo Mortensen in the movies).

The significance of apparently similar adornments for Elladan and Elrohir is not explained—given that they are riding with the Dúnedain (the only Elves in the company), one may conjecture that these are some kind of lesser stones that may signify a high position subordinate to Aragorn's command of the Northmen (it is to be noted that the sons of Elrond remained after Elrond left, and may eventually have decided themselves to share the fate of Aragorn and the Rangers). On the other hand, when Arwen appears for her wedding, Frodo sees her with "stars upon her brow," evidently the same tressure of gems that she wore in Rivendell: "Above her brow her head was covered with a cap of silver lace netted with small gems, glittering white"—so this all may be nothing more than the custom, or prerogative, of Elrond's house to wear such gems.

For another, mostly unrelated, instance of the same image in Tolkien's writing, see "Smith of Wooton Major." The image of a man with "a star on his brow" was evidently something that stirred Tolkien's imagination especially.

—Ostadan

Q29: There are a few things about Boromir's journey to Rivendell that don't make sense to me: 1) Why didn't anyone in Gondor know where Rivendell/Imladris was? Didn't they have maps in their archives? 2) Why did Boromir's journey take so long? At one point

Aragorn says that it would take him 12 days to walk from Weathertop to Rivendell, a distance of about 214 miles, which averages out to 18 miles a day. Boromir takes 110 days to travel from Minas Tirith to Rivendell, a distance of about 1275 miles, averaging 12 miles a day. He traveled on horseback for the first 705 miles, as far as Tharbad, so the daily average distance for the second part of the journey must have been much slower. Admittedly Aragorn was used to walking long distances, had less to carry and knew where he was going, but it still seems odd. 3) Why did Boromir lose his horse at Tharbad when Gandalf and all nine Black Riders seem not to have had any trouble? The horse returned to Rohan, so it wasn't killed. Looking forward to hearing from you,

A: We must remember that the location of Rivendell was kept very secret. The Enemy would never easily find it, and also it was difficult for allies and friends to locate unless they had specific knowledge of its whereabouts. In *The Hobbit*, Tolkien states: "It was not so easy as it sounds to find the Last Homely House west of the Mountains." I am surprised that Boromir managed to find Rivendell at all. However, it's very likely that Elven scouts found Boromir wandering around, and thus led him into the valley after learning his identity. As for why it took so long for Boromir to get there? Well, it seems he just took his time—unlike Strider and the Hobbits, he was not forced to travel swiftly across the land with the Enemy chasing after him. Boromir had never traveled north of Rohan, and knowing absolute zero about the lands beyond, he would necessarily have to be slow and careful. The loss of his horse cannot be explained with any supportive information from Tolkien's text. I only assume that the fording of the Greyflood was a treacherous business for those less skilled on horseback than Gandalf and the Nazgûl.

—Quickbeam

Q30: At the council of Elrond, when Aragorn is speaking of the secret and thankless watch the Rangers keep on the Shire and other Northern regions, he comments on the derision cast his way by people like Barliman, around whom there are enemies that would work great devastation if he were not guarded by Aragorn and the other Rangers. I have always wondered which "foes" specifically he is speaking of? I can't seem to think of any heart-freezing foes that lie within a day's march of Bree and would destroy it, aside from the Barrow-wights, but

I was always under the impression that they could not or would not leave the Downs. If you could offer some explanation as to who exactly these foes might be, I'd be greatly appreciative.

A: I don't assume the wild lands of the North (which were once part of Arnor) were safe and comfy just because they were "mostly empty." We can find several instances of dangers and evil creatures causing problems in the northern stretches of Eriador. During the Fell Winter of T.A. 2911 the terrifying White Wolves came down from the North and attacked everyone, including the Hobbits. There were Stone-trolls and Hill-trolls occasionally, looting and pillaging across the land. You know there could be Orcs too. Let us not forget the evil power of the Witch-king, for although the power of Angmar in the north was at its height many centuries before the War of the Ring, there was still some remnant of his malevolence lingering about the lands (Treebeard makes a sly reference to it). Considering that the Rangers knew more than anyone about such wandering creatures and evils, and had to deal with them at a great price, it seems reasonable for Aragorn to complain about Barliman's complacency.

—Quickbeam

Q31: After seeing *The Two Towers* movie my sister asked me, "Why is the Forbidden Pool forbidden?" I was quite chagrined to realize that after decades of reading the books, I didn't have a clue. Even more chagrined to realize I'd never even questioned it... At any rate, do any of you know just why?

A: There is a very simple explanation: the water basin below Henneth Annûn was part of the secret refuge controlled by Gondor. It was not a "forbidden pool" because of any properties of the water itself. Rather, it was a secret military installation and the entire location—cave, waterfalls, paths, and pool—was secret. To keep it secret from any and all, a law was written to kill any trespassers who discovered the place without being bidden there by representatives of Gondor. That was the law, plain and simple. According to this strict system, there was no other 100 percent failsafe measure to keep the location of Henneth Annûn a secret. It is all the more remarkable that Faramir chose to circumvent the law in the instance of Gollum's capture, even though Gollum clearly knew nothing about the military use of the locale.

—Quickbeam

Q32: This idea has haunted me for quite some time now, and others have confronted me with it as well. I have tried to defend the honor of *LotR*, but I have failed to see any explanation for my idea. Why did Frodo not simply dispose of the Ring in Moria? He could have cast it down into the great fires (lava/magma) of the great abyss of Moria, and surely not even the most elite of Sauron's forces would ever be able to retrieve it, would they?

A: A similar question was asked in the Council of Elrond about casting the Ring into the ocean. Gandalf replies that it would not be safe forever even there and that they should look for a way to end the threat of the Ring forever.

The same answer can be applied to the pits of Moria. Mountains crack, valleys are upraised, underground rivers change their course, lava dries up and cracks open, revealing fossilized secrets ... and there are many things in the deeps. Gandalf's objective, and the Council's, was to destroy, not hide, and the fires of Moria would not have done the trick.

—Anwyn

Q32: I'm confused about whether or not you can kill a wizard. I know of what happens to Saruman. The book says that his spirit leaves his body and disappears with the wind. Does this mean that he actually dies, or is it more of a reference to just his soul ending life in Middle Earth?

A: This is a confusing issue. There are references that seem to state the spirit (of Sauron) was "rejected" by the Valar, and one would assume that what's sauce for the goose would be sauce for the gander—that Saruman, being the same kind of spirit, would be subject to the same treatment. But the question then becomes, "What happens to a spirit when it is 'rejected?'" It either continues to exist as itself or it does not. If it continues to exist, then clearly it is formless and powerless for all the time it remains in Middle-earth. Personally, I believe that it's plausible that with this "rejection" comes dissipation—that when the wind took the spirits of Sauron and Saruman, it scattered their essence to the four corners of the earth.

—Anwyn

Q33: How knowledgeable was Aragorn regarding the Palantíri and the willpower of Sauron? How did Aragorn know that Sauron would not be able to read his mind if he used the Palantíri, at least enough to learn of the Fellowship's quest to destroy the Ring in Mt. Doom? After all, his ancestor Isildur was corrupted. Denethor was corrupted by Sauron through the Palantíri, as was perhaps Saruman, and Gandalf feared using it. Who does this Aragorn fella think he is, anyway?

A: He is the heir to Elendil and Isildur. The Palantíri are his by right. As Tolkien wrote in the essay on the palantíri (in *Unfinished Tales*): "In the case of Denethor, the Steward was strengthened, even against Sauron himself, by the fact that the Stones were far more amenable to legitimate users: most of all to true 'Heirs of Elendil' (as Aragorn), but also to one with inherited authority (as Denethor) as compared to Saruman, or Sauron." Aragorn was "naturally" stronger than Sauron in the use of the Stones. In the same paragraph, he clarifies that Denethor was *not corrupted*: "Denethor remained steadfast in his rejection of Sauron, but was made to believe that his victory was inevitable, and so fell into despair."

—Ostadan

Q34: I have a question about why the men of Gondor named the pass that they themselves built into Mordor (I think) Cirith Ungol. For, assuming "ungol" refers to Shelob, how did the men build the pass if Shelob was there? Surely they would have been eaten?! But if Shelob wasn't there, why name the pass "the spider's cleft?" Were there other spiders there? Or was there another name for it?

A: Of course, men did not build the pass, but the tower above it. The passage giving Shelob's history suggests that she had indeed been present even before Sauron, and a danger to Men using the path and tunnel when Minas Ithil was a fortress of the South Kingdom. It also appears that Shelob herself made the main tunnel. The passage that describes it also suggests that the straight and winding stairs were also Orc-work, to complete the path to Minas Morgul. Presumably the Gondorian guards only used the main road to Minas Ithil.

It seems plausible that the Gondorians knew of Shelob quite early on, and named the cleft (and lair, Torech Ungol) accordingly. Mordor was never a wholesome land, and guard duty within Mordor was doubtless considered "hazard duty" by those hardy souls who undertook to man the tower. For as the passage above suggests, yes, it does seem that the occasional unfortunate Man of Gondor strayed too close to her lair and became supper.

—Ostadan

Q35: I see many times throughout the books the words "wizard" or "wizardry." Now, Saruman and Gandalf are wizards, right? So I always thought that wizards were good (with the exception of Saruman who turns to evil, but he was good in the beginning.) What confused me was in the book *Return of the King*, a little while before Aragorn takes the Paths of the Dead, he looks into the palantir. When he tells the others what he did, Gimli reprimands him for looking into a stone of "wizardry." It makes it look all of a sudden like wizardry is evil, or did Gimli just not know what he was talking about? One other time I saw it was when Gandalf said (and I can't remember exactly where in the book) "If you meddle in the affairs of wizards you will face consequences" or something like that. What exactly is this whole wizard concept?

A: As with any other special power, "good" or "evil" depends on the use of the power, not upon the power itself (the exception being, of course, the power of the One Ring, which was irrevocably evil because that was the nature of the power put into it as an object). "Wizardry" is rather a catch-all term spoken by mortals or Elves who don't necessarily understand (or who perhaps, like Elrond, do understand all too well) the nature of the power entrusted to Gandalf and Saruman and Radagast. It simply refers to the feats they can accomplish with their powers as Maiar that are not available to mortals. So as you state, Gandalf remained "good," Saruman turned to "evil," and the "wizardry" of the palantiri could be used for good or evil, depending on the user. As for "Do not meddle in the affairs of wizards, for they are subtle and quick to anger," well, that could be said of a good many persons other than wizards, but the difference is that the wizard can use his power to make life particularly unpleasant for you if he so chooses, as we see with Wormtongue.

—Anwyn

Q36: I have read that the Barrow-wights were influenced by Sauron's return to power in the Third Age. Why didn't the Dead Men of the Haunted Mountain (Paths of the Dead) also serve Sauron instead of Aragorn? Weren't they wraiths, too?

A: They were not wraiths as we know the use of the word in connection with the Ringwraiths, no. They were ghosts chained to the mortal plane by a task left unfinished (not an uncommon legend about spirits). They had vowed to fight AGAINST Sauron, back in the earlier wars, but they broke their vows and skulked into the hills. Broken vows are a very serious matter, holding their own special power, in Tolkien's legendarium. Thus with a vow broken, the spirits were left to skulk forever until they fulfilled their vow, so if they had served Sauron in this new conflict, their vows would have remained broken and their spirits harnessed to the physical plane. When they served Aragorn and fought against Sauron, they were released from their vows and able to take their eternal rest away from the plane of Middle-earth.

—Anwyn

Q37: If Elves are so pure and one with nature and perfect, how do you explain the Wood-elves in *The Hobbit* getting drunk on wine and passing out? It doesn't seem like a very Elvish thing to do.

A: It is curious that people assume the entire race of Elves were somehow morally superior, without fault or frailty, nobler in nature, and at all times devoted to peace, love, and happiness. What seems like "an Elvish thing to do" is a peculiar way of looking at things. Perhaps it is a notion some readers get from limited exposure to the Third Age Elves as presented in *The Lord of the Rings*: where they concerned themselves with healing the hurts of the world and living in a mummified "faux peace" brought forth by the Three Rings. Thus one might walk away from the book thinking Galadriel and Legolas are shining examples of how selfless and wonderful Elves must all be. Their waybread is good for the soul! Their miruvor is even better! They taught the Ents to speak and use language for heaven's sake! All Elves must therefore be "green and good." Well, wake up and smell the Oath of Fëanor, my friend, because it hurts like a sack full of bricks upside your head. After reading *The Silmarillion* you will have a whole new concept about what the Eldar were capable of, both positive and downright horrid. Although most Elves were wonderfully divine and pure of "soul," their history is not one of perfect bliss. They killed their own brethren in cold blood, they stole property not theirs, they swore vengeance and death that flew in the face of the Valar's laws, they were suspicious and spiteful, they treated Dwarves poorly just because they were ugly (or too different from them)—and dare I say it—one Elf was consumed by an unwholesome lust for his own first cousin. To my mind it seems of little consequence that Wood-elves would enjoy the fruit of the vine and maybe get a little sloppy from time to time. It does nothing to taint their "clean living" image, for I never thought they had one, really. Haven't they earned themselves a good, stiff drink though? After so many centuries of grief, I wouldn't mind a little bit of merlot to take the edge off!

—Quickbeam

Q38: The Wise always say that using the Ring would be folly, even if Sauron were successfully overthrown through use of it, because the new Ringmaster would simply replace the old one. My question is: if someone of sufficient strength, say Gandalf or Saruman or Galadriel, were to master the Ring, could they control the Nazgûl with it? Obviously Frodo could not, but he never mastered the Ring. To what extent did they serve the Ruling Ring, and to what extent Sauron himself?

A: There is something specific in *Letters* (No. 246) that gives us some explanation. Frodo could not have controlled the Nazgûl at that point in the story where he claimed the Ring—very true indeed—and Tolkien muses that if the story's events did NOT unfold as he wrote them, specifically if Gollum did not get the Ring and fall into the Crack of Doom, if Frodo had continued to wield the Ring as a new "power," then the Nazgûl would have soon arrived at the Sammath Naur and "they would have obeyed or feigned to obey any minor commands of his that did not interfere with their errand—laid upon them by Sauron, who still through their nine rings (which he held) had primary control of their wills." This type of rumination Tolkien considered "an interesting problem," and reflects on your main concern. The Ringwraiths served the Dark Lord Sauron as he was the one entity wielding enough of his power (through the nine rings) to control them. They had given their wills up to him a long time before. It would not seem to me that a Hobbit or Elf or Man bearing the Ring could reverse this channel of power. But for one possible exception: since Gandalf was of the Maiar himself, equal (and yet opposing) to Sauron's power, there might have been an eventuality where he wielded the Ring and rendered Sauron "completely overthrown" and neutered. Not a very fun idea, but if you can imagine a One Ring-wielding and terribly altered Gandalf rising to power at Barad-dûr to overthrow Sauron and replace him, then you can imagine the one instance where the Nazgûl could be brought to "heel" and obey a new master.

—Quickbeam

Q39: Whose idea was it to send Boromir to Rivendell?

By Boromir's account at the Council of Elrond, he went there of his own free will, and Denethor did not want him to go. Did I misinterpret that? Peter Jackson's movies suggest otherwise, that Denethor had ordered Boromir to go to Rivendell against Boromir's will.

In chapter 4 of book 5, "The Siege of Gondor," Faramir says something that would make more sense if the latter were true. He says that Denethor himself gave the quest to Boromir.

A: Having read the passages you mention, you're right that they seem to contradict each other at face value. But perhaps they can be interpreted so as to remove the conflict. At the Council, Boromir says that Faramir was eager to take on the challenge of the dream himself, but that since the way was dangerous, Boromir claimed the right to go instead. I would guess that if there was a conflict between them on it, they may have appealed to Denethor, who would have wanted to give Boromir his way because he was his father's favorite, and yet still have not wanted him to go. So it may have been like a catch-22 for Denethor; he judged in Boromir's favor because he wanted to make him happy, but was still "loth" to let him go at all.

—Anwyn

Q40: Something that's always bothered me is the poem that Treebeard sings to the hobbits about all the free peoples and the animals. On the upper tier are elves, men, dwarves, ents, and eventually hobbits. My first question is why is it not just men and elves, not dwarves? Men and elves were the only ones intended to live in Arda and the dwarves were just thrown in after Aule made them. Second, if you're going to throw Ents into the list of free peoples, why aren't the eagles there too? I thought that they were created by Manwe and Yavanna at about the same time for about the same purpose.

A: Just because the Dwarves were not in Eru's original plan does not mean that he did not make plans for them once they came into existence. Though Aule "created" them, he could not give them true life and freedom; this was granted by Eru, and once done, they would then count among the free peoples.

As for Ents and Eagles, well, Eagles are animals, however intelligent. Remember that Tolkien gives speech to other animals than the Eagles but does not include them as "people;" the fox in the Shire, for example, as well as Smaug, and Shadowfax, though he did not speak, certainly possessed intelligence out of the ordinary for his kind. Lastly, remember who's making the list! The Ents certainly would not consider themselves animals, and though they may not be "people" from our perspective, they are free and intelligent and sentient, and therefore it's not surprising that they include themselves in a list like that. We've not seen a list made by the Eagles; who knows how their list would start?

—Anwyn

Q41: 1) It's apparent that the "blood of Westernesse" became "diluted" over time, both in Arnor and Gondor, although this happened at different rates. In Arnor and the north, it seems like most of what was left of the Dunedain remained more or less pure-blooded Numenorean. On the other hand, it seems like only a small elite nobility of Gondor remained so. Why is that?

2) Gandalf mentions in *RotK* that Denethor and Faramir had mostly Numenorean blood but Boromir didn't. How can this be possible if Boromir and Faramir had the same parents?

A: Arnor dwindled swiftly, apparently before there was time for the Numenorean bloodlines to be mixed with that of humans who had stayed in Middle-earth all along. Gondor, on the other hand, was a prosperous, bustling nation for a long time. In essence, there were lots of people down there who didn't come from Numenor, and as time went on, things happened naturally and these people's lineage became mixed with that of the Numenoreans.

As for Denethor, Faramir, and Boromir—I have always thought that Tolkien was using a little poetic license here, mixed with only a little biology. Yes, they had the same parents, but that doesn't mean they had to look or act anything alike; it may be that Denethor or his wife carried genetic material from some of these "native Middle-earth dwellers" and not Numenoreans, and that that material was more strongly expressed in Boromir than in Faramir, whose genes thus retained more of the "pure" Numenorean strands. Poetically speaking, however, I have always thought it just meant that Faramir and Denethor, through whatever quirks of nature, looked and acted more like their Numenorean forefathers while Boromir bore a stronger resemblance to some of these other strains of folk.

—Anwyn

Q42: Just finished reading the appendices to *LotR*. One thing noted was the fact that Cirdan gave Gandalf the Elven ring Narya when the Istari came to Middle-earth.

Now it is clearly noted that Saruman was the head of the Istari and Gandalf's superior in that order. If I recall correctly, Saruman was also head of the White Council.

But I wonder how Saruman would be able to overcome Gandalf enough to imprison him in Orthanc in 3018 T.A.? As one of the Istari, Gandalf certainly had some inherent magical powers without the ring Narya. Not really knowing too much about the magical properties of Narya, one would think it would help Gandalf at least equal, if not surpass, Saruman's powers. Gandalf had a ring of power; Saruman did not. Advantage Gandalf!

It does not seem consistent that Saruman, although very learned and powerful, would be able to best another Istari who also possessed a ring of power.

A: A mistaken concept about these rings is that one of their purposes is advantage in a fight. We clearly see time and time again that this is not the case. Cirdan even says flat out to Gandalf that with Narya, he may "rekindle hearts in a world that grows chill." Given that Gandalf and Saruman were both Istari/Maiar, as you say, the advantage would likely lie with Saruman as Gandalf's "superior," until Gandalf was remade.

Besides, we are not told exactly how Saruman restrained Gandalf. *Fellowship* does not even say there was a fight! Gandalf just says they took him and put him on top of Orthanc. Either Gandalf thought that it was not an appropriate time for fighting, or he was outnumbered by Saruman's thugs and perhaps knew what power Saruman might bring to bear if he did attempt resistance. We're simply not told. Even Gandalf, obviously, cannot fly off towers...at least not under his own steam.

—Anwyn

Q43: I've always been curious about the date in which the Fellowship left Rivendell on the Quest—December 25. Do you believe this to be of any significance given that Tolkien was a Roman Catholic, and if so how?

A: In a 1953 letter (#128 in *Letters*), Tolkien wrote that "The Lord of the Rings is of course a fundamentally religious and Catholic work; unconsciously so at first, but consciously in the revision." Not only does the Quest begins on December 25, but it reaches its fulfillment on March 25, in medieval England considered the date of the original Good Friday, and celebrated by the Church as the Feast of the Annunciation, the conceiving of Jesus in the womb of the Virgin Mary. There can be no doubt that this is part of the "conscious revision."

—Ostadan

Q44: Since the balrog of Moria was destroyed by Gandalf, why didn't the dwarves reinhabit the mine after the war of the ring? Wasn't there still mithril to be had there?

A: This has been the subject of much speculation. Robert Foster's encyclopedic Guide points out that Tolkien never mentions such an activity. Fantasy author Dennis McKiernan began his career by writing a Lord of the Rings sequel recounting the Dwarves' attempt to reoccupy Moria; it was legally unpublishable, and was eventually rewritten into a different, but congruent, fantasy world of McKiernan's own and published as the "Silver Call" duology (I do not personally care for McKiernan's writing, but you may be interested in seeing his "take" on the subject).

In any case, it now seems likely that the Dwarves did eventually reinhabit Moria. In the genealogy of Durin's house that appears in Appendix A, we see an undated reference to "Durin VII & Last". This would hint of the fulfillment of the prophecy of the re-awakening of Durin to once again be Lord of Khazad-dûm. It is given, perhaps, greater weight by a passage that Tolkien wrote for Appendix A, but did not appear in the published version; it can be found in *The Peoples of Middle-earth* (*History of Middle-earth XII*):

"And the line of Dáin prospered, and the wealth and renown of the kingship was renewed, until there arose again for the last time an heir of that House that bore the name of Durin, and he returned to Moria; and there was light again in deep places, and the ringing of hammers and the harping of harps, until the world grew old and the Dwarves failed and the days of Durin's race were ended."

Christopher Tolkien notes, "It is impossible to discover whether my father did in fact reject this idea, or whether it simply became 'lost' in the haste with which the Appendices were finally prepared for publication. The fact that he made no reference to 'Durin VII and Last', though he appears in the genealogy in Appendix A, is possibly a pointer to the latter supposition."

For my part, I like to think of this passage as "true", a joyful finish to the story of the Dwarves, mixed, as always with Tolkien, with that melancholy for things that must pass from the world.

—Ostadan

Q45: What is the difference between a wizard and a sorcerer? In *The Silmarillion* and other places it references the men "who used the Nine Rings became mighty in their day, kings, sorcerers, and warriors of old." All other references I can find to sorcery and wizardry relate only to the Maiar. Were there Men who became wizards or sorcerers, or were there defining differences between the two? Thanks for help in explaining.

A: The first distinction that must be made is that Tolkien intended the word "wizard" to apply only to the Five Istari that were sent as emissaries of the Valar. They were indeed Maiar spirits given a physical incarnation. The idea is linguistic, as with most everything in Tolkien's world. The translation of "Istar" into the common tongue gives you a word that sounds very much like "Istar"—"Wizard." Just say it out loud to yourself several times and you'll see what I mean. The words "sorcerer" and "sorcery" do not apply to these five Maiar, but rather to any other creature, Maia or mortal, that attempts to practice magical arts. So if a man attempted to learn and execute the power of the Unseen world, practicing sorcery or black magic, Tolkien would never refer to him as a "wizard" (not in the Hogwarts sense of the word). Some of the Black Numenoreans that Sauron seduced with the power of the Nine Rings were supposedly practitioners of such sorcery. Sauron himself was once referred to as a Sorcerer.

—Quickbeam

Q46: After having finished reading *The Lord of the Rings* yet again, and watching *The Two Towers* on DVD (again!) I was wondering:

When Gandalf gets "reborn," how come he comes back as an old man again, and not a younger (perhaps stronger?) man? Did Eru decide his physical form had to stay the same, or could he have been given the form of something stronger, i.e., a Balrog or something?

A: It seems that Tolkien wanted Gandalf to still be the same, recognizable Gandalf (in a human form) that had already existed for so long. After all, how does one continue to build such strong relationships with the denizens of Middle-earth, if you show up again with a completely different physical form? You couldn't pick up with your friends right off the bat, for they wouldn't recognize you at all. You can't build allegiances with kings if you're a completely different physical person "claiming" to be Gandalf. How could one prove that declaration if he was a physically different individual? I don't see it working out that way, personally. Much more can be learned (beyond my subjective musings) in Tolkien's *Letters*, No. 156, where the Professor explains that Gandalf's purpose, as with all the Istari, was to be an old man, and do the things an "old man" would be able to do without exhibiting too much power. There was a very specific limitation on the Wizards' power, as most of you will know—they were never allowed to run around challenging Sauron with greater force or power than he. Their job was to "train, advise, instruct, arouse the hearts and minds of those threatened by Sauron to a resistance with THEIR OWN STRENGTHS" (emphasis mine), and not just to do the job for them. So you see, Gandalf would never have come back as a giant, mega-powerful, shape-changing, ball-busting, super warrior with Balrog powers. Instead, Tolkien sought to serve his story with the new Gandalf providing careful and persistent encouragement, as a sage old man, with his powers actually "enhanced" just enough to deal with the situations that had worsened since Saruman's unexpected corruption.

—Quickbeam

Q47. On the slopes of Orodruin, Gollum attacks Frodo. Sam watches Frodo fend off Gollum, and there is a moment where Sam seems to see them with an altered vision. As Gollum grovels at Frodo's feet, Frodo appears like a stern figure robed in white, his hand clutching what seems to be a wheel of fire. Out of that wheel of fire comes a voice:

"Begone, and trouble me no more! If you touch me ever again, you shall be cast yourself into the Fire of Doom." (*The Return of the King*,

Chapter 3 "Mount Doom.") It seems that Frodo has made this pronouncement with the power of the Ring. Shortly thereafter, after Frodo has claimed the Ring for his own and put it on, Gollum bites off his finger and finally gets back the Ring. He then takes a step too far and falls into the Crack of Doom.

Was Gollum obeying Frodo's command? He did indeed touch Frodo, and ended up casting himself into the Fire of Doom.

A: There's two ways to look at it. Yes, Gollum did obey Frodo's command, pure and simple. But there's more going on than that: Tolkien was shaping the narrative so that we have a dramatic foreshadowing of what *will* happen. Think how many things in the book did turn out exactly as the prophecies said: The King *did* return, the Sword that was Broken *was* reforged. The manner in which the prophecies are fulfilled still surprise us, yet feel instinctively "right" because Tolkien has laid it out before us already in the scenes like the one you describe. This kind of foreshadowing is one things Tolkien does supremely well. He's already hinted—Gandalf says it right back in Bag End—that Gollum might have some crucial part to play in the story of the Ring. He mentions at it again at the Council of Elrond.

You make the point that Frodo makes his pronouncement over Gollum with the power of the Ring. When Frodo commands Gollum to leave him alone, the Ring seems to be lending Frodo some of its power. Gollum has been under the spell of the Ring for so long that there is no way he can resist the command of one who calls on its power. It's interesting that at the moment he does that, Frodo seems dominated neither by good nor evil. Something in his will is still striving to carry out his Quest, to destroy the Ring. If he's using the Ring it's to clear away an obstacle to that quest, and you could say that he is acting on the side of Good. But on the other hand, he's also removing a rival who take the Ring from him—so the Ring's evil is directing him to do whatever he has to in order to keep it. This scene catches Frodo point where he is completely neutral—the Ring's control of him and his own self-control seem completely balanced against each other, and neither has yet won. So when Sam sees Frodo shining with light and power (and I think we're meant to understand that he is seeing his spiritual being, not his physical body), there is no way we can know whether he's shining with the power of his own will and faith, or by the power of the Ring which comes ultimately from Sauron.

—Tehanu

Q48. If one Silmaril is cast into the earth and one is cast into the sea and one is on Eärendil's brow, why can't the Valar take the Silmarils and reconstitute the two trees? Bearing in mind that Aulë is master of the earth, Ulmo is master of the seas, and Eärendil wants a favor from the Valar. (Fëanor doesn't have to give them freely since he's now in the halls of Mandos.)

A: I think the answer has to do with the responsibility that the Valar feel towards the other creatures in Middle-earth. When the only light in the world came from starlight and the Two Trees in Valinor, most of Middle-earth was in virtual darkness, for the land of Aman was far to the West and the light of the Two Trees couldn't cover all the earth. The Two Trees apparently illuminated just the area around them where the Valar lived. When the Elves awakened in their part of the world, they were content with only starlight—in fact they loved it. But after Melkor destroyed the trees, the Valar decided to "illumine Middle-earth and with light to hinder the deeds of Melkor." And indeed Melkor feared and hated the new light of the Sun, which traveled over the whole of Middle-earth.

By the time Men had entered the history of the world, the world had come to expect and depend on the sunlight and moonlight made for their benefit.

The chapter in *The Silmarillion* called "Of Men" describes how coming of the sun made things quicken into growth and the earth teemed with life and grew green. "In that time the air of Middle-earth became heavy with the breath of growth and mortality, and the changing and aging of all things was hastened exceedingly...the Eldar increased, and beneath the new Sun Beleriand grew green and fair." And with the first rising of the Sun, the first Men awoke.

The remaining light of the Two Trees, gathered into the Sun and Moon, did more good spread across the whole world. Seeing this, the Valar may have decided that the Silmarils, too, could do more good by remaining in the sea, earth and sky where their force could spread around further.

—Tehanu

Q49: Among the agents of Sauron, the Mouth of Sauron is introduced to us relatively late in the book. I'd assume that Sauron would send forth from the Black Gate his *topmost* lieutenants in only a very necessary situation, as he seems to do with the Mouth of Sauron.

However, the dreaded Ringwraiths are running amok all the time, perhaps indicating a less prestigious position among Sauron's forces. How powerful in strength, rank, and intelligence do you think the Mouth of Sauron is in comparison to the Nazgûl?

A: I think they have different powers and Sauron uses them for different things. The Nazgûl are more supernatural, and as such they are untiring and have the power to intimidate or compel their victims. They're ideal for sending out on a long quest to hunt for the Ring, for instance. But their weakness is that they exist only by the will of Sauron and the Ring, and their own nature seems reduced to being almost puppets of Sauron. Also they don't see well. When they are hunting for the Ring in the Shire, they seem badly organized and easily distracted. One imagines them existing for long periods of time at an instinctive level, hunting rather mindlessly, following Sauron's instructions unquestioningly. Occasionally they seem roused to think and speak and make decisions, but one almost gets the sense that they exist as real personalities only in brief flashes. Sauron wouldn't want to rely on them in anything that involves too much talking or independent decision making. They can manage to interrogate the old Gaffer, but that's about as much as they can do, and I suspect the interrogation is not very subtle.

Their magical power is great—enough to challenge Gandalf, even, for that is the confrontation that Gandalf fears during the battle of Minas Tirith. The Lord of the Nazgûl has magic to confront him, and his incantations help shatter the gate of Minas Tirith. We don't know how a battle of wills between them would have ended, for the Lord of the Nazgûl is drawn aside to attack the Rohirrim and Theoden instead. The Ringwraiths are powerful—but not, I think, cunning. Sauron uses them, but they are no more than appendages to his will.

When it comes to dealing with people face to face, bargaining with and commanding and observing them, the Mouth of Sauron seems to be more useful. He's better at politics. Tolkien tells us that he served Sauron for a long time, and learned a good deal of his own sorcery, and knew Sauron's mind. In other words, he and Sauron actually converse, as opposed to just transmitting orders. He has his own power and cunning and can argue with and taunt Aragorn and Gandalf in front of the Black Gate. Somehow one cannot imagine the Black Riders holding such a sustained conversation. The Mouth of Sauron notices the reactions of his listeners and plays cruelly with them, using Frodo's discarded cloak to make them believe that the hobbits and the Ring have been captured.

The Mouth of Sauron is also called the Messenger, and I wonder whether it was he, and not one of the Nazgûl, that was sent to question the Dwarves about the finding of the Ring. At the Council of Elrond, Glóin describes him merely as a horseman, and says that when he threatened them his breath hissed like snakes.

He is called the Lieutenant of Barad-dûr and at the Black Gates, the watchers read his thought, that he means to be the tyrant that Sauron sets up to command them all. Sauron will place him in Isengard, to watch over and rule the West. I think he is definitely higher up in the pecking order of Barad-dûr than the Nazgûl.

—Tehanu

Q50: When Gandalf tells Frodo that he was meant to have the Ring, I think we see this idea recurring a lot throughout *LotR*, that things are just meant to happen. Right? So Bilbo was meant to stumble upon this ring, just as Déagol was meant to find it in the river and be murdered. Then how is it that Gandalf comes to Bilbo in the beginning of *The Hobbit*? From what I understand, they didn't know each other prior to that. Was Gandalf just using his wizard's sixth sense or foresight, knowing that Bilbo and his relative were destined for great things, and that's why he was compelled to come to him at Bag End? Like he was just doing his job as an Istar to make sure some lazy hobbit gets out the door on time without a handkerchief so that the world would be saved?

A: Personally, I think that destiny is largely a matter of hindsight. Gandalf is wise and gifted with a certain amount of foresight, but if he knew where the Ring was, he could have gone into the tunnels himself at any time. No, I believe Gandalf realizes that he himself, like other created beings, is an instrument in the hands of Iluvatar, and that if Bilbo was "meant" to find the Ring, then Gandalf was "meant" to help him along the way.

—Anwyn